SUBJECTIVITY AND OTHERNESS

SHORT CIRCUITS
Slavoj Žižek, editor

The Puppet and the Dwarf: The Perverse Core of Christianity, by Slavoj Žižek

The Shortest Shadow: Nietzsche's Philosophy of the Two, by Alenka Zupančič

Is Oedipus Online? Siting Freud after Freud, by Jerry Aline Flieger

Interrogation Machine: Laibach and NSK, by Alexei Monroe

The Parallax View, by Slavoj Žižek

A Voice and Nothing More, by Mladen Dolar

Subjectivity and Otherness: A Philosophical Reading of Lacan, by Lorenzo Chiesa

SUBJECTIVITY AND OTHERNESS

A Philosophical Reading of Lacan

Lorenzo Chiesa

THE MIT PRESS   CAMBRIDGE, MASSACHUSETTS   LONDON, ENGLAND

© 2007 Massachusetts Institute of Technology

MIT Press books may be purchased at special quantity discounts for business or sales promotional use. For information, please email special_sales@mitpress.mit.edu or write to Special Sales Department, The MIT Press, 55 Hayward Street, Cambridge, MA 02142.

This book was set in Joanna MT and Copperplate 33bc by Graphic Composition, Inc. Printed and bound in the United States of America.

Library of Congress Cataloging-in-Publication Data

Chiesa, Lorenzo.
    Subjectivity and otherness : a philosophical reading of Lacan / Lorenzo Chiesa.
      p. cm.—(Short circuits)
    Includes bibliographical references.
    ISBN-13: 978-0-262-53294-5 (pbk. : alk. paper)
      1. Lacan, Jacques, 1901–1981. 2. Subjectivity. 3. Other (Philosophy) I. Title.
    BF109.L23C45 2007
    150.19'5092—dc22

                                            2006029831

10 9 8 7 6 5 4 3 2 1

CONTENTS

A short circuit occurs when there is a faulty connection in the network—faulty, of course, from the standpoint of the network's smooth functioning. Is not the shock of short-circuiting, therefore, one of the best metaphors for a critical reading? Is not one of the most effective critical procedures to cross wires that do not usually touch: to take a major classic (text, author, notion) and read it in a short-circuiting way, through the lens of a "minor" author, text, or conceptual apparatus ("minor" should be understood here in Deleuze's sense: not "of lesser quality," but marginalized, disavowed by the hegemonic ideology, or dealing with a "lower," less dignified topic)? If the minor reference is well chosen, such a procedure can lead to insights which completely shatter and undermine our common perceptions. This is what Marx, among others, did with philosophy and religion (short-circuiting philosophical speculation through the lens of political economy, that is to say, economic speculation); this is what Freud and Nietzsche did with morality (short-circuiting the highest ethical notions through the lens of the unconscious libidinal economy). What such a reading achieves is not a simple "desublimation," a reduction of the higher intellectual content to its lower economic or libidinal cause; the aim of such an approach is, rather, the inherent decentering of the interpreted text, which brings to light its "unthought," its disavowed presuppositions and consequences.

And this is what "Short Circuits" wants to do, again and again. The underlying premise of the series is that Lacanian psychoanalysis is a privileged instrument of such an approach, whose purpose is to illuminate a standard text or ideological formation, making it readable in a totally new way—the long history of Lacanian interventions in philosophy, religion, the arts (from the visual arts to the cinema, music, and literature), ideology, and politics justifies this premise. This, then, is not a new series of books on psychoanalysis, but a series of "connections in the Freudian field"—of short Lacanian interventions in art, philosophy, theology, and ideology.

"Short Circuits" intends to revive a practice of reading which confronts a classic text, author, or notion with its own hidden presuppositions, and thus reveals its disavowed truth. The basic criterion for the texts that will be published is that they effectuate such a theoretical short circuit. After reading a book in this series, the reader should not simply have learned something new: the point is, rather, to make him or her aware of another—disturbing—side of something he or she knew all the time.

Slavoj Žižek

SUBJECTIVITY AND OTHERNESS

INTRODUCTION

"What will you do with all that I say? Will you record it on a little thing and organize soirées by invitation only?—Hey, I've got a tape by Lacan!"[1] This passage from Seminar XVII shows that Lacan was well aware that his teachings would, sooner or later, be incorporated into what he disdainfully named the "university discourse." However, one fundamental question remained open at that time and still remains at least partly open today: in what way would such an assimilation occur? Despite the pessimism expressed by the above cynical remark, we now know that academic philosophy has been able to recuperate Lacan's work while at the same time preserving its subversive power. It is on the basis of such a productive compromise that, for example, a rigorous thinker like Badiou reads Lacan through the latter's self-professed role of "anti-philosopher," and does not hesitate to call contemporary philosophers "only those who have had the courage to work through Lacan's anti-philosophy without faltering."[2] Having said this, I believe that the risk of a belated fashion for "Lacan soirées" and the hegemonic imposition of a "soft"— or simply mistaken—approach to his oeuvre is presently higher than ever in Anglophone university circles.

The starting point of this investigation into Lacan's theory of the subject must therefore coincide with the explicit assertion of a polemical program that tacitly informs this book from beginning to end: in contrast to what some commentators have recently suggested, the time for a "simple" exegesis of Lacan's work—which is often problematically opposed to its "dynamic usage"—has not passed. On the contrary, precisely insofar as certain quarters of academia have of late conferred citizenship upon Lacan and, despite the current renaissance of Lacanian studies, Lacan's (philosophical) reception has thus far been less than satisfactory, one is inclined to propose that the time for—serious—exegesis can now finally begin. . . .

Lacan has acquired the reputation of being unreadable, and while he is indisputably difficult to understand, it has rightly been observed that he is perhaps not so difficult. The present work takes its impetus from the disquieting supposition that incessant gibes about his irreverent style and openly contradictory pronouncements are usually nothing but an alibi for mental laziness; the inconsiderate critic who has not yet found the "unfaltering courage" advocated by Badiou should at least be humble enough to admit what two of Lacan's friends had the intellectual honesty to admit: as Lévi-Strauss confesses, despite sensing the importance of Lacan's theories, "I'd have had to read everything five or six times. Merleau-Ponty and I used to talk about it and concluded that we didn't have the time."[3] Interestingly enough, the position according to which "Lacan is impenetrable" (even after five or six readings) is adopted by two diametrically opposed types of scholars: aprioristic anti-Lacanians, for whom, as Chomsky stated, "Lacan was a conscious charlatan,"[4] and aprioristic pro-Lacanians, for whom Lacan is a kind of prophet who should be interpreted in a rhapsodic, semipossessed manner. In both cases, what is symptomatically rejected is the working hypothesis, if not the assumption, that Lacan is a paradoxically *systematic* thinker.

To paraphrase Žižek's defense of the Cartesian subject, one could therefore argue that the foreclosure of Lacan's "open system" forms the "silent pact of all [or at least some of] the struggling parties of today's academia."[5] Indeed, it is precisely this problematic aspect of Lacan's work that the "pro-Lacanian" call for an end to exegesis induces one to overlook by disdainfully bypassing any meticulous interpretation. Certainly, it would be naïve to suggest that there is a "true" Lacan who is waiting to be discovered; reducing the obscurities of his oeuvre does not mean eliminating them. But, above all, we should avoid detecting in Lacan's—astutely maneuvered and self-conscious—*pas-à-lire* any form of consent toward "wild interpretation," whether textual or clinical. (His profound aversion to Dostoyevsky's "God is dead; everything is permitted"[6] is well known, and forgetting it is simply inexcusable. . . .)

So why is Lacan a *paradoxically* systematic thinker? Because, despite formulating a highly elaborate and consistent theory, he decides to present it to us through the work-in-progress that leads to its emergence and to its continuous, fertile rediscussion (in his Seminars) as well as the inherent questions, doubts, and dead ends that *all* consistent, "closed," and completed philosophical systems end up silently confronting (in the Écrits and other written articles). After all, this is equally the reason why Lacan can appropriately define himself as an "anti-philosopher"; insofar as he demonstrates that "philosophy, while using much of the methodology of the sciences, has a tendency to gloss over incompleteness in its results [and] lacks the scientific ability to bear incompleteness,"[7] he exposes the hidden side of all philosophical systems. In parallel, it follows that, from this standpoint, an antiphilosopher is ultimately more "scientific" than a philosopher.

Against the background of such debates and controversies, the principal aim of this book is to analyze the evolution of the concept of subjectivity in the works of Jacques Lacan. More specifically, it endeavors to carry out a detailed reading of the Lacanian subject in its necessary relation to otherness according to the three orders of the Imaginary, the Symbolic, and the Real.[8] Although a significant part of this work shall be reserved for a detailed confrontation with the gestation of the notion of the subject of the Real (other) in the years between 1956 and 1963, it is nevertheless my intention to follow the chronological development of Lacan's theory of the subject from his first writings on the paranoiac status of the imaginary subject's knowledge (*connaissance*) in the early 1930s to his final formulations of the real subject's identification with the symptom in the mid-1970s.

If, on the one hand, it is clearly possible to divide Lacan's examination of the subject into three consecutive stages (imaginary subjectivity in the 1930s and 1940s; symbolic subjectivity in the 1950s; real subjectivity in the 1960s and 1970s), on the other hand, this book is mainly interested in emphasizing the continuity underlying these seemingly incompatible phases. Each "old" theory of the subject is recuperated within the framework of a "new" elaboration, and its fundamental tenets are retroactively reassessed—often without being refuted—from the perspective of a general psychoanalytic discourse which becomes increasingly complex.

Thus, the centrality of the so-called mirror stage in the formation of the subject's alienated imaginary identity (treated in Part I) is later subsumed under the linguistic reinvention of Freud's Oedipus complex as the precondition for the subject's symbolic identification (analyzed in Part II). Similarly, as we shall examine in Part III, the prevalence of the symbolic subject of the signifier is in turn both preserved and reevaluated when it begins to be measured against the stumbling block of the Real as that which is irreducible to the Symbolic. The same may be said for the role of otherness with respect to the subject: the function of the imaginary other is progressively subsumed under that of the symbolic Other, and the self-sufficiency of the Other is itself rethought in terms of a necessary interaction between symbolic and real otherness; yet, at the same time, these new contextualizations do not prevent the imaginary other and the symbolic Other from retaining most of their original characteristics.

"'So what about the subject? Where is he?' . . . Since it was a philosopher who asked this question . . . I was tempted to answer: 'I return the question to you, on this point I give the floor to philosophers. After all, it's not fair that all the work should be up to me.' The notion of the subject surely demands revision starting from the Freudian experience."[9]

On the basis of Freud's discoveries, Lacan outlines a revolutionary theory of the subject and, despite his relentless attacks against philosophy, repeatedly invites it to collaborate with psychoanalysis in order to build on his groundbreaking investigations. Unfortunately, such a call has largely gone unheard. Derrida's reaction is, in this case, paradigmatic; although he mistakenly criticizes Lacan for promoting a reactionary "phallogocentric" subject which supposedly reintroduces the metaphysics of presence, and unhesitatingly calls Lacan's thought a "system," he nevertheless deems it unnecessary to expose such a system.[10] This book moves from the opposite premise according to which, especially in light of the recent and widespread debate over a return of the subject in contemporary European philosophy, Lacan's psychoanalytic theory of subjectivity must be reconsidered as an innovative point of reference—one that was never satisfied with any structuralist or poststructuralist talk of a "death of the subject"—and, what is more, must carefully be expounded.

So what about the *Lacanian* subject? Where is he? In very general terms, one could suggest that, from the early 1960s onward, Lacan's subject amounts to an irreducible lack—the real other as the inherent impasse *and* precondition of the Symbolic—which must *actively* be confronted and assumed. Therefore, this notion of subjectivity is profoundly incompatible with any philosophy—from deconstructive *doxa* to certain mistaken readings of Lacan[11]—which limits itself to delineating the contours of a vanishing substanceless subject "at a safe distance": the Lacanian subject is a *subjectivized* lack, *not* a *lacking* subject or subject of impossibility, even though he presupposes the assumption and overcoming of a purely negative moment. As we shall see in the final chapter, this is valid both at the level of the child's entry into the symbolic order—the moment at which the purely negative lack of demand is reversed and positivized into the being of desire as lack-of-being—and at the level of the end of psychoanalytic treatment understood as a "deeper" assumption of lack.

The present work is primarily concerned with the subject who has attained a "normal" symbolic identification by successfully resolving his Oedipus complex. The most noticeable consequence of this approach is that it will not be possible to carry out a detailed comparison of the different models of subjectivity which Lacan deduces from the clinical categories he elaborates; this is particularly the case with regard to the separation of the two kinds of neurosis (hysteria and obsessional neurosis) and the way in which they should both be opposed to perversion. On the other hand, the necessity clearly to demarcate successful subjectivation from its complete failure will require a thorough consideration of the way the notion of psychosis evolves throughout Lacan's oeuvre.

There are two main reasons for my choice to restrict myself primarily to a study of the "normal" subject: first, the belief that any theoretical claim concerning specific clinical conditions should be supported by adequate psychoanalytic experience—which I do not possess and whose evidence would in any case lie beyond the scope of a book of philosophy. Here the reader should be reminded that whenever Lacan scrutinizes a clinical distinction, for example the distinction between neurotic and perverse forms of subjectivation, he unfailingly avails himself of case studies; despite their incontestable importance, philosophical, purely abstract formulations are in these instances usually confined to marginal remarks.

Secondly and more importantly, this book acknowledges that Lacan progressively questions the very existence of a "normal" subject. The border between "normality" and "abnormality" is gradually blurred; thus every inquiry into the former inevitably leads to the latter. In a sense, one might well argue that Lacan has left "normality" behind insofar as the "standard" version of subjectivation is made to overlap with what could be named a "forced neurotization."[12] Yet this universalization of neurosis does not alone suffice to account for the "abnormal" character of the "standard" subject. As we shall closely examine at the beginning of Chapter 4, after the recovery of a structural lack in the symbolic Other, Lacan also believes that all subjects are potentially psychotics, and can obviate this condition only by means of a "suture" which is epiphenomenal. From the standpoint of the symbolic structure, psychosis logically precedes "normality." In addition to this, in his late work Lacan regards perversion as a generalized hegemonic social structure (epitomized by the capitalist discourse) while, at the same time, the "standard" neurotic resolution of the Oedipus complex should itself be considered as a "père-version," a veiling of the lack in the Other.[13] To cut a long story short, one could conclude that the increasing difficulty of accurately delimiting a "normal" subject in Lacan's work is compensated for by the awareness that, for him, "normality" necessarily partakes of neurosis, perversion, and even psychosis.

On this point, the vicissitudes of the notion of desire are exemplary: throughout Seminars V and VI, although not without oscillations, Lacan still seems to rely on an underlying idea of "normal" desire which he often evokes but never fully elucidates.[14] Here "normal" desire is definitely opposed to neurotic desire—insofar as the latter is subjected to the demand of the Other—and as such tacitly overlaps with a no better specified notion of "pure" desire. When, in Seminar VII, "pure" desire is explicitly posited as "tragic" desire, Lacan is obliged to reassess his implicit identification of "normal" and "pure" desire. From this point on, the former will always be associated more openly with neurotic desire, and the neurotic subject will be normalized.

With these specifications in mind, Part I of this book focuses on the subject of the Imaginary, and provides a precise account of the way in which the ego comes to be defined as an imaginary function by Lacan. The ego corresponds to the subject's identifying alienation in the imaginary other and, given its narcissistic-specular nature, should not be confused with the subject of the unconscious. Although such an imaginary alienation is a noneliminable precondition of the subject as such, its utterly (self-)destructive tendencies can nevertheless be overcome only by the subject's introjection of the symbolic agency of the ego-ideal. Here, it is my intention to emphasize the way in which, according to Lacan's anti-Darwinian stance, the subject's disordered Imaginary is, first and foremost, proof of man's—contingently successful—"dis-adapted" evolution. On this general basis, in this part I also attempt a systematic confrontation with Lacan's early text "Les complexes famili-aux" (1938) which, ingeniously combining Hegelian dialectics with evidence drawn from ethological and psychological experiments, offers both a plausible psychological explanation of the child's chronological "stages" of psychosexual development and an initial, albeit fragmentary, thematization of the unconscious as an essentially symbolic structure.

Part II contains a systematic analysis of the subject of the Symbolic. In one and the same gesture, Lacan relates subjectivity to language understood as a structure, the symbolic order as the legal fabric of human culture, and the Freudian uncon-scious. The first chapter is concerned above all with the exploration of the famous Lacanian motto according to which "The unconscious is structured like a lan-guage." Here, I endeavor to illustrate the precise reason why, despite being articu-lated like language, the unconscious is not the same as ordinary conscious discourse. After this confrontation, the second chapter investigates in detail the way in which Lacan explains the individual subject's active entry into the Symbolic as the funda-mental Law of society and how, before such an entry, the child is completely sub-jected to the Other. This will also be the place to assess Lacan's thorough linguistic rethinking of the Oedipus complex, engaging in a close reading of Seminars IV and V; despite all successive theoretical innovations—most noticeably the preemi-nence given to the Real—Lacan's exhaustive discussion of the three forms of lack (frustration, privation, castration) as necessary preconditions for correctly under-standing the subject-object relationship accomplished by these seminars repre-sents one of the most important milestones of his theory.[15]

Although it is certainly the case that a—more or less convincing—description of the influence of structural linguistics on Lacanian psychoanalysis and of in-tricate notions such as the "quilting point," the "Name-of-the-Father," and the "phallus" is already available in countless introductory books, the originality of Part II of this book lies in its attempt to elucidate further the way in which these concepts systematically coalesce around a number of problematic questions. What is the difference between conscious-diachronic and unconscious-synchronic me-tonymy? Why is metaphor also said to represent a vertical quilting point? Is there a way to pinpoint appropriately the distinction between the Name-of-the-Father and the phallus?

Part III is the most extensive part of the book, and deals with the subject of the Real; more specifically, it attempts to demonstrate the way in which, after realiz-ing that the symbolic Other is structurally incomplete, Lacan gradually—and not without hesitations—reorganizes his theory of the subject of the unconscious on the basis of the notion of the fundamental fantasy as inextricable from the object *a*, the leftover of the Real in the Symbolic. In other words, the subject is now considered to be a "middle term between the real and the signifier."[16] The first chapter begins with a detailed analysis of the meaning of the formula "There is no Other of the Other," and argues strongly in favor of the suggestion that, in this case, Lacan radically reverses his previous "structuralist" reliance on a transcendent "Other of the Other," namely, the Name-of-the-Father as the "signifier of signifiers." This examination is paralleled by a meticulous scrutiny of the changing status of the order of the Real in the late 1950s; one can plausibly argue that, for Lacan, the "holing" of the symbolic Other results from, among other things, the necessity finally to thematize the Real in a more direct and convincing way. Here the focus of my analysis will be on the productive inconsistencies of Seminar VII, whose contradictory statements allow us to regard it as "in-between two Lacans." Moving on from these considerations, the second chapter investigates the subject of the Real as the subject of the fundamental fantasy, then raises the open question of how Lacan proposes individually to subjectivize the real lack beyond the dimension of collective (ideological) fantasies. This will first involve an examination of the notions of (death) drive and desire around the pivotal point of the object *a* as remainder and reminder of the Real (here, key passages from Seminars V, VI, and X will carefully be analyzed) and will finally lead, in the last two sections, to the issue of the "pleasure in pain" of *jouissance* to be understood primarily as the subject's structural enjoyment of the object *a*.

This book presupposes that Lacan's teachings subsequent to Seminar X should, first and foremost, be labeled under the heading of *jouissance*, and that such a classification makes it impossible to dissociate any serious consideration of his late theory of the subject of the Real from issues that are essentially ethical and political. Although the concluding sections pay considerable attention to the innovative aesthetic and ontological coordinates of the ethics of psychoanalysis as an ethics of the *ex nihilo*, as well as to the related deadlock of "pure" desire and its possible superseding through an antitransgressive individuation of *jouissance*, I am well aware of the fact that they function solely as a platform, albeit an indispensable one, for future research.

"Nothing goes unmarked by that powerful articulatory necessity that distinguishes [Freud's texts]. That's what makes it so significant when one notices places where his discourse remains open, gaping, but nevertheless implying a necessity."[17] This observation leads Lacan elsewhere to render explicit one fundamental methodological tenet of his exegetical approach to Freud's oeuvre: "To interpret even what is implicit in Freud is legitimate in my eyes."[18] In a similar fashion, I am convinced that any rigorous interpretation of Lacan's own works requires an equally legitimate "filling in of gaps": this is precisely the point at which a dedicated exegetical reading demonstrates its compatibility with considerable creativity.

It is well known that Lacan always defended his subversion of the psychoanalytic establishment by advocating a "return" to the true spirit of the Freudian revolution. Yet at the same time, he was also unequivocally working on a reinvention of psychoanalysis. Here the paradox is only apparent: his innovations were first and foremost based on a meticulous reading of the writings of the father of psychoanalysis; Lacan's inventive additions originated from his insistence on stubbornly confronting and overcoming the many deadlocks of Freud's oeuvre. In the same way, it is high time that "committed" Lacanians should acknowledge the need to *return to Lacan*.[19] Although such a return should not aim at dogmatizing his work—it is indeed essential to encourage a "dynamic usage" of Lacan in several contexts precisely in *opposition* to its "soft" dogmatization in feminist/cultural/ cinema studies—what is nevertheless indispensable in order properly to (re)direct this interdisciplinary endeavor is a detailed analysis of Lacanian concepts; in all likelihood this will also show that they are less deliberately elusive than they may initially seem. To sum up, it is important to persevere in a rigorous exegesis of Lacan's work precisely in the name of a loving fidelity to Lacan's *open oeuvre*, and of the theoretical respectability that must be accorded to its divulgation.

PART I

THE SUBJECT OF THE IMAGINARY (OTHER)

God gave them eyes so that they could not see.
Isaiah 29:10

CHAPTER 1

THE SUBJECT OF THE IMAGINARY (OTHER)

Lacan's first theory of subjectivity, as developed in the years between the publication of his doctoral thesis on "self-punishing paranoia" (1932) and the beginning of his famous seminar at Saint Anne's Hospital in Paris (1953), revolves around the subject's imaginary dimension. It is based upon a fundamental, aprioristic distinction, one that, despite many changes, will remain present in all of Lacan's successive theories of subjectivity: the ego is an imaginary construction, and it must be differentiated from the subject of the unconscious. As Lacan unequivocally asserts in Seminar I: "If the *ego* is an imaginary function, it is not to be confused with the subject."[1] Two elements clearly emerge from this straightforward statement: (1) the subject cannot be limited to the Imaginary; (2) one has to comprehend the manner in which the ego *qua* imaginary function works in order to avoid inadvertently confusing it with the subject (of the unconscious). A third, basic conclusion that remains implicit here but is often clearly expressed elsewhere should be drawn: the fact that the subject should not be "confused" with the ego *qua* imaginary function does not indicate that they are unrelated. On the contrary, it is Lacan's main objective to demonstrate how the ego is nothing but a *necessary* imaginary function of the subject, while arguing that the subject cannot be reduced to his imaginary dimension.

In this chapter, dedicated to the subject of the Imaginary as it is described in Lacan's early work, it is therefore my primary intention to provide a precise account of how the ego comes to be defined as an imaginary function. At this early stage of my discussion, it is also important to add that, in his first theory of the subject, Lacan is more concerned with disclosing the functioning of the ego than he is with delineating the structure of the subject of the unconscious that is irreducible to it: the latter emerges only in an indirect, negative manner as a consequence of what is attributed to the former. It is in fact only in the mid-1950s that the subject of the unconscious will be treated directly by Lacan in the context of a new theory of subjectivity that will shift the axes of his research from the order of the Imaginary to the Symbolic. From then on, despite the subsequent preeminence acquired by the order of the Real in the early 1960s, the subject of the unconscious will remain central to Lacan's later theory of subjectivity.

If on the one hand, in Lacan's early work, the distinction between the ego and the subject of the unconscious is, as I have pointed out, an a priori working hypothesis that is yet to be proved, on the other hand, it may properly be grasped only if it is considered from the very beginning as a critique of mainstream post-Freudian psychoanalysis (especially the so-called "ego psychology"). Authors such as Hartmann, Kris, and Loewenstein seemed in fact to maintain a substantial equation between the subject and the ego, to the detriment of the unconscious; in other words, in general, they appeared to understand psychoanalysis as a means of enabling the ego's "colonization" of the unconscious's "irrational" drives and instincts. This reading of Freud also allowed the invention of a socially "adaptive" function of psychoanalysis that Lacan often associates with what he defines as the "American way of life": the analysand's ego had to be "cured" and reinforced by being reshaped in the image of the analyst's strong ego.[2]

Lacan considers ego psychology to be a tacit but radical betrayal of Freud's theoretical subversion, whose main tenet, according to him, is the subject's predominantly unconscious nature, and the consequent displacement of the ego from the central function in psychic activity attributed to it by both Cartesian philosophy and classical psychology. Freud's view that the ego is not a mental substance is supplemented by Lacan with the assertion that neither does it correspond to the supreme synthesizing psychic locus of what Freud named the "perception-consciousness system."[3] In other words, according to both Freud and Lacan, the psychic agency of the ego has to be subordinated to the logic of a more primitive "layer" of subjectivity. This is precisely what the experience of psychoanalysis manages to show empirically: that there is an unconscious subject whose reasoning, far from simply being identifiable with sheer irrationality, does not coincide with the ego—nor, as will later become clearer, with the ego-related dimension of self-consciousness—and which manifests itself in phenomena such as dreams, bungled actions, slips of the tongue, and psychosomatic symptoms.

It is therefore within this historical framework that Lacan's unrelenting call for a "return to Freud" should be understood—a return that intends first and foremost to emphasize the narcissistic-specular and consequently alienating and derived nature of the ego, together with the impossibility of constraining the subject within its boundaries. The ego is not the subject tout court; on the contrary, it corresponds to the subject's identifying alienation in the imaginary other (an other that initially corresponds to the subject's specular image): in parallel, psychoanalysis does not aim at strengthening the ego but instead at realizing the subject of the unconscious through the overcoming of imaginary alienation. The next two sections of this chapter will deal primarily with the ego as the site of such an alienation, while the final section will outline the contours of Lacan's first and as yet only fragmentary thematization of the unconscious to be understood as a symbolic structure.

1.2 "JE EST UN AUTRE": THE (DE)FORMATIVE FUNCTION OF THE IMAGE AND THE MIRROR STAGE

At this stage, the distinction between the ego and the subject outlined above should be reformulated in more specific terms: in the first place, it is correct to maintain that Lacan recognizes that the subject's imaginary identity lies literally outside of himself. It corresponds to a paradoxically alienated identity. In other words, the ego lies outside (what is generally thought to be) the (self-contained identity of the) ego.[4] This is why, in these years, Lacan often refers to Rimbaud's motto "*je est un autre.*" Consequently, the ego, to be understood as the subject's imaginary identity, cannot directly be equated with the individual: the ego *qua* imaginary identity individuates the subject only by way of a detour through the other.

Two fundamental issues have to be raised in order to clarify this point: (1) How is this imaginary *alienation* of the subject in the other achieved? (2) In what sense does it provide the subject with his imaginary *identity*? These two questions could be expressed in one: how can the image (of the other) be considered as a source of alienating psychic identification for the subject? In "On Narcissism: An Introduction,"[5] Freud had already emphasized how the baby's psychic development depends upon his being captured by images (both of his mother's body and of his own body). Lacan reworks this Freudian theme and attributes a "morphogenetic" function to images—that is to say, he believes that certain images are able to exercise a (de)formative power over the subject's psyche; given their importance, he also deems these images—or, more correctly, *imagos*—to be the precise object of psychoanalytic theory.[6] According to Lacan, imaginary identification occurs in the subject through the unconscious assumption of an external image (initially of the subject's own body as reflected in a mirror) in which he recognizes himself. Therefore, identification does not imply the mere influencing of the subject by an external image or an imitative relationship between the latter and a preexisting ego: on the contrary, the ego can first be created only because the image irremediably "traps" the subject. It is in this sense that Lacan defines imaginary identification as *psychically causal*: the ego is a psychic agency caused in the subject by his alienating identification with a series of external images. The ego is an other, since the *imagos'* (de)formative power absorbs and captures the subject. Lacan uses the term "*captation*" to describe this process: as Evans has noted, this term could be rendered in English as both capture—the subject is in fact *necessarily* attracted by the external image that alienates him—and captivation—given that, as we shall later see in more detail, this inevitable capture *fascinates* the subject by providing him with a primal, though alienated, form of identification.[7] The ambivalent status of the Imaginary is recognized by Lacan himself when he states that the ego is a "*vital dehiscence* that is constitutive of man":[8] in his first theory of the subject, this is the principal paradox upon which both subjectivity and human life *tout court* are based.

In order to produce a more precise account of the genesis of the ego, it is convenient to refer to Lacan's famous theory of the mirror stage (dating back to 1936), which rigorously delineates his notion of the subject's alienating imaginary identification. According to Lacan, an original alienating identification occurs for the child during the so-called mirror stage: such a primordial experience founds what both Freud and Lacan define as the Ur-Ich, the primal basis upon which the ego will later emerge. The mirror stage establishes a structural psychic dialectic between the subject and the other that serves as a model for the entirety of the subject's many chronologically successive imaginary identifications: the ego is nothing but their sum total at a given point in time. Therefore, it is not too much of an exaggeration to maintain that, by means of the continuous acquisition of new imaginary identifications corresponding to different crucial moments in the subject's psychic life, the mirror-stage experience is repeated indefinitely throughout one's existence due to the imaginary relationships that are established with other human beings.[9]

Lacan's theory of the mirror stage relies primarily on evidence drawn from various psychological experiments.[10] These have shown that a child of between six and eighteen months old recognizes himself in the image of his own body as it is reflected in a mirror. Moreover, this recognition produces a clearly observable "jubilation" in the child. The subject recognizes himself in the otherness of the specular image: in so doing, he undergoes a redoubling through which he is able to objectify himself in the mirror, to identify himself with an imaginary other. It is important to note that this specular image does not need to be provided by a mirror: the image of another child of approximately the same age will also be perceived by the subject as a specular image, that is to say, without recognizing the other as other.

Imaginary identification can consequently be said to be alienating by definition; in addition to this, the alienated ego also fails to recognize its own functioning. Thus, a double misrecognition (méconnaissance) takes place: in fact, the ego not only, as it were, "finds itself" at the place of the other (the first misrecognition: the ego is alienated) but also provides the subject with a deceptive impression of unity (the second and most fundamental misrecognition: the ego does not recognize itself as alienated). According to Lacan, it is the ego that makes me accept as true that I am myself and the other is the other. This was Descartes's conclusion in the Meditations, and it explains his statement that madness consists in believing oneself to be other than one is ("they think they are kings when they are really quite poor, or that they are clothed in purple when they are really without covering").[11] Lacan undermines this argument on its own grounds by asserting that it is no more crazy to believe oneself to be a king when one is not than it is to believe oneself to be oneself.[12] The ego makes us believe that we are isolated, solitary spherical beings, deaf and dumb as planets, as Lacan suggests elsewhere.[13]

At this stage, we should be able to clearly demonstrate why the subject cannot be reduced to the ego. The latter is a (false) unity consisting of an extensive macro-image in which various (ideal) images are overlaid and amalgamated, and which the child comes to confuse with (what turns into) "himself"; this self/ego has thus to be considered as a passive, mental *object*. The ego becomes an *inertial* object, since it fails to accept its dialectic.[14] Hence, we can conclude that the subject cannot be reduced by any means to the ego, simply because the latter is actually an object. This unreceptive hypocrisy, this primordial autism, corresponds to the "madness" of the ego; consequently its paradoxical truth emerges precisely in "ordinary" madness, where any dialectic between the subject and the other is even more radically put into question: the most succinct definition of a psychotic in Lacan's first theory of the subject would be someone who is stuck at the mirror-stage, and therefore fails to recognize the other as other. Lacan thus includes madness in the basic structure of human subjectivity: psychosis is no longer understood as an organic deficiency but as a possibility open to all human beings.

But why is the subject captivated by the image of his own body in the first place? It is only by answering this question that we can truly understand the genesis of the ego. I shall now provide a detailed description of the theoretical reasons which, according to Lacan, justify his explanation of the phenomena observable in the mirror stage:

(1) Lacan accepts one of the principal tenets of *Gestalt* theory according to which an animal is instinctively predisposed to recognize the image of the body of another animal of the same species as a whole, and is consequently attracted by it. It is only thanks to *Gestalten* that an animal's sexual reproduction is made possible: reproduction is necessarily associated with the lures of the Imaginary.[15] Lacan thinks that human instincts also function via *Gestalten*, but in a distorted way: in fact, such a distortion makes it impossible to consider human drives as mere natural instincts. In other words, man has a "disordered imagination":[16] his later claim according to which there is no human sexual relationship should also be related to such a disorder. These arguments constitute the only significant biological reference of Lacan's psychoanalytic theory.

(2) In what way is the functioning of *Gestalten* distorted in human beings? In general, Lacan thinks that man is, by definition, a disadapted animal: this is a view he will never abandon, and one which leads him to criticize Darwin. Human beings' astounding psychic development and the emergence of language and culture that it made possible are far from being the result of a particularly successful adaptation of the species:[17] on the contrary, "man's relation to nature is altered by a certain dehiscence at the heart of the organism."[18] More specifically, according to Lacan, human disadaptation is primarily due to the fact that all human beings are born *prematurely*; as he remarks, such a physiological prematurity of birth is especially noticeable in "the objective notion of the anatomical incompleteness of the

pyramidal system [of babies]."[19] In other words, human babies cannot walk, and are absolutely dependent on adults to carry out all basic vital tasks: adopting Freud's terminology, Lacan defines this prolonged "primordial Discord" as a state of helplessness (*Hilflosigkeit*). In parallel, human babies demonstrate a precociously refined power of vision. It is precisely against this background that the peculiarly (de)formative function of the human *Gestalt qua* specular image has to be understood: the completeness of the subject's body image as reflected in the mirror provides him with a form of unity that compensates for human helplessness. Yet at the same time, the attraction exercised on man *qua* animal by the *Gestalt* acquires for him a completely different meaning: animals instinctively "recognize" other animals, and are thus able to carry out basic vital processes, but they do not alienate themselves in the image. On the other hand, man identifies himself with the specular image in order to make up for his original helplessness.[20] This is why Lacan states that "the mirror stage is a drama whose internal thrust is precipitated from insufficiency to anticipation":[21] that is to say, *organic* insufficiency (helplessness) is supplemented by an *ideal* imaginary unity. Such an anticipated form of mastery— which makes the baby rejoice—is a "drama," as Lacan says, if not a tragedy, since it necessarily superimposes alienation upon identification, thus making it forever impossible for the subject to achieve the perfect self-identity of the external alienated image with which he identifies. To put it differently, the imaginary alienating identification that attempts to remedy original helplessness renders man an even *less* adapted animal: in order to carry out his species-oriented sexual functions, he will then need to undergo a readaptation that, as we shall see later, can only be culturally mediated by what psychoanalysis calls "complexes."

(3) The alienating identification with the specular image is rapidly "precipitated," as Lacan says, since, in concomitance with the capture or captivation operated by the mirror image, the baby also experiences a simultaneous image of his own body's fragmentation; this can be understood either as a transposition of the baby's organic deficiencies into the Imaginary or as an intraimaginary comparison between the completeness of the specular image as perceived by the baby and the *partial* vision that he necessarily has of his own body—indeed, one can never directly look at one's own body as a whole. This particular point of Lacan's theory of the mirror stage is usually overlooked, if not misunderstood: the "orthopedic" action of the unity provided by the specular image of the body does *not* follow a stage in which the baby experiences his body as fragmented. The two *imagos* can only emerge together.[22] The baby recognizes the fragmentation of his real body only when he starts to be attracted by the completeness of his specular image. The anxiety provoked by the experience of his real fragmentation accelerates the subject's alienating identification with the mirror image. But it is precisely in the psychic

dialectic between the fragmented body and the unity of the specular image as experienced by the subject that the genesis of the ego is to be sought: the primordial ego (Ur-Ich) as the alienating *identification* with the specular image corresponds to the misrecognizing stagnation of such a dialectical process, which nevertheless continues its activity. This is why fantasies of fragmentation may reemerge in some formations of the unconscious such as dreams and, at an organic level, in certain hysterical psychosomatic symptoms.[23]

(4) The primordial ego as a mental object is thus the product of a reification that follows—if not chronologically, then at least logically—the first movement of a psychic dialectical process. The specular image in which the subject alienates himself in order to acquire a unity is *introjected* by him and forms the primal basis of his ego. However, the relationship between the subject and the external perfection of the specular image will always presuppose an irreducible dialectical tension. All this means that if, on the one hand, the mirror stage allows the subject to individuate himself as ego, on the other, the emergence of the ego constitutes the primary source of the subject's alienated status, since it is based on an alienation in the other, that is to say, a structural disjunction between the ego and the subject. The image that institutes the subject as an ego is the same image that separates the subject from himself. Despite the achievement of an (alienated) identification, the specular image thus represents an unattainable ideal image for the subject: the Lacanian name for this ideal image is *ideal ego*. Given that what takes place at this point corresponds to the repetition at a higher level of psychic development of the first dialectical relation between the fragmented subject and the specular image, one could also state that the ideal ego is nothing other than the specular image as experienced by a subject whose ego is by now at least partially formed. As we shall now see in more detail, if the ego is introjected by the subject, the ideal ego is in its turn *projected* by the subject *qua* ego onto all other subjects as well as onto all objects.

1.3 HAINAMORATION, IDEAL EGO AND EGO-IDEAL

The primordial ego corresponds to the first alienated stratum of our imaginary identity, the product of an original alienating redoubling of the subject caused by his capacity to identify himself with his mirror image (or with the imaginary other understood as a mirror image). Such an identification relies on the fact that the subject is captivated by the image of the human body that functions as a *Gestalt*. The Ur-Ich thus attempts to realize an impossible coincidence with the ideal image reflected by the mirror: given such an impossibility, this relationship ends up in a permanent rivalry of the subject with himself, with the narcissistic image of himself that the lure of the mirror creates. Such a rivalry is already evident at the level of the dialectic between the subject's perception of his fragmented body and his parallel vision of the completeness of the specular body:[24] it continues after the constitution of the Ur-Ich and successively consolidates itself in concomitance with the progressive reinforcement of the ego's alienating identifications. In other words, from the beginning of his psychic life, the subject both eroticizes and vies with his own image, since it constitutes the ideal perfection which the subject does not have. Narcissism and aggressivity are thus one and the same thing; in later years, Lacan creates a neologism in which "being in love/enamored" (enamouré) and "hate" (haine) are fused in a single term: he speaks of hainamoration.[25] Narcissism can generally be defined as the (self-loving) relationship between the subject and his own ideal image; aggressivity differs from sheer aggression, which is merely violent acting: the latter is just one of aggressivity's possible outcomes. Aggressivity itself is, rather, a precondition of the subject's imaginary dimension, and can never be completely eliminated.[26] "Aggressivity is the correlative tendency of a mode of identification that we call narcissistic, and which determines the formal structure of man's ego and of the register of entities characteristic of his world."[27] As a consequence, the augmentation of aggressivity will be proportional to the narcissistic intensity of the subject's relationship with his own ideal image; this is why Lacan writes that aggressivity (especially) "underlies the activity of the philanthropist, the idealist, the pedagogue, and even the reformer."[28] The subject who, when considered as an ego, is nothing but the consequence of an alienating identification with the imaginary other, wants to be where the other is: he loves the other only insofar as he wants aggressively to be in his place. The subject claims the other's place as the (unattainable) place of his own perfection. It goes without saying that, for the same reason, this ambivalent relationship is also self-destructive.

Lacan had already pointed this out in his doctoral thesis on self-punishing paranoia: in certain forms of paranoia, by attacking an admired person with whom she ideally identifies, the psychotic is actually attacking herself: in this way she punishes herself for not being able to achieve her ideal image. In self-punishing paranoia, the psychotic "strikes in her victim her own exteriorized ideal. . . . With the same blow that makes her guilty before the law, [she] has actually struck herself."[29] As we have already seen, psychosis provides us with the clearest evidence of a psychic process that is effectively operative, to different degrees, in all subjects. According to Lacan, the ego is essentially paranoiac because it always necessarily mistakes itself for the other. The same applies for all knowledge that is related to the ego:[30] imaginary, ego-logical connaissance—which Lacan will later clearly distinguish from symbolic savoir—is in fact based on a structural misrecognition (méconnaissance) which precedes it. However, a nonpsychotic subject obviously differs from a psychotic who remains caught in the mirror stage for the entirety of his life: this is due to the fact that a nonpsychotic subject can also transcend the imaginary alienation of his ego—which will nevertheless always remain present in the background—and interact with other subjects through the mediation of a reciprocal symbolic recognition made possible only by speech.

Some further points must now be developed:

(1) The subject directs narcissistic and aggressive feelings toward his ideal image both during and after the mirror stage: in other words, an ambivalent love–hate relationship between the subject and his ideal image is established independently of whether or not he is able to recognize the other as other. After the formation of an Ur-Ich in the mirror stage, the subject is still not able to recognize the other as other: therefore he directs his ambivalent desire either toward the specular image provided by the mirror or toward another subject of the same age who is actually perceived as a mere mirror image (this is clearly observable in phenomena of so-called transitivism: a child who slaps another child on his right cheek can then start to cry while touching his own left cheek). Once a more developed form of ego emerges through repeated introjections—through a more permanent stagnation of the dialectical process between fragmented body and ideal image which contemporaneously allows the subject for the first time to superimpose on his ego a sense of (fake) self-consciousness—the subject is finally able to recognize the imaginary other as other. (This change, as I shall later specify, is highly problematic and ambiguous in Lacan's early thought.) From then on, despite this newly acquired capacity, the ego will nevertheless continue to be involved in an ambivalent relationship with the other. Despite recognizing the other as other, the ego will nevertheless, to a certain extent, continue to confuse him with his ideal image. The subject qua ego continuously competes with the other by projecting his ideal ego onto him. The ideal ego always accompanies the ego. In everyday life, what I see in the other is nothing but my own ideal image (ideal ego), which I both love and hate: the eyes of the other indeed reflect my own specular image. . . . Lacan is particularly interested in highlighting, beyond the mirror stage and the intrasubjective phases of the subject's psychic development, the intersubjective, sociopolitical dimension of aggressivity: in our preeminently aggressive society, "war is proving more and more to be the inevitable and necessary midwife of all progress."[31] As he emphasizes in the concluding section of "Aggressivity in Psychoanalysis" (1948), it is fundamentally in terms of radical narcissistic aggressivity that key political events of the twentieth century such as the Nazis' search for Lebensraum and the race for the conquest of (outer) space must be understood. In one of the most intense passages of Seminar I, Lacan thus concludes that, at the imaginary level, "every human function would simply exhaust itself in the unspecified wish for the destruction of the other as such."[32]

(2) The fact that the subject *qua* ego continuously projects his own ideal image—that is to say, his ideal ego—onto the external world not only affects his relationship with other human beings but also heavily conditions his (mis)apprehension of all external objects. As I have already said, imaginary knowledge (*connaissance*) is for Lacan structurally paranoiac: this is "the most general structure of human knowledge," and "constitutes [both] the ego and its objects with attributes of permanence, identity and substantiality, in short, in the guise of entities or 'things.'"[33] Lacan can therefore speak explicitly of a "*hominization of the planet*"[34] that is valid for both natural and manufactured entities. It is indeed clear that by continuously projecting his own ideal image onto the external world, man "anthropomorphizes" animals and other organic beings; for Lacan, an animal can be individuated only by man's imaginary projections—that is to say, only if man manages to see the image of man in the animal, as it were. On the contrary, an animal *qua* individual is in itself "always already dead," in that it exists only to serve the reproduction of its species.[35] With regard to "the world of [man's] own making," Lacan reminds us that "it is in the automaton that [it] tends to find completion."[36] This clearly epitomizes the basic "hominizing" character of technology. The imaginary dimension that determines technological production should at this point also throw new light on the way in which technological progress is inevitably bound for aggressivity and war. More generally, according to Lacan, the entirety of the external world, both manufactured and natural objects, should be considered as a "statue in which man projects himself."[37] The individuation of organic and inorganic beings alike is possible only on the basis of an underlying imaginary anthropomorphization.

(3) In his first theory of the subject, Lacan clearly distinguishes the notion of *ideal ego* from that of *ego-ideal*: such a difference was already indicated by Freud, but he failed fully to elucidate it. In general, if the ideal ego is a projection of the ego's ideal image onto the external world (equally onto human beings, animals, and things), the ego-ideal is the subject's introjection of another external image that has a *new* (de)formative effect on his psyche. In other words, the ego-ideal adds to the ego a new stratum that provides the subject with a secondary identification. The subject reiterates here the first dialectical movement which he had initially carried out by introjecting the specular image that gave rise to the primordial alienating identification of the Ur-Ich.[38] More specifically, the ego-ideal is, in the first instance, the consequence of the subject's identification with the *imago* of the father, which alleviates the aggressive-narcissistic solipsism of the ego by making the subject enter the symbolic plan of the Law; thus Lacan can state that the ego-ideal lies at "the joint of the imaginary and the symbolic."[39] Secondary identification (post-

Oedipal identification) has a "pacifying function."[40] The highly sophisticated functioning of this process cannot be described in detail here; it will be described in Chapter 3, where I shall analyze the importance of (the resolution of) the Oedipus complex as it is more rigorously reelaborated in Lacan's later theory.[41] For the time being, it must be noted that the ego-ideal necessarily remodels any further projections of the ideal ego: if, on the one hand, the ideal ego is logically prior to the ego-ideal,[42] on the other, it is inevitably reshaped by it. This is why Lacan, following Freud, says that the ego-ideal provides the ideal ego with a "form."[43]

(4) The distinction between ideal ego and ego-ideal enables us to make some points regarding narcissism and love. Commentators have often stated that Lacan's early works present us with a uniquely pessimistic notion of love, which is easily reducible to imaginary narcissism. I would claim, rather, that, already in his first theory of the subject, love transcends the imaginary order due to its proximity to the emergence of the ego-ideal. More specifically, I believe that, even though it is legitimate to speak of imaginary narcissistic love, it is nevertheless important to point out how, for Lacan, the object of narcissism is not, strictly speaking, the same as the object of love. This may be seen from the straightforward observation that we do not indiscriminately fall in *love* with every imaginary other that we encounter.[44] Lacan manages to provide this empirical phenomenon with the outline of an explanation. He suggests that the loved object does not merely correspond to the object upon which I project my ideal ego (the latter is indeed projected onto *all* objects, since it constitutes them), it is not simply the object toward which my aggressive narcissism is directed. On the contrary, *the loved object is that object which causes the ideal ego to be projected in a particular way.* The loved object is introjected by identification: it is thus connected to the ego-ideal which modifies the ego, adding a "new stratum" to it and readjusting each of its further projections, each new ideal ego. In Seminar I, Lacan states that the ego is an onionlike object which "is constructed out of its successive identifications with the loved objects which allowed it to acquire its form": the pertinence of this metaphor is self-evident.[45] In the same Seminar, Lacan also unequivocally suggests that there is an "exact equivalence" between the love object and the ego-ideal.[46] To put it in simpler terms, we could conclude that at this stage, for Lacan, to love somebody means to expose one's narcissism to the influence of the beloved: in other words, the consequence of loving is being narcissistic in a particular manner, that is to say, projecting our newly reshaped ideal ego onto all outer objects after it has undergone an alienating identification with the beloved. . . . It is therefore correct to maintain that love ultimately superimposes a new ego-ideal onto a preexisting ideal ego (in love "the *Ichideal*, considered as speaking, can come to be placed in the world of objects on the level

of the Idealich").[47] For the same reason, it is also correct to maintain that love disturbs the symbolic functions of the ego-ideal ("Love provokes . . . a perturbation of the [symbolic, pacifying] function of the ego-ideal").[48] Consequently, if, on the one hand, love is not, strictly speaking, identical with narcissism, on the other, it is nevertheless the case that the subject remains entrapped in a narcissistic psychosexual economy (even after he has entered the Symbolic/Law). Having identified with the beloved, the lover aggressively projects the image of the beloved—which is never "pure," since it is added to a preexisting ideal ego—onto all other objects, including the beloved herself.

The entirety of Lacan's imaginary dialectic should now be more intelligible; the introjection of the ego as an alienating identification with the specular image is followed by the projection of the unattainable perfection of this specular image as an ideal ego onto all outer objects, which in its turn is followed by the introjection of an ego-ideal (initially provided by the imago of the father): the ego-ideal symbolically reconfigures all successive projections of the ego. Clearly, the subject can then be attracted by a new love object after he has entered the Symbolic/Law. Every new love will correspond perfectly to the intervention—at the imaginary level—of a new ego-ideal. The opposite is not true: a new ego-ideal is not merely loved since it operates primarily at the symbolic level, and it is only because of its original symbolic status that it can successfully reshape the subject's Imaginary, which would otherwise remain immutable. To conclude, we must note that the secondary identification provided by the father embodies only the first of several possible ideals (according to Lacan's later elaborations, any symbolic object can function virtually as an ego-ideal—and as a love object). However, the first ego-ideal, that provided by the father, remains a fundamental one—and all others depend on it—in that it allows the subject to enter the symbolic dimension of the Law, to recognize the other through speech and, as a consequence, partially to transcend imaginary (self)-destruction.

(5) The notions of narcissism and imaginary love also serve as a background for Lacan's first resumption of the Hegelian–Kojèvian dictum according to which "Desire is the desire of the other." At this early stage, the formula can already be interpreted in a variety of ways. As one of Lacan's students efficaciously points out in Seminar I: "You say the desire of the other. Is it the desire which is in the other? Or the desire that I have for the other? For me, they are not the same thing. [This formula can relate to the] desire in the other, which the ego can recapture by destroying the other. But at the same time it is a desire which it has for the other."[49] Lacan promptly acknowledges that the formula "is not valid in only one sense,"[50] and can mean that desire is both (a) an imaginary desire on the basis of which the subject qua ego desires what the other desires, and consequently aims at aggressively destroying the other

("desire in the other"); and (b) a symbolically mediated desire which makes the subject desire the other: *he desires that the other recognize and desire him*—his desire—and in order to do so he can recognize the other only by temporarily overcoming aggressivity, by entering/accepting the mediation of the symbolic Law through speech ("desire *for* the other").[51]

And the formula has yet another sense—one that Lacan tends not to distinguish explicitly from the first, but one that is nevertheless presupposed by his overall theory of the imaginary subject. "Desire is the desire of the other" should also be referred to a *primitive* desire which would be a desire for the other at the imaginary level: I desire the other since the other is the locus of my alienating identification (my primordial ego), he usurps my place and I want to eliminate him. This level is strictly related to the first, but the first does not map onto it exactly. Why? Because in this last case I do not want to destroy the other because he *has* the object of my desire; on the contrary, I want to destroy him because he *is* the object of my primordial desire: the other *qua* specular image literally stands in my place, there where I desire to be a unity, and supersede alienation. In other words, the first two readings of the formula that Lacan provides us with both presuppose a clear distinction of the ego from the other, while this last reading—logically the first— presents us with the subject's desire at a stage when he cannot yet make such a distinction (the mirror stage). Desiring what the other desires (the first reading of the formula) corresponds to a narcissistic, destructive desire that nevertheless presupposes an initial, minimal recognition of the other as other: such a recognition can occur only when desire is enacted according to the second reading of the formula. Indeed, in this case, I desire what *the other* desires; we could define this desire as an intrasymbolic imaginary desire. To put it in simpler terms: having recognized the other as other, I do not desire to *be* the other—with whom I identify— but I desire what the other desires, or, I contradictorily desire to be exactly like the other *without* wanting to be (the) other.[52]

All this amounts to emphasizing once more the problematic status of the passage from the purely narcissistic reality of the mirror stage to the point at which the child is for the first time able to recognize the other as other. I believe that in his early theory of subjectivity Lacan is not able to solve this deadlock satisfactorily, mainly because his notion of the Symbolic is here only embryonic. His arguments on this topic are often incongruous. For example, in Seminar I he seems to suggest that the child becomes able to distinguish his ego from the other as other when he is around eighteen months old, at the moment of the dissolution of the mirror stage, that is, long *before* recognizing the desire of the other through (the resolution of) the Oedipus complex.[53] From what we have just seen, logically this cannot be the case. I believe Lacan is obliged to adopt this position since, here, he is still attempting to reconcile his philosophically indebted theory of the Imaginary with a plausible psychological explanation of the child's chronological "stages" of psychic development: for instance, he has to defend his dialectical claims against the empirically evident fact that a child seems to be able to distinguish himself from his siblings well before reaching the age of five (when, according to psychoanalysis, the Oedipus complex is usually resolved). It is therefore not surprising that in his later theories of identification, Lacan will always consider the discussion and, more specifically, the temporalization of pre-Oedipal phenomena as senseless if they are not retroactively understood on the basis of the Oedipus complex qua permanent symbolic structure of the subject. More generally, it is important to note how, despite its marginal thematization in Lacan's early works, desire clearly constitutes the primary force underlying all the subject's imaginary dialectical movements. This is why Lacan speaks of a "see-saw of desire"[54] made of successive projections and introjections.

1.4 Consciousness, the Unconscious, and the Complexes

One last dialectical movement still awaits explanation in Lacan's theory of the subject's imaginary psychic development. It is indeed clear that the subject's introjection of the ego as the primary (alienating) identification (Ur-Ich) has to follow—if not chronologically, at least logically—a primordially unconscious projection/representation of the (other's) body image as such. Imagos must somehow be "produced" by the subject: as a matter of fact, Lacan defines them as "unconscious representations."[55] It might be useful to observe here that in his early work Lacan seems to understand the unconscious in terms of intentionality (even though he never fully develops this). This is why, whenever he contends with Freud's statement according to which the ego should be considered as a synthesizer of the "perception-consciousness" system, he is implicitly suggesting that such a system should instead be understood primarily in unconscious, intentional terms. Referring to Merleau-Ponty's *Phenomenology of Perception*, Lacan proposes that one of the primal tasks of psychoanalysis is phenomenologically to "consider all [unconscious] experience lived before any objectification as well as before any reflexive analysis that mixes objectification with experience."[56] Lacan rethinks phenomenological intentionality in terms of un-*conscious*, anti-objectifying experience.[57] In other words, the un-conscious cannot be limited to what is excluded from self-consciousness, and is consequently somehow dependent on it: on the contrary, psychic activity is *in general* un-conscious and only limitedly self-conscious—that is to say, the unconscious *qua* specific locus of the repressed is only a subset of the un-conscious *qua* general psychic activity.

Lacan is proposing nothing less than the un-consciously intentional nature of the Freudian perception-consciousness system *tout court*. For this same reason, he thinks it is impossible to reduce consciousness (that is, un-conscious "lived experience") to the opaque nature of the ego as an object. What about *self-consciousness*? Does it have to be equated with the ego? At this stage it should be clear that, according to Lacan, there is no self-consciousness if by "self-consciousness" we mean a kind of consciousness that is fully present to itself. We could say that the ego is identical to self-consciousness only if we specify that this "self" is achieved exclusively through an alienating identification with the other. Lacan's often apparently contradictory statements with regard to this topic must therefore always be referred to the following conclusion: either there is no self-consciousness at all (as fully present to itself), or "self"-consciousness corresponds to the *alienated* ego. On these same grounds, Lacan is also able to speak of consciousness in terms of a "polar tension between an *ego* ['self'-consciousness] alienated from the subject and a perception which fundamentally escapes it, a pure *percipi*":[58] in other words, consciousness *qua* un-conscious perception continues its activity even after the initial formation of the ego (this is in fact how the ego-ideal can be introjected). We could suggest that the unconscious *stricto sensu*, the unconscious to be understood as the locus of what is expelled from self-consciousness, is precisely the product of such a "polar tension" between the ego and the unconscious as "pure *percipi*."

As I have just proposed, *imagos* as (exceptional) images cannot obviously exist independently from the subject, and must therefore initially be represented by him. We should now more specifically explain just how this occurs *despite* their (de)formative power. One could say that, according to Lacan, they are more constitutive than constituted: in other words, if he does not deny that they are constituted by the subject, the fact remains that they are substantially different from normal images (which is why psychoanalytic theory uses the Latin term to designate them). Only very few particular images correspond to unconscious representations that have a (de)formative power over the subject's psychic development. But from where does such a (de)formative power derive? It is obtained from complexes to be understood as fundamental, unconscious structures of interpersonal relationships: this is how Lacan understands the rational nature of the unconscious in his early work.[59] The subject finds his place in this pregiven symbolic structure through the action of *imagos* as unconscious representations. Freud tended to consider complexes as (phylo)genetically transmitted from generation to generation, that is, as innate; Lacan refuses to relegate the efficacy of *imagos* to the sphere of instincts, even though, as we have seen in the case of the Gestaltic nature of the specular *imago*, instincts undoubtedly have a certain relevance. Not without oscillations, Lacan regards the (de)formative power of *imagos* as *culturally mediated*.[60] The subject unconsciously "possesses" and projects a privileged image—an *imago*—that in its turn (de)forms him, since it is already embedded in the Symbolic: "*Imagos* are images which are already assumed in the symbolic order and are consequently capable of 'symbolic efficacy.'"[61] This is certainly true for the *imago* of the father on which Lacan's first theory of the Oedipus complex depends.

In "Les complexes familiaux," Lacan discusses three basic and successive complexes, all revolving around the (de)formative function of three different *imagos* that dictate the subject's early social interactions in the context of his family: the weaning complex, the intrusion complex, and the Oedipus complex. The weaning complex involves the primordial relationship established between a newborn baby and his mother. This structural interpersonal relationship is based on the maternal attentions that aim to compensate for the helplessness of the baby caused by the prematurity of his birth; thus the birth is considered by Lacan as an "ancient weaning" to be distinguished from weaning *stricto sensu* (that is, delactation).[62] The baby accesses the complex by way of an alienating identification with the *imago* of the breast. It is clear that Lacan transposes here the logic with which he has already explained the mirror stage. By identifying with the breast, the baby attempts to continue intrauterine life after having been born prematurely;[63] in parallel, he initiates "a metaphysical mirage of universal harmony"[64] that will always accompany him. In other words, through this identification the baby both establishes a feeding relationship which allows him not to starve and finds himself irremediably alienated in the other. If, on the one hand, the relationship between baby and mother is implicitly thought by Lacan in terms of *Gestalten*—and therefore as instinctual—on the other hand, he is interested primarily in underlining how the mother's attentions go well beyond satisfying the baby's essential needs, and should therefore be understood in cultural terms.[65]

With the intrusion complex, Lacan provides further proof of the importance of the mirror-stage theory while relocating it to a wider context. This complex finds expression in the relationship that is established between the child and his sibling, whom he considers as a rival. As a result, the structure of the interpersonal relationship on which the complex is based is jealousy; the subject accesses it by an alienating identification with the *imago* of the counterpart (*semblable*) understood as a specular image. I must emphasize that it is only with the resolution of the intrusion complex that the child is able to recognize the other as other, to acquire a "self"-conscious ego. Lacan thus distinguishes an "identifying jealousy" (*jalousie par identification*)—the intraimaginary rivalry between the subject and his specular image provided either by the mirror or by another human being—from a (minimally) extraimaginary jealousy between two subjects when they relate to a third object, that is, intrusion *stricto sensu*. Jealousy is in this last case described as the "archetype of all social feelings," given that by recognizing the other "with whom either fights or contracts are started," the subject "finds at the same time . . . the socialized object."[66] Even in this text, Lacan fails to demonstrate clearly how such a fundamental change occurs.

Finally, the Oedipus complex takes place between a child of three to five years of age and those persons around him who embody the maternal and paternal function. Its basic structure involves love for the parent of the opposite sex and rivalry with the parent of the same sex. If, on the one hand, Lacan, unlike Freud, recognizes the cultural relativity of the conjugal family on which this relationship is based in modern and contemporary Western societies, on the other, he reaffirms the universality of the resolution of the Oedipus complex to be understood as the prohibition of incest and consequent emergence of Law (together with a concomitant possibility of transgressing it).[67] The subject resolves this last complex by an alienating identification with the *imago* of the father from which he derives his ego-ideal; the ego-ideal is only one consequence of the subject's entry into the Law, the other being the superego as repressive agency, which is also brought about by the *imago* of the father.

In his early works, Lacan repeatedly and explicitly speaks of psychoanalysis in terms of a *dialectic*: I believe this claim must be taken quite at face value. In fact, not only does Lacan attempt to read Freud's psychoanalytic *technique* in dialectical terms,[68] he also develops a new psychoanalytic *theory* that audaciously combines Hegelian philosophy with the evidence drawn from ethological and psychological experiments to provide us with a highly original theory of the subject's psychic development. The strict, if not forced, dialectical geometry of such a process is generally overlooked by Lacanian commentators. On the contrary, I believe that its rigor is strikingly evident in the succession of the three complexes as presented in "Les complexes familiaux." According to Lacan, the introduction of a complex—which in different guises compensates for the subject's persistent helplessness—always follows a biopsychical crisis,[69] and precedes the resolution of the complex itself to be understood as a new crisis. To use Hegelian terminology, it is possible to state that every complex qua synthesis (*Aufhebung*) that allows the unfolding of a particular stage of psychic development (*qua* thesis) follows a crisis *qua* antithesis/negation and precedes a new, "higher" crisis (*qua* new antithesis). Prematurity of birth must consequently be considered as a primordial crisis/antithesis; the weaning complex, which compensates for it, provides the subject with an initial synthesis and an initial development of the psyche, whereas weaning stricto sensu (delactation) introduces a new crisis/antithesis (which corresponds to the resolution of the weaning complex—weaning in the broad sense of the word). The intrusion complex which follows it—"identifying jealousy," the aggressive narcissistic relation of the subject with the specular image, equally directed toward other siblings of the same age—must be understood as a new synthesis/thesis which is then interrupted by intrusion *stricto sensu*, the recognition of the other as other. Intrusion *stricto sensu* thus constitutes a new crisis/antithesis and the solution of the intrusion complex. Finally, the Oedipus complex is a new synthesis/thesis that implies the love for the parent of the opposite sex from the standpoint of a subject whose (alienated) ego is by now clearly able to separate itself from the other. The resolution of this complex in the prohibition of incest achieved by the threat of castration—which Lacan refuses to read in terms of a real threat and understands, rather, as a resumption of the image of the fragmented body[70]—constitutes a new crisis/antithesis. This is in turn followed by a new synthetic identification with the *imago* of the father (the introjection of the ego-ideal).

It is evident that, throughout this process, psychic synthesis (*Aufhebung*) simultaneously annuls, preserves, and raises to a higher level a permanent psychic opposition. The subject's psyche develops in parallel. Imaginary alienation, originally determined by prematurity of birth, never ends. Man remains a disadapted animal. He never attains the homeostatic zero at which the animal's psyche is set, a zero that should also be applied to the animal's sexual life: animal instincts are in direct relation to their object, while man breaks the "immediate adaptation to the environment that defines the animal's world by its innateness [*connaturalité*]," he interrupts the "living being's unity of functioning which, in the animal, submits perception to instincts."[71] However, man's disadaptation—which is also sexual— is equaled by his outstanding psychic capacities; as Hyppolite notes in one of his numerous interventions in Seminar I: "Knowledge, that is to say humanity, is the failure of sexuality."[72] Lacan believes that readaptation, a—never complete—redirection of man's narcissistic and (self)-destructive ego libido toward the genital object (and therefore to the accomplishment of his animal task with respect to the species), is made possible only by the mediation of (the resolution of) the Oedipus complex, that is to say, culturally. In Seminar I, Lacan distinguishes primary narcissism from secondary narcissism, and indicates the way in which they correspond to two forms of libido. Primary narcissism depends on *Gestalten*, and is therefore valid for animals and man alike: it corresponds to sexual libido. Secondary narcissism is, rather, the consequence of the alienating identification(s) produced by the *Gestalt* of the human body for the human psyche: thus it corresponds to ego libido, that is to say, narcissism *stricto sensu*. Here Lacan is making two fundamental claims: (1) *all* libido (even animal, sexual libido) is narcissistic in essence insofar as it depends on the imaginary function of the *Gestalten*; (2) more importantly, man can carry out the tasks of his animal, sexual libido only if he partially overcomes the self-destructive tendencies of his ego libido (directed toward the ideal ego). This can be achieved culturally only by the introjection of the ego-ideal that resolves the Oedipus complex: the ego-ideal can be said to represent a paradoxically symbolic readaptation of man's disadapted libido, a symbolic palliative for a "disordered imagination." For the early Lacan, man's uniqueness is determined more by the Imaginary than it is by the Symbolic.

But what does Lacan mean more precisely when he claims that the Oedipus complex is both cultural and structural?[73] As we have seen, he is denying that it is based on instincts. If, on the one hand, natural instincts are universal by definition—man's defective Imaginary obviously constituting an exception to this rule—and, on the other, all cultures are particular—being characterized by particular laws—Lacan's main issue regarding complexes could be circumscribed by the following question: is there a universal Law of culture? He thinks he can answer this positively by indicating the prohibition of incest: all cultures—despite their particular laws—have somehow to universally distinguish themselves from nature. The prohibition of incest as universal Law of culture not only distinguishes culture from nature but also somehow "naturalizes" culture, provides culture with a universal *structure*. However, Lacan refuses to accept Freud's idea according to which cultural structures (the Oedipus complex and its possible variations) are transmitted (phylo)genetically from one generation to another. He agrees with Freud that the transmission of the Oedipus complex cannot be dependent upon the specific contingencies of a given familial situation (otherwise the structure would risk not being universal), but he also believes that if transmission were genetic, then culture would become nature and complexes would be mere instincts. For Lacan, culture structurally modifies human nature, "naturalizes itself," as it were, by becoming universal, while at the same time preserving its distinction from nature (this is another way of viewing the fact that the gap between man and animal can never be completely filled); holding such a view is possible only if one hypothesizes the existence of an unconscious cultural structure, the Oedipus complex, upon which the functioning of human instincts (drives) depends. As Miller writes: "It is as if he—Lacan—said to himself 'Freud thought he could ground his concept of complexes in instinct, and I'm going to do just the opposite. I'm going to take the concept of complex as primary and clarify the concept of [human] instinct on its basis.'"[74]

To conclude, it must be noted that, in "Les complexes familiaux," the uncon-scious as a symbolic structure is not yet explicitly thematized in terms of language. It is also clear, however, that such a thematization, which is the main topic of my next chapter, is prepared by Lacan's work on complexes: this work undoubtedly presents us with his first formulation of the symbolic order understood as a *rational* unconscious structure. In the mid-1950s, Lacan's overall psychoanalytic theory undergoes a radical reformulation which can be summarized by the dictum "The unconscious is structured like a language." In this new context, only the Oedipus complex will be preserved. However, *imagos* will still be considered to have a (de)formative function: despite all the changes in Lacan's theory, this will remain the only explicit biological reference of his teaching as a whole.[75]

PART II

THE SUBJECT OF THE SYMBOLIC (OTHER)

To read coffee grounds is not to read hieroglyphics.
Lacan, Seminar III

CHAPTER 2
THE UNCONSCIOUS STRUCTURED LIKE A LANGUAGE

"From the small to the big Other": this is how Jacques-Alain Miller—editor of the Seminars—entitled a fundamental series of lessons that Lacan gave during the first semester of 1955. Such a motto deserves special consideration, since it effectively captures a much more general turning point in Lacanian thought. Beginning with Seminar II (1954–1955), Lacan capitalizes the Other, and proceeds to elaborate an innovative theory of the subject. In brief, the big Other may be equated with: (a) *language* as a structure (as in structural linguistics); (b) *the symbolic order* as the legal fabric of human culture (in accordance with Lévi-Strauss's anthropology); (c) *the Freudian unconscious* as reformulated by Lacan in his widely promoted return to its original, subversive signification. Despite their mutual superimpositions, it would be misleading to immediately assume that these three notions perfectly overlap. The subject of the Other can appropriately be grasped only by clearly defining these three vertices. This is the main aim of the present chapter and the one that follows.

With particular reference to the notion of subjectivity, Lacan's new interest in the big Other corresponds to a shift in emphasis from the formula "The ego is an other" to the formula "I is an Other."[1] Having almost exclusively concentrated on what the subject was *not* (the ego), Lacan's theory becomes more constructive: first and foremost, the subject is now positively identified with the subject of the Other. On the basis of my initial claim, the latter should be understood equally as: (a) the subject of language; (b) the subject of the Symbolic; and (c) the subject of the unconscious. If, on the one hand, it is relatively easy to see, even at this early stage, how the first two relate to each other (how could the symbolic Law that founds human society not be related to human language as something uniquely distinct from a mere animal code?),[2] on the other, the link between language (along with the Symbolic) and the unconscious is not so immediately apparent.

Let me attempt to provide a preliminary, partial explanation of this relation here. The subject of the unconscious is, for Lacan, both the *unconscious* subject, a psychic agency that is opposed to the agency of consciousness (or, better, self-consciousness), and the subject *of* the unconscious, the subject *subjected* to the unconscious. The fact that the conscious subject is subjected to the unconscious can initially be explained by answering the following naïve question: why does psychoanalysis take the trouble to think about the unconscious in the first place? The answer is to say that an unconscious *topos* separated from consciousness must exist because something which is not conscious tangibly manifests itself within consciousness. What is more, these manifestations, the so-called "formations of the unconscious," are far from "irrational": they can be seen to follow certain regular patterns, which Freud had already considered to be fundamentally linguistic.[3]

Consequently, we could at least infer that the conscious subject is partially subjected to an unconscious structure (the Other) that appears to be closely related to language (qua Other).

In parallel, we should recall how everyday conscious experience shows us that the subject is normally subjected to language: the subject finds himself always-already immersed in language. In other words, the specular, alienating identification of the subject with the imaginary other necessarily presupposes an earlier, original—and perpetual—alienation in the Other qua language. This fact does not obliterate Lacan's earlier explanation of imaginary alienation: the subject's imaginary alienation is, rather, redoubled by an alienation in language which—logically, if not chronologically—precedes it. To cut a long story short, the mirror stage occurs after the baby has been given a name and the persons surrounding him have started to talk about him (which indeed they do even long before the child's birth).[4]

Moving from these broad premises, my analysis of the subject of the Other will proceed as follows: in the present chapter, I shall primarily be concerned with the exploration of the famous Lacanian dictum according to which "The unconscious is structured like a language." In stark contrast to what is implicitly proposed by those commentators who restrict themselves to a superficial analysis of Lacan's appropriation of the Jakobsonian linguistic laws of metaphor and metonymy, I will try to demonstrate that, despite being regularly articulated like language, the unconscious is not the same as ordinary (conscious) discourse. The unconscious "isn't a language in the sense in which this would mean that it's a discourse . . . but is structured like a language."[5] In Chapter 3, I shall move on to confront in detail the ways in which Lacan explains the individual subject's active entry into the Symbolic as the fundamental Law of society. In other words, this will be the place to assess Lacan's thorough linguistic rethinking of the Oedipus complex.

These two chapters can be said roughly to correspond to the two main axes of Lacan's investigations during his so-called "structuralist" period. I shall, for my part, generally refrain from labeling this phase of his production in such a way. It is my intention, however, to show by other means how it remains possible to circumscribe this part of Lacan's oeuvre. This will be done at the beginning of Chapter 4. Clearly, the notion of structure has a huge importance for Lacan, especially during the period between 1953 and 1958, but I believe his militancy in the structuralist movement is, at best, a heterodox one. The reason for this is simple: as Lacan unambiguously states in Seminar V, precisely at the apex of his alleged involvement with structuralism, "subjectivity is not eliminable from our experience as analysts."[6]

As a result of the shift in focus from imaginary alienation in the small other to linguistic alienation in the big Other, Lacan is able to propose the thesis that the subject undergoes a "twofold alienation."[7] That is to say: "There is the other as imaginary. It's here in the imaginary relation with the other that traditional *Selbst-Bewusstsein* or self-consciousness is instituted. . . . There is also the Other who speaks from my place, apparently, this Other who is within me. This is an Other of a totally different nature from the other, my counterpart."[8] One could correctly argue that Lacan deals with the issue of the subject's alienation in the big Other in two significantly different manners during the 1950s. This dissimilarity does not necessarily amount to an incompatibility between two alternative speculations but should, rather, be regarded as proof of a theoretical evolution in Lacan's theory of the subject of the Other. Particularly in his seminal article "Function and Field of Speech and Language" (1953), Lacan suggests that alienation in language can successfully be overcome; this achievement would also enable the subject to overcome imaginary alienation and its narcissistically destructive tendencies. According to this text, the function of so-called "full speech" would consist in actively overcoming *individual* alienation in *universal* language through psychoanalytic treatment.[9] The key reference for Lacan here is Hegel's dialectics as mediated by Kojève. On the other hand, a few years later, in his article "The Agency of the Letter in the Unconscious" (1957)—as well as in Seminars IV and V—Lacan appears to assume that alienation in language cannot be overcome. In other words, the subject's individual speech is irremediably subjected to the universal field of language, and to its laws. Lacan's key reference for this second phase—which will be treated in the next two sections of this chapter—is Saussure's structural linguistics, largely in the form of Jakobson's reelaboration.

It is now important to analyze in greater detail what, according to Lacan, alienation in language consists of. I shall begin by considering this issue from the standpoint of speech. In the early 1950s, Lacan is primarily interested in explaining the relationship between language (*langage*) and speech (*parole*). To put it succinctly, speech (*parole*) corresponds to the actual execution of a language in an individual subject. As we have already noted, Lacan believes that the subject is necessarily alienated in language insofar as language already exists before his birth and insofar as his relations with other human beings are necessarily mediated by language. But how is the fact that language precedes the subject—and, above all, imposes itself as an irreducible mediator of the subject's relation with other subjects—automatically linked to the fact that he is *alienated* in language?

(1) Lacan begins from a very clear-cut empirical observation. First of all, the subject is alienated in language because he never manages to say exactly what he really wants to say. His interlocutor is unable to grasp fully what the subject actually means to tell him: words do not suffice to convey the subject's desire appropriately, and consequently fully to satisfy it. At the same time, the subject's individual speech—his perpetually addressing a counterpart in discourse[10]—also always says *more* than the subject wants to say. The counterpart can read in the subject's words something that he did not intend to tell him. (Furthermore, the counterpart is usually unaware of his interpreting beyond the subject's conscious intention.)[11] Lacan believes it is precisely the thematization of such a surplus of speech with respect to conscious intention that led Freud to discover the efficaciousness of the "talking cure," psychoanalytic treatment. Before Freud, Lacan argues, "intention was confused with the dimension of consciousness, since it seemed that consciousness was inherent to what the subject had to say qua signification [*signification*]."[12] In simple terms: before Freud, it was assumed that the subject could consciously say what he wanted to say. The mistaken equation between intentionality and consciousness (the fact that the unconscious was overlooked) relied precisely on the unquestioned equation between consciousness and signification. On the basis of Freud's confutation of both these equations, Lacan deduces the existence of a (universal) "wall of language" that prevents each subject from fully speaking with the Other. For the time being, the phrase "speaking with the Other" should be understood both as the subject's unconscious *full speech* about his true desire, and as the subject's speaking to the Other unconscious subject. I shall later attempt to elucidate how, from the standpoint of the unconscious, this is a spurious distinction.

(2) From the same empirical recognition of the misunderstandings caused by language in speech, Lacan comes to the conclusion that linguistics is correct in distinguishing a subject of the *statement* (roughly attributable to language) from a subject of the *enunciation* (roughly attributable to full speech). To put it bluntly, the "I" which functions as the grammatical subject of a given statement may not be identified with the "I" which carries out this *act* of speech. The former is nothing but the linguistic correspondent of the ego. The alienating "wall of language" overlaps with imaginary alienation: it is nothing but the latter's transposition into words. That is, the subject of the statement corresponds to the objectified *pendent* of the ego in the realm of language. More precisely, as Fink has lucidly observed, "the personal pronoun 'I' designates the person who identifies his or herself with a specific ideal image. Thus the ego is what is represented by the subject of the statement."[13] Lacan defines the speech of such an I as *empty speech*: consequently, empty speech is nothing but speech alienated in language, subjugated to its imag-

inary deformation. In everyday life, human beings communicate through empty speech.[14]

(3) Lacan extends to every subject the Freudian concept of the Ich-Spaltung (confined by Freud to the pathological sphere of fetishism and the psychoses) precisely by referring to the linguistic distinction between the subject of the statement and the subject of the enunciation. The subject undergoes a split (Spaltung) "by virtue of being a subject only insofar as he speaks."[15] In speech and because of speech, the subject is never fully present to himself. That which is not present in the statement but is presupposed and evoked by it (the enunciation) indicates the locus of "another scene" in the subject: the subject of the unconscious which, as I have already indicated, depends on specific linguistic laws, and sustains a particular "thought."

(4) The discovery of a structural split in/of the subject subverts the Cartesian cogito while, at the same time, revealing its intimate relation to psychoanalysis. As Lacan repeatedly states, "I think where I am not, therefore I am where I do not think."[16] This is to say that the unconscious I, the subject of the enunciation, really thinks at the unconscious level: it (ça) thinks where the I qua ego and qua subject of the statement is not (conscious). Conversely, the I qua linguistic ego is (conscious) where it, the unconscious subject, does not think. Most importantly, the subversion of the Cartesian ego shows that its illusion of unity is possible only because of its strict interdependence with the Spaltung. There is no self-consciousness without the unconscious, and vice versa. Descartes's formulation of a fundamental principle of self-consciousness could be said contemporaneously to decree, at the level of the history of thought, the formal birth of the unconscious (although this birth will remain implicit until Freud). Consequently, it is strictly speaking senseless to speak of a pre-Cartesian notion of the unconscious.[17]

(5) The strong interdependence between the Cartesian ego and the Freudian unconscious indicates, for Lacan, that the subject of the unconscious is not simply an alternative ego,[18] concealed by repression. Neither does the subject of the unconscious correspond to any sort of "unknowable substance"[19] that would represent the buried core of one's repressed desires, and would simply be awaiting liberation from the constraints of Cartesian self-consciousness.

In "Function and Field," Lacan affirms that the subject's alienation in language—empty speech as delineated above—can be superseded by full speech. The latter's emergence coincides with the subject's assumption of his unconscious desire. It is also clear that, in this article, Lacan superimposes truth upon unconscious desire.[20] How can this realization of the unconscious be achieved? Lacan opposes the specular dialectic of a desire based on the ego's imaginary alienation to the symbolic dialectic of a desire conveyed by the function of full speech. To cut a long story short, full speech is able to offer the subject a different, non-narcissistic satisfaction of his desire. Beyond the emptiness of speech that accompanies ego-logical imaginary objectifications, the subject is constantly speaking with his unconscious, even if he is unaware of it. One should then ask the following naïve question: what does the unconscious subject say, and what does he want? He (unconsciously) addresses the Other (subject) so that the truth about his speech—the specificity of his unconscious, repressed desire—may be recognized by the Other. This is what full speech fundamentally is: more precisely, it corresponds to the subject's full assumption of a speech which he normally utters without being aware of it. Consequently, full speech is inextricable from symbolic intersubjectivity,[21] which is indeed in turn—as I have already outlined in Chapter 1—inseparable from mutual recognition of one's desire and the related dimension of pact as the instauration of the Law. To quote Lacan: (a) "[Full] speech is the founding medium of the intersubjective relation"; (b) "We must start off with a radical intersubjectivity, with the subject's total acceptance by the other subject"; (c) there exists a common "function of recognition, of pact, of interhuman symbol."[22] It is therefore clear that, in the early 1950s, Lacan's notion of the Symbolic is profoundly indebted to the Hegelian-Kojèvian principle for which human desire corresponds to the desire to be recognized by the Other.

It should equally be clear by now why, according to Lacan, an actual return to Freud's original discoveries entails a resumption of the often underestimated *practical* importance of speech in psychoanalytic treatment, in contrast to the importance bestowed on the subject's physical reactions during the course of treatment by many psychoanalytic schools. Psychoanalysis aims to symbolize through full speech the imaginary identifications that objectify the subject in his ego.[23] More precisely, in the specificity of the analytic setting, the general, apparently unspecified symbolic desire for recognition—which implicitly underlies all everyday intersubjective interactions insofar as they presuppose the symbolic dimension—is transformed by the analyst into a recognition of the analysand's particular imaginary alienating identifications that ensnare his individual unconscious desire. Psychoanalysis should therefore dis-identify the subject from his imaginary identifications. Dis-alienation can be attained only through dis-identification. Dis-alienation—from imaginary identifications and, therefore, also from the imaginary "wall of language"—will ultimately coincide with an integration of the individual's desire (for symbolic recognition of his unconscious desire) into the universal Symbolic. At this stage, Lacan appears to believe that unconscious desire can be fully realized: it is enough for it to be recognized by the

Other (subject). A calibrated orthopedics of (mutual) recognition is thought to suffice to dis-alienate desire. As I shall soon attempt to show, such an optimistic solution seems, at least partially, to contradict Lacan's continual warnings against ingenuously conceiving of the unconscious as a "true" substance which should be substituted for the ego.

2.3 THE NOTION OF MESSAGE

Lacan relates the notions of full and empty speech to his well-known dictum according to which "The sender receives his own message back from the receiver in an inverted form."[24] Here I intend to demonstrate, through a close reading of this formula, that for Lacan what is really at stake in its varying significations is the gradual passage from an *individual* conception of the unconscious revolving around the notion of speech to a *transindividual* one revolving around the notion of language.

On an initial level, one could simply argue that the sender (subject 1) automatically receives his message back insofar as, as a matter of fact, the sender always hears himself speaking. As Lacan himself states, "the sender is always a receiver at the same time, . . . one hears the sound of one's own words."[25] No doubt this is a direct consequence of the subject's linguistic *Spaltung*, his being split between the subject of the statement—who "intentionally" sends the message to another subject—and the subject of the enunciation—who always hears and records the "full" message expressed in the statement, even though "it's possible [for the subject of the statement] not to pay attention to it."[26] Such an explanation of the formula, however, fails to account for the "inversion" which, according to Lacan, is imposed on the message when it is received back by the sender. What does "inversion," a term which in his early work Lacan normally applies to the imaginary phenomenon of transitivism, stand for in this context?

According to a first *intersubjective* interpretation of the formula of message, we can suggest that inversion corresponds to the fact that the symbolic message of the Other (*qua* Other unconscious subject 2) is necessarily received by subject 1 through the imaginary inversion of the ego-other relation. The symbolic relation conveyed by full speech is interfered with by the "wall of language," which derives from the imaginary relation. To put it differently, the unconscious message of subject 2 is not normally assumed by subject 1: it remains latent. In this sense, inversion is *negative*. It corresponds to the alienation in language to which the subject is relegated in everyday life. As Lacan writes: "The imaginary relation, which is an essentially alienated relation, interrupts, slows down, inhibits and . . . inverts . . . the relation of speech between the subject and the Other, the big Other, insofar as it is *another subject*."²⁷ In other words, here inversion means that the subject can receive the message of the Other only as an ego founded on an alienation in the imaginary counterpart.

Having said this, I believe that inversion does not necessarily have to be negative. According to Lacan, there is a *positive* form of inversion, one that has to be related to the specific context of the psychoanalytic setting. In parallel, I would claim that positive inversion should be associated with the formula of the message in the precise wording which Lacan gives to it: "The sender receives his own message back from the receiver in an inverted form." Positive inversion applies to an *intrasubjective* interpretation of this formula.

But let us proceed with order. Let us be more precise as to what occurs in the psychoanalytic setting. Why can inversion also be considered as positive? Briefly, the analyst enables the analysand to receive his own unconscious repressed message (his desire) back by suspending the "wall of language." This can be achieved by the analyst's refraining from occupying the position of the imaginary counterpart. The analyst sends back to the analysand the latter's own (initially empty) message in an inverted, full form—that is, he makes the analysand assume his full speech. One could thus suggest that, for Lacan, successful analysis manages to *invert imaginary inversion*: the analysand's own message as empty, imaginary, inverted speech is itself inverted by the analyst who places himself in the position of the Other. It is important, however, to underline how the (analyzed) subject will still receive his own message with his ego. This is the only way in which the subject, as an individuated subject, can receive any message whatsoever. Despite this, analysis achieves the temporary suspension of the alienating mediation provided by the imaginary counterpart. The subject *qua* ego receives his message directly from the Other, to be understood as the subject's own unconscious embodied and refracted back by the analyst due to the suspension of the latter's own ego during analytic treatment.

To recapitulate: I have attempted to show how the fact that, according to Lacan, all messages are invariably received by the subject in an inverted form has to be interpreted in two different ways:

(1) at an *intersubjective* level, the message of the Other is always received in an inverted form. This corresponds to negative inversion;

(2) at an *intrasubjective* level, thanks to psychoanalytic treatment, the sender is able to receive back, to assume, *his own* unconscious message. This corresponds to positive inversion.

In addition to this, it is important to indicate how the formula "The sender receives his own message back from the receiver in an inverted form" is also valid outside the psychoanalytic setting. If, on the one hand, it is only at the end of psychoanalytic treatment that the subject is able to assume his message after it has been intentionally sent back to him by the Other (qua analyst), on the other, in everyday life he continuously receives his message back from the Other, but is unable to assume it. Who is this Other who (unintentionally) sends the message of the subject back to the subject, without the latter's being aware of it? This question is only apparently banal; it actually deserves particular consideration, since it lets us grasp how, according to Lacan, the unconscious message exists independently of any clear-cut distinction between sender and receiver (subject 1 and subject 2).

Ultimately, for Lacan, beyond the imaginary dimension, one can never be said transitively to communicate a meaning. Communication (of a message) and meaning are superimposed on one another: there is no meaning as an independent object circulating in the communication (of a message) established between two subjects.[28] Conversely, there is no communication (of a message) which is not always-already inscribed in meaning. In other words, we are dealing here with a *transindividual* unconscious that differs from both intrasubjectivity, the unconscious as the "Other who is within me," and intersubjectivity, the unconscious of the Other subject. As Lacan points out in Seminar III, "the unconscious . . . *this sentence*, this symbolic construction, covers all human lived experience like a web . . . it's always there, more or less latent."[29] The idea of an "individual" unconscious—on which both intra- and intersubjective accounts of the unconscious are based—makes sense only if the Symbolic is associated with the Imaginary. More importantly, we should emphasize that what is finally at stake in the notion of message is the passage from an unconscious understood as the *Other of speech* (which always presupposes the individual subject) to an unconscious understood as the universal, nonindividuated *Other of language* (which, as we shall see in the next section, relies on the linguistic notion of the signifier and the structural laws that govern it). As Žižek has noted: "It is the decentered Other [language as such] that decides the true meaning of what we have said."[30]

I suggest that the gradual imposition of a transindividual notion of the unconscious has important repercussions for another well-known Lacanian dictum of the 1950s, according to which "The unconscious is the discourse of the Other":[31]

(1) When the Other still refers to the (unconscious of the) Other individual subject, the formula means that the subject's unconscious is the product of the *speech* that individual subjects, including the subject in question, have addressed to him.

The child's unconscious is formed by the speech of those who surround him as well as by his own.

(2) As soon as the Other is understood as a nonindividuated locus, the formula means that what appears—from an imaginary standpoint—to be the "individual" unconscious of one given subject cannot actually be dissociated from *language as such*. It is in this sense that the unconscious is at times said to lie "outside" the subject. As a consequence, "The unconscious is the discourse of the Other" can equally be rendered as "The unconscious (which is structured like a language) is the Other." It would, however, be wrong to equate Lacan's transindividual unconscious with any sort of quasi-Jungian archetypal unconscious—"collective" by definition. The former corresponds to a symbolic *signifying* structure; the latter coincides with the pregiven *signification* of a set of primordial images. For Lacan, the unconscious as signifying structure produces conscious signification. Jungian psychoanalysis reverses this Freudian principle: it is the unconscious as primordial signification that produces the linguistic structure.

In the final part of this section, I intend to argue that the emergence[32] of the notion of a transindividual unconscious—as universal structure of language—renders explicit the covert paradox on which Lacan's conception of the aim of analysis as the individual subject's realization of his own true, unconscious desire through full speech was implicitly based. In fact, if on the one hand Lacan repeatedly warns us against misinterpreting the unconscious as a subjective hidden substance, on the other, at this stage of his production, he does not seem to realize that the full realization of the subject's substanceless unconscious would inevitably correspond to its utter desubjectivization into a substantial structure. Adopting Lacan's own contemporaneous definition of psychosis, we could argue that this would inevitably correspond to a "being passively spoken by language," language to be understood as the transindividual locus of the unconscious. In other words, Lacan's notion of an individual unconscious that would be equated with full speech seems to give rise to a vicious circle: the aim of analysis is to overcome empty speech and the imaginary wall of language, but, in parallel, the more one's *individual* speech is symbolized, the more it is integrated into the *transindividual* symbolic dimension of language. Language is never imaginary *per se*: the wall is erected solely by the individual subject's own imaginary identifications. Once these are fully revoked, the subject is absorbed by language, the transindividual unconscious. I do not believe it is possible to reconcile this dis-identifying de-subjectivization with the optimism evoked by the pseudo-Hegelian "humanist" leitmotiv of dis-alienation as presented by Lacan in "Function and Field."[33]

It is important, however, not to oversimplify Lacan's notion of full speech (as subjective unconscious truth). In "Function and Field," as well as in the first two Seminars, full speech as truth is a *retroactive* creation which did not exist prior to psychoanalytic treatment. As Lacan puts it, full speech corresponds to a *secondary historicization* that actualizes the symbolic meaning (*sens*) of repressed signifiers, not to the banal recovery of a preexistent imaginary forgotten signification (*signification*) already organized in the form of a conscious sentence.[34] Nevertheless, truth is instituted only insofar as repressed signifiers are recovered. Truth, which is the realization of the subject's desire, merely depends, for Lacan, on the elimination of repression, on the analyst's recognition of full speech through interpretation. If this is the case, then we are again dealing here with the paradox I mentioned above: the complete overcoming of repression, the subject's complete assumption of his own unconscious full speech, entails the disappearance of the individual unconscious and, in parallel, the disappearance of individual self-consciousness. To the best of my knowledge, Lacan never openly problematized this serious impasse in his work from the early 1950s. He does not point out the way in which the recovery of repressed signifiers and the consequent psychoanalytic articulation of truth via retroactive historicization has a meaning, both theoretical and therapeutic, only if we assume that *something has to remain repressed*; without repression, fully symbolized individual speech would transform itself into transindividual language.

In his concise and generally accurate description of full speech, Evans seems to propose a way out of this impasse: according to him, Lacan is aware that "full speech is not the articulation in speech of the whole truth about the subject's desire, but the speech which articulates this truth *as fully as possible* at a particular time."[35] On that basis, one could easily infer a viable explanation of how full speech differs from psychotic "being spoken by language." In psychotic "speech," the unconscious turns out to be fully "out in the open,"[36] which means, strictly speaking, that the psychotic has no unconscious, given that, by definition, the unconscious is constituted by a gap between what is repressed and what is "out in the open."[37] On the other hand, in full speech the truth about unconscious desire can only *partially* be assumed, and in no way can this assumption ever be fully completed. This would coincide with the asymptotic point at which full speech becomes psychotic delusion.

Evans's isolated statement is substantially correct, but a chronological problem persists; his argument cannot properly be applied to "Function and Field." This is irrefutably demonstrated by the terminology of the notions that the article adopts and promotes: if Evans's argument could be applied to "Function and Field," the very notion of "full speech" would prove to be self-refuting. In fact one would be obliged to conceptualize a full speech which is never actually full. . . . A rather senseless question would then follow: when does empty speech stop being empty and become partially full? What does "as fully as possible" mean? I believe Lacan will confront the deadlock generated by the notion of full speech, and will consequently discuss the importance of primal repression, only in later years, having reassessed the Other *qua* language through the linguistic notions of signifier and signified.[38]

2.4 SIGNIFIER, SIGNIFIED, LETTER

In an apparently trivial passage of Seminar III, Lacan summarizes in rapid succession what he believes to be three fundamentally divergent notions of language. According to the first, which Lacan defines as "naïve," "there is a superimposition, like a tracing, of the order of things onto the order of words." As for the second, "it's thought that a great step forward has been made by saying that the signified only ever reaches its goal via another signified, through referring to another signification [*signification*]." This notion of language is implicitly made to correspond with Saussure's. The third notion of language is Lacan's own: "This [the second notion] is only the first step, and one fails to see that [another] is needed. It has to be realized that without structuring by the signifier no . . . meaning [*sens*] would be possible."[39] Lacan thus both recognizes his debt to Saussure and marks his distance from the linguist. Saussure is correct in claiming the mutual dependency of signifieds, the differential structure of language, but he is incorrect insofar as he fails to emphasize the supremacy of the signifier over the signified.

In this section, I shall begin by explaining the Saussurian notions of signifier and signified, and the way in which Lacan reformulates them. I shall then proceed to clarify the way in which the link between signifiers and signifieds is, for Lacan, organized by the (Jakobsonian) laws of metaphor and metonymy. Finally, and most importantly, I shall attempt to clarify what the dictum "The unconscious is structured like a language" means if one assumes that the unconscious consists of signifiers. Here, I shall primarily be interested in analyzing the way in which the unconscious "structured like a language" functions. In Chapter 3—focused on Lacan's rereading of the Oedipus complex as the subject's active entry into the big Other *qua* symbolic order of Law and culture—I shall explore how the unconscious is formed in the individual subject.

The second part of Seminar III—and, above all, the article "The Agency of the Letter"—suggests that by 1956 Lacan's return to the Freudian discovery of the unconscious no longer revolved primarily around the pseudo-Hegelian dialectical function of speech, but instead became increasingly dependent on the structuralist notion of language as initially formulated by Saussure. As Lacan states: "Firstly there is a synchronic whole, which is language as a simultaneous system of structured groups of opposition, then there is what occurs diachronically, over time, and which is discourse."[40] (The reader should be reminded that, at this stage, the notions of speech and discourse tend to overlap insofar as (a) discourse stresses the intersubjective dimension of language; and (b) "what distinguishes speech from . . . language" is the fact that "to speak is first of all to speak to others.")[41] More specifically, what is at stake is a reelaboration of the Saussurian notion of the sign as the basic unity of language. According to Saussure, the sign is composed of two interdependent components: (1) the signified, corresponding to the *conceptual* element—and not to the real object denoted by a referent; (2) the signifier, corresponding to the *phonological* element—however, the signifier does not simply correspond to the sound of an actual act of speech but is, rather, an "acoustic image" of that sound. Signifier and signified are linked together in a *bi-univocal* way, and thus form a sign. Saussure represents this relationship with the following schema:

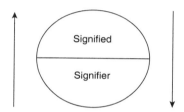

Schema 2.1

Furthermore, Saussure attributes two fundamental characteristics to the sign:

(1) The sign cannot be isolated from the system of which it is part—that is, as Lemaire notes, "only the entire system of language gives the sign its specificity [its linguistic value] as opposed to the other signs."[42] (The same applies to the signified and the signifier considered independently of one another.) In other words, language is a *differential* system in which the signification inherent to one sign emerges exclusively through the *opposition* that exists between all signs.

(2) The phonological and the conceptual components of the sign—the signifier and the signified—are linked together in an *arbitrary* way. Since it is the linguistic structure as such that confers on the sign a specific linguistic value, the link between the two components of the sign can be only epiphenomenal, correlative

to the link between the phonological and the conceptual elements of all other signs.

Despite adopting this notion of the sign, Lacan simultaneously subverts it in three fundamental ways:[43]

(1) The signifier logically precedes and causes the signified. This is clearly exemplified by Lacan's rectification of the Saussurian schema which he in fact represents by means of the algebraic notation S/s (signifier over signified). This means that the conceptual nature of the signified is the product of the signifying action of the signifiers. Lacan calls *signification* the process whereby the concatenation of signifiers generates the signified: "The signifier doesn't just provide an envelope, a receptacle for signification. It polarizes it, it structures it, and brings it into existence."[44] In other words, the notion of linguistic value cannot directly be applied to the signified as such, but only to signification insofar as it is structured by the signifier.[45] In parallel, the supremacy of the signifier over the signified corresponds to the autonomy of the differential, oppositional order of the Symbolic that transcends the apparently unitary and static order of the Imaginary.

(2) The link between signifier and signified ceases to be bi-univocal. Lacan indeed affirms that "the relationship between signifier and signified is far from being one-to-one."[46] This is inextricable from the preeminence attributed to the signifier, and can easily be demonstrated by two straightforward matters of fact: first of all, we know that language evolves over time; a given signifier of a given language can historically adopt different functions.[47] Secondly, the discrete elements, the signifying words that compose a sentence, do not generate any signification *per se* if considered at the level of the sentence; they do so only retroactively, after the sentence is terminated.[48] This demonstrates that the signified can never be referred to one single signifier but is, rather, the product of a complex interrelation between signifiers: "It is in the chain of the signifier that meaning [*sens*] insists but none of the elements of the chain *consists* in the signification [*signification*] of which it is at that moment capable."[49] Elsewhere, Lacan is therefore able to conclude that "the relationship between the signified and the signifier always appears fluid, always ready to come undone":[50] it would be profoundly mistaken to believe that the signifier merely represents the signified. To cut a long story short, one could argue that Lacan destroys the unity of the Saussurian sign: the bar in the algebraic notation S over s marks an actual division that is overcome only in an indirect way.

(3) Structure and subject are not mutually exclusive concepts. For Lacan, the structuralist approach to language is important insofar as it implicitly assists us in track-

ing down the existence of a *subject of the signifier*. Safouan correctly observes that "Lacan's reflection on the signifier is in constant interreaction with his reflection on the subject. . . . The gap which can never be filled between signifier and signified causes the fact that the subject is not only a subject of the signified, but also and above all, a subject of the signifier."[51] The subject is split because of the action of the signifier or, more precisely, because the signified continuously slips beneath the bar of the signifier as an effect of the concatenation of signifiers. In a sense, Lacan complicates the distinction between (conscious) subject of the statement and (unconscious) subject of the enunciation by proposing the following proportion: (subject of the) signified : (subject of the) statement = (subject of the) signifier : (subject of the) enunciation. As he writes in Seminar IV, there is "a sort of superimposition between the course of the signifier . . . and the course of the signified"; thanks to the signified, "the continuity of lived experience, the flux of the tendencies in a subject and between subjects is given."[52] This is to say that if, on the one hand, the signified sides with the conscious "continuity of lived experience," on the other, the signifier sides with the unconscious. What is more, these two courses are "superimposed": each word the subject utters resonates and is inscribed in two different "scenes," the ego and the unconscious. I propose that, for the time being, the dictum "The unconscious is structured like a language" should simply be interpreted as "The unconscious is made of signifiers" or, rather, as "Signifiers form the unconscious": this is essentially due to the fact that signifiers transcend the conscious dimension of the signified. Signifiers are linked in many *synchronic* unconscious signifying chains, which ultimately *are* the unconscious. These chains are created according to the laws of metaphor and metonymy, and are responsible for generating signification at the conscious level. In parallel, self-consciousness corresponds to nothing but *one* continuous, uninterrupted chain, formed both by the signified that results from my speech and by that which I associate with the speech of other subjects:[53] this single chain may be equated with the *diachronic* "lived experience" of the individual subject from his birth to his death.[54]

Following this subversion of the Saussurian sign, Lacan is able to offer three new interlinked definitions of the notions of signifier, sign, and subject:

(1) "The signifier is a sign that doesn't refer to any object." It "is a sign which refers to another sign, which is as such structured to signify the absence of another sign, in other words, to be opposed to it in a couple."[55] What is more, the signifier does not necessarily correspond to a word (in a sentence): oppositional units at all hierarchical levels of language, from the phoneme to the sentence, can function as

signifiers. Human body language—for example, shaking one's head, nodding, waving, and so on—insofar as it is equivocal, can also work as a signifier.

(2) A sign is, strictly speaking, something that overlaps with the notion of code or "biological sign," with the Gestaltic/imaginary—bi-univocal—relation between an index and a referent. This is the domain of animal communication. (Think, for example, of the way in which the appearance of a certain color in an animal can automatically trigger a certain sexual response in its partner.)[56] Animal communication is thus "significant," while human communication is "signifying," which means never bi-univocal, as the ineradicable possibility of lying—the quintessence of the symbolic dimension—concretely attests.

(3) "There's no other scientific definition of subjectivity than one that proceeds from the possibility of handling the signifier for purely signifying, not significant ends, that is, expressing no direct relation to the order of appetite."[57] This definition already provides the basis for Lacan's well-known formula of the early 1960s according to which a subject is that which is represented by a signifier for another signifier.[58] The subject cannot be reduced to the signified—indeed, the subject of the signified corresponds to the ego; on the other hand, he cannot even be identified with a signifier, given that it is the very action of signifiers that splits him between statement and enunciation. No signifier fully signifies the subject, even though there are "privileged" signifiers.

Having surveyed the notion of signifier, we should now move on to analyze the way signifying chains are formed in the unconscious and, above all, according to which linguistic laws they produce conscious signification. In other words, what does "The unconscious is *structured* like a language" really mean?

Lacan derives from Jakobson's linguistics[59] the idea according to which language is divided into two main axes (horizontal or diachronic, and vertical or synchronic), each of which is ruled by a specific linguistic law (metonymy for the horizontal axis, metaphor for the vertical axis). Furthermore, following Jakobson's suggestion, Lacan believes that Freud's description of the dream-work as dependent on the principles of displacement and condensation anticipates the formulation of the linguistic laws of metonymy and metaphor. As in the case of Freud's *Verschiebung* (displacement), metonymy indicates the combination of one signifier with another. On the other hand, echoing the idea of *Verdichtung* (condensation), metaphor is constituted by a process whereby one signifier is substituted for another. Substitution produces signification.

First of all, let us briefly summarize Jakobson's notions of metaphor and metonymy.[60] Jakobson believes that speech presupposes two basic procedures: selection and combination. Selection is the choice of one linguistic unit (at different levels of the oppositional hierarchy of language) among other possible units. This operation presupposes the possibility of substituting one term for another; selection and substitution rely on the associations that can be made between two linguistic units because of their similarity (e.g. the association between the word "thesis" and the word "dissertation"). Similarity also includes oppositions between two linguistic units: in other words, substitution functions in accordance with the association of both synonyms and antonyms (e.g. the word "thesis" can also be associated with/substituted for the word "antithesis").[61] Combination is the putting together of many linguistic units (e.g. words) into a larger linguistic unit (e.g. the sentence "I am writing my thesis"): "These connexions of an increasing level of complexity are governed by phonological, grammatical and syntactic laws of decreasing constraint."[62] The two axes of substitution and combination are closely related; Saussure had already illustrated such a relation by means of the following comparison: "Each linguistic unit is like a column in an ancient building. This column is in relation of contiguity with other parts of the building: the architrave, for example (illustrating the plan of combination). On the other hand, the column which may, for instance, be Doric reminds us of other architectural styles: Ionic, Corinthian (illustrating the plane of selection)."[63] By referring to schema 2.2 below, it is easy to see how the axis of substitution may be said to be "vertical" and "synchronic" (two linguistic units are virtually present at the same time), while the axis of combination is said to be "horizontal" and "diachronic" (one linguistic unit follows another unit in time). Finally, Jakobson names the vertical axis after the rhetoric trope of metaphor (in which one object is used to describe another object, and is thus substituted for it); the horizontal axis after the rhetoric trope of metonymy (which may refer to relations of contiguity between two objects).

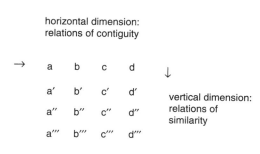

horizontal dimension:
relations of contiguity

→ a   b   c   d   ↓

a′   b′   c′   d′   vertical dimension:
a″   b″   c″   d″   relations of
                       similarity
a‴   b‴   c‴   d‴

Schema 2.2

At the risk of stating the obvious, it is important to insist on the fact that Lacan adapts Jakobson's laws of concrete *conscious* language, the object of linguistics, to his thesis of the *unconscious* structured like a (conscious) language, the object of psychoanalysis. For Lacan, the unconscious is structured *like* a language, it follows the linguistic laws that Jakobson attributed to conscious language. Strictly speaking, however, the unconscious is *not* a language as we normally understand it, and as Jakobson theorizes it. The signifiers of the unconscious possess a symbolic (oppositional/differential) *meaning* that causes signification to emerge in consciousness, but they do not possess, *per se*, any signification. Signification can only be conscious, and the unconscious is, by definition, not conscious. In other words, as I have already observed, there is no archetypal unconscious signified for Lacan. Such a specification is essential if we are not to misread Lacan's appropriation of the notions of metaphor and metonymy.

One could correctly object, as I myself did earlier, that from the standpoint of the Symbolic, language as structure and the transindividual unconscious are identical: consequently, any attempt to distinguish them would be artificial. I accept such an objection but, at the same time, wish to emphasize that for Lacan the Symbolic is never, in *practice*, completely detached from the Imaginary.[64] Hence (conscious) language and the transindividual unconscious are not simply the same thing. More importantly, this distinction should help us to avoid the confusion between two different applications of the notion of metonymy. According to Jakobson, the vertical axis of metaphor holds in *absentia*, its units are mutually exclusive in concrete discourse, while metonymy holds in *presentia*, the combination of signifiers is diachronic; on the other hand, for Lacan, *metonymy holds both in presentia and in absentia*. Against those commentators who often use examples derived from positive language to illustrate the metonymic function of the unconscious, I argue that Lacan implicitly distinguishes between:

(1) metonymy as combination in *conscious* speech, that is, the grammatical/syntagmatic rules of positive language as studied by Jakobsonian linguistics. Lacan fully accepts them;

(2) metonymy as combination in the *unconscious*. Lacan's belief in the existence of an unconscious level of metonymy is proved by the fact that the two formulas of metaphor and metonymy are *both* explicitly presented as a "topography of the unconscious" in his seminal essay "The Agency of the Letter."[65] Jakobson had already admitted the existence of some metonymic combination within the vertical associations, which, by definition, hold in *absentia*, synchronically. *Lacan transforms the logical necessity of the vertical axis* (made of *both* metaphors and metonymy)—the existence of a linguistic *structure* which, according to Saussure and Jakobson, concrete dis-

course continuously presupposes—*into the actual reality of the unconscious.* Unconscious metonymy has therefore to be referred to the vertical/synchronic axis of language; more specifically, it consists of a *combinatory association by contiguity*—and not of a substitutive association by similarity, as in the case of metaphor—*that is ultimately linked to the conscious/diachronic/horizontal axis of speech at a specific point by a metaphoric substitution*—that is to say, by repression. Unlike the diachronic chain formed by conscious metonymy, unconscious metonymy is continually fragmented and "redirected" by metaphor.[66] Hence, unconscious metonymy cannot constitute a "straight" axis of speech perpendicular to conscious speech, another alternative ego; on the contrary, it forms several overlapping unconscious signifying chains (see schema 2.3).[67] The unconscious is thus ruled by both metaphor *and* metonymy. Metonymy in the unconscious is based on the principle of combination but, clearly, as Freud was already aware, the unconscious does *not* follow the combinative grammatical conventions of positive language; in fact it is atemporal, and does not obey the law of noncontradiction. Conversely, it is impossible to justify

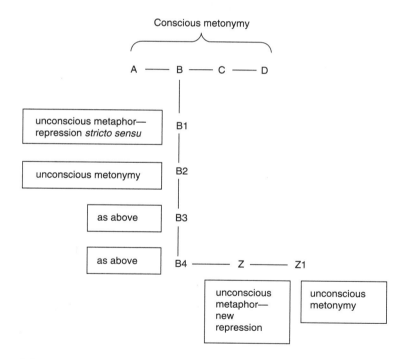

Schema 2.3

the process of displacement in the dream-work by resorting to grammar: after all, this is why a dream seems so "unreal."

Let us now attempt to analyze in detail the way in which metaphor and metonymy operate in the unconscious and, more precisely, how they generate *new* signification—and thus indirectly also the combinative laws of grammar that structure conscious language.

It is initially correct to state that self-consciousness corresponds to the signified whose continuous metonymic flow can be depicted as one straight diachronic chain that accompanies the individual subject from the mythical utterance (or hearing) of his first signified to his death as the definitive loss of self-consciousness. In parallel, it is correct to maintain that the unconscious is made up of signifiers that form multiple synchronic chains due to metaphoric substitution. Such a clear-cut dichotomy between two distinct scenes or *topoi* must, however, be supplemented with a more complex explanation: on its own it would fail to explain how the unconscious is related to self-consciousness. As we have seen, their actual connection is an empirical fact witnessed by the existence of the formations of the unconscious, such as symptoms, jokes, and slips of the tongue. In other words, on a closer inspection, one should observe how, for Lacan, it is also the case that *conscious* language itself is composed of both the signified *and* the signifier: this is precisely the discovery of the structural linguists. As I have already pointed out, Lacan fully accepts this common cornerstone of their otherwise often divergent theories. Structural linguistics teaches us that, in conscious language, any given signified (e.g. "thesis") is related to a signifier (e.g. 'θi:sIs) thanks to the (metaphoric/"vertical") notion of linguistic value. Conversely and more importantly, according to Lacan, the unconscious can be considered as a "potential" signified. It is the unconscious that is ultimately responsible for the process of signification *tout court*. But the signified produced by signification can only be conscious. As we have just seen, in the unconscious there is no "privileged" chain of signifiers, no "straight" diachronic chain. The necessary link between the unconscious and self-consciousness (as different *topoi*)—that is, the actualization of unconscious meaning (*sens*) in conscious signification (*signification*)—is provided by the formations of the unconscious. Unconscious meaning is therefore nothing but signification *in potentia*.[68] The formations of the unconscious both actualize unconscious meaning (in consciousness) and, at the same time, their linguistic *modus operandi*—metonymic combination and metaphoric substitution—shows how conscious signifiers (to simplify, the sounds that we utter or hear) have wider repercussions in the unconscious. The formations of the unconscious are *new* effects of signification which, one could suggest, "give form" to the unconscious by turning it into consciousness: this is possible only as a result of the presence in the unconscious of a structural arrangement of signifiers, that is, unconscious meaning.

All this leads us to conclude that signifiers are simultaneously inscribed in both consciousness and the unconscious. As we shall see in more detail toward the end of Chapter 3, double inscription is a consequence of primal repression. Primal repression mythically occurs as soon as desire—or, better, demand—is alienated in language, as soon as the individual subject uses language—or initially disorganized sounds—to attain the satisfaction of his instinctual needs. The primordial signifying cry that accompanies the attempt to fulfill one's need causes primal repression which, in turn, marks the birth of the unconscious. Therefore, the fact that every signifier is doubly inscribed means simply that once one signifier has been repressed in the unconscious, all successive signifiers will be linked to the repressed signifier, the nucleus of repression, and will form chains *even though they are not themselves directly repressed*. The simple inscription of a signifier in the unconscious corresponds to a metonymic combination in the unconscious: this occurs whenever a signifier is uttered or heard in consciousness, which means at the same time as a new "segment" is added to the conscious signifying chain.

On the other hand, repression *stricto sensu*, that is, repression of a specific signifier from consciousness—(secondary) repression is by definition, for Lacan, the repression of a signifier—corresponds to a metaphoric substitution which "redirects" the multiplicity of unconscious signifying chains; topographically speaking, it imposes on them a 90-degree turn.[69] Lacan is extremely clear on the following points: (a) repression is a metaphor; (b) repression cannot avoid the return of the repressed; (c) the return of the repressed—the formations of the unconscious— functions according to metaphoric substitutions; (d) signification is produced exclusively by metaphor. Hence, one should argue that if signification, and thus the signified, arises only as a result of metaphoric substitutions, then signification is necessarily related to both repression and the return of the repressed. In other words, repression (of a signifier) engenders new signification in consciousness; the formations of the unconscious are nothing but neologisms, "signifiers that escape the code": this is particularly evident in the case of jokes.[70] Finally, it is important to add that Lacan himself emphasizes that *all* signifiers composing the battery of signifiers of a given positive language, the code equivalent to the vertical/substitutive axis of Saussure and Jakobson, and thus their signification, were originally neologisms.[71] Metaphor creates new signification by substituting one signifier for another, and this can occur only in concomitance with repression.

My stress on the dependence of new (neologistic) signification on repression and the return of the repressed makes it necessary to specify how my claim differs from Laplanche's anti-Lacanian argument according to which unconscious metaphoric substitutions are *always* responsible for the connection existing in consciousness between the signifier and the signified. This view distorts the notion of double inscription by rendering it inextricable from repression *stricto sensu*. The fact that *new* signification necessarily emerges through metaphoric substitution (repression *stricto sensu*) does not entail that, at the conscious level, already existing signification cannot function autonomously of the unconscious—cannot, that is, function according to the laws of grammar alone. Furthermore, for Laplanche, at the *individual* level of the child's pre-Oedipal psychogenesis, it is the always-already metaphorical structure of the unconscious that allows the acquisition of language; while for Lacan, language precedes the unconscious. More specifically, language can be said to precede the complete structuring of the unconscious inasmuch as primal repression—the metonymic uttering of the first cries, phonemes, or words—occurs in the individual without any metaphoric substitution. Unlike Laplanche, Lacan thinks of elementary signifiers as mere oppositional couples— such as the *Fort–Da* described by Freud that attempts a primal symbolization of the trauma provoked by the mother's absence. Metaphoric substitution—and the parallel possibility of repression *stricto sensu*, together with a fully articulated language—will successively be effected only by the resolution of the Oedipus complex. Having said this, I also more generally argue, in agreement with Lacan, that language (and grammar) is *historically* produced only in concomitance with repression: all the words that we use in conscious language—and initially acquire as children independently of metaphoric substitutions—were once neologisms.[72]

These remarks should also throw some light on the reason why Lacan believes that metonymy logically precedes metaphor. The child starts to speak (in a nonarticulated way) precisely by naming what he demands. Demand is at this stage simply accompanied by a nonarticulated metonymic slide of phonemes or words.[73] Hence it is not metonymy in the sense of the syntagmatic rules of conscious speech that precedes metaphor. Grammar is coextensive with signification, which is made possible by metaphor. In other words, signification ultimately relies on a primal metaphor—the paternal metaphor that resolves the Oedipus complex—thanks to which metonymy as syntagmatic speech may arise. The primal metaphor is also a precondition for any clear distinction between the unconscious and self-consciousness. Before the advent of the paternal metaphor, language (as nonsyntagmatic metonymy) already alienates the child's demand—which is therefore also somehow repressed—but both the unconscious and self-consciousness are not yet completely structured.[74] Primal repression is effectively repressed only retroactively through the resolution of the Oedipus complex.

One final point needs to be discussed before moving on to the analysis of the Other, and of the unconscious, from the standpoint of the individual subject's active entry into the Symbolic as Law (the Oedipus complex). The linguistic structure of the unconscious is often defined by Lacan in terms of the "letter." His most important article on the distinction between the signifier and the signified is indeed entitled "The Agency of the *Letter* in the Unconscious." What is a letter, and how does it differentiate itself from a signifier? As Lacan states, a letter must always be taken literally,[75] and if one takes it so, one immediately realizes that a letter is material, it is the "material support that concrete discourse borrows from language."[76] On an initial level, a letter thus corresponds to the written materialization of a phoneme (e.g. the ink that occupies a certain space and is taken to represent a sound). More importantly, on a second, broader level, *a letter is nothing but a signifier as it materially exists per se in the unconscious, independently of its effects of (conscious) signification.* As Miller clearly states, a letter is "a sign, defined not in its effect as signified, but in its nature as an object."[77] In other words, a letter is a meaningless signifier, the *real* structure of language. This is why it is fundamentally imprecise, if not incorrect, to fully equate the—oppositional, differential—order of the Symbolic with that of language. In a sense, the triad Imaginary, Symbolic, Real is reflected within language in the triad signified, signifier, letter.

Moving from these premises, one has to emphasize how Lacan understands the unconscious in terms both of the *signifiers as symbols*, as responsible for creating effects of signification, and of the *signifiers as letters*, the *pure* signifiers, the dimension of the Real-of-language. From this it also follows that the unconscious *qua* letter/Real-of-language can present itself to the subject independently of the individual subject's own active participation in the Symbolic. In other words, the subject can passively "be spoken" by language to be understood as the transindividual unconscious. According to Lacan, this is what happens in psychosis and explains why, as he states repeatedly, in psychosis what is not symbolized returns in the Real. It returns in the *Real-of-language*, for instance as auditory hallucinations.

Given that every individual human being is surrounded by language long before he can actively manipulate it, one must assume that, logically, the literal, real character of the signifier precedes its symbolic value. In other words, the letter precedes the unconscious, or rather, precedes the symbolic shaping of the unconscious in the individual subject—which is parallel to the emergence of self-consciousness. If, on the contrary, one defends the logical priority of the un-conscious over the letter, one inevitably falls back into proto-Jungian positions for which the "other scene" has as such some imaginary signification.

In Seminar III, Lacan provides us with a key definition of the letter by stating that "every real signifier is, as such, a signifier that signifies nothing."[78] This state-ment can be read in two complementary ways:

(1) As we have already noted, a signifier differs from a (natural) sign in that it is signifying and not significant. Only significant (Gestaltic/imaginary) signs signify something *per se*—a red feather signifies ejaculation—whereas *one* signifier, a real letter, does not signify anything: it has no effects of signification since there is no bi-univocal relation between the signifier and the signified. A signifier is signify-ing and produces an effect of signification only when considered in a differential/ oppositional relation with all other signifiers: this is what a symbol is for Lacan.

(2) Even if taken as a set, signifiers are, *per se*, just letters that do not signify any-thing as long as they are considered separately from the effect of signification they generate. In other words, symbolic signifying chains—the association of unconscious signifiers by metaphor and metonymy—may properly be so named only from the perspective of the signified they produce in the Imaginary. In themselves, they are a mere association of meaningless letters as material sup-port of signifiers.

To clarify this difficult point, Lacan perpetuates Freud's passion for hieroglyphics. Lacan believes that hieroglyphics provide perfect evidence of the level of the Real-of-language. As he puts it, the signifying chain as letter "is found to survive in an alterity in relation to the subject [the individual subject's self-consciousness] as radical as that of as yet undecipherable hieroglyphics in the solitude of the des-ert."[79] Here Lacan is implicitly suggesting that one should consider the role of hier-oglyphics before they were deciphered as that of a paradoxical *signifying chain without signification*.[80] Western archaeologists attempted to decipher hieroglyphics because they supposed them to signify something for another civilization, but they did not signify anything for the archaeologists themselves. This proves that the letter, the Real-of-language, underlies the dimension of the signifier as symbol. It would be wrong, however, to assume that when the symbol (the hieroglyphic) is deci-phered, the letter simply disappears: on the contrary, it remains there as a neces-sary material support of the signifier/symbol; it is also in this sense that the letter is said to "insist." The same point can also be demonstrated *per negativum*: what if the hieroglyphics had turned out to be a fake, and only *seemed* to signify something? In this case, archaeologists would have been mistaken in inferring the existence of a signification where there was only a randomly marked stone or papyrus, the purely material dimension of the alleged signifying chain—which normally remains concealed in everyday discourse. In the end, what is at stake in the notion of letter is a dimension of meaninglessness that is constitutive of the process of signification as such, a lack of signification that is structurally linked to signification and does not merely amount to non-signification. Lacan will see the radical consequences of this conclusion—the end of the autonomy of the symbolic order— only in the late 1950s, after the notion of the Real had come to occupy the center of his theoretical interests.

CHAPTER 3

Oedipus as a Metaphor

Lacan's convoluted account of the Oedipus complex is based on three clear-cut a priori assumptions: (a) a baby is always-already immersed in the Other *qua* language, long before he acquires the ability to speak. This is because from the moment of his birth, and probably even earlier, he hears other human beings speaking. What is more, other human beings may be speaking about him; (b) the Other *qua* language cannot but be structured in a symbolic way: human beings are speaking beings insofar as they establish a culture governed by a fundamental Law which distinguishes them from animals. More concretely, we could say that the people the baby hears speaking most at the beginning of his life—his mother, father, brothers, and sisters—are already symbolically related to each other in a family; (c) symbolic relationships can never be phylogenetically transmitted from one generation to another.[1] Precisely insofar as the Symbolic may, broadly speaking, be understood as a successful "reaction" against the disadaptation of man as animal, it is impossible for the Law to be "naturally" inherited. A baby is born as a totally helpless animal surrounded by and belonging to a species which has transformed its helplessness into a formidable tool that allows it to dominate all other "adapted" animals.

On these premises, the entire issue of the Oedipus complex according to Lacan could be summarized as follows: if, on the one hand, from the standpoint of the big Other, language and the Symbolic perfectly overlap, on the other, this is far from being the case for the newborn child. Language is always-already there for him, but the symbolic relations that structurally accompany it remain utterly enigmatic. As a consequence, the child has to "learn" how actively to enter the Other *qua* Symbolic, and to enter it as an individual since, at first, he is only passively alienated within it. The child is initially an "a-subject"[2] (*assujet*) entirely subjected to the Other. The pre-Oedipal child is an individuated subject only for the Other: with the resolution of the Oedipus complex, however, the child individuates himself symbolically. The process of symbolization is, for the child, a gradual one: however, it is fully actualized only by the resolution of the Oedipus complex. Therefore, although Lacan admits the existence of symbolizations that precede the Oedipus complex, these pre-Oedipal processes are, strictly speaking, only *retroactively* symbolized with the resolution of the Oedipus complex. This means that if the Oedipus complex does not occur, or if it does not function properly, the child does not (properly) enter the Other *qua* Symbolic as an individual subject. Nevertheless, given the existence of pre-Oedipal protosymbolizations, the child is not necessarily prevented from acquiring a certain ability to speak (indeed, a child learns to speak well before the age of five, when the Oedipus complex declines); in other words, he may be able actively to enter the Other *qua* language despite his inability to enter the Other *qua* Symbolic. It must, however, be noted that, strictly speaking, for Lacan, the full structuration of speech in the individual is always brought about by the resolution of the Oedipus complex: language as *speech* is fully structured for the child only when he has properly located himself in the symbolic order.

As we saw in Chapter 2, the less language is symbolized, the more it remains at the level of the letter. This remark is particularly useful in describing the original position of the child with respect to the Other: before his active entry into the Symbolic through the (resolution of the) Oedipus complex, the child is in relation to language as letter, the Real-of-language. One is obliged to conceive a primordial point at which he is fully alienated in language, like a pet. Although this represents a merely mythical beginning, it is nevertheless the case that the child continues to be spoken by language (as letter) even after he begins to learn how to speak. It is useful to compare the situation in which children can speak without their speech being properly symbolized with that of the psychotic subject, who can also usually speak. As we have seen, even in the latter case there is in fact a privileged relation with letters. In psychosis, language materializes itself as letter—for example, in the guise of auditory hallucinations—insofar as symbolization has not succeeded; unsurprisingly, Lacan thinks that psychosis is due to the foreclosure of the signifier responsible for resolving the Oedipus complex, the Name-of-the-Father.

When we attempt to delineate the crucial distinction between the Other *qua* language and the Other *qua* Symbolic as experienced in the child's early years, we must always remember that the same language perceived by the child as letter—even when he is partially capable of mastering it in a protosymbolic way—constitutes, at the same time, a fully articulated symbolic system for the adults who surround him. The parallel with hieroglyphics is very useful here: we could suggest that the child has to decipher a series of hieroglyphics as enigmatic letters. Their overall signification may remain obscure to him even after he has detected some clear patterns and is able to replicate them (by speaking). In other words, the child from very early on begins to suppose that what appears to him as language *qua* letter is actually a fully articulated symbolic system for the Other—for example, as I will show in greater detail later, this occurs when he questions himself after his appeal to his mother has been neglected. However, it is absolutely vital to underline once again how these early stages of symbolization can be defined as symbolic only in a retroactive way: the child cannot, strictly speaking, question "himself," since his questioning is not yet symbolically individuated. . . . What at the outset should be considered as *virtually* symbolic for the child—and is *actually* symbolic for the Other that surrounds him—*will have become* actually symbolic for the child after the resolution of the Oedipus complex.

The retroactive character of pre-Oedipal symbolic processes is equally valid for pre-Oedipal *unconscious* life. Freud always insisted on the retroactivity of the trauma: a traumatic experience that occurred very early on in one's life—for example, the witnessing of parental copulation—is actually repressed only years later, that is, paradoxically, when it is possible for the subject to make some (unconscious) sense of it. In other words, proper repression requires proper individuation, and the unconscious may properly be so named only in concomitance with the emergence of self-consciousness. (As I attempted to demonstrate in Chapter 1, despite the early constitution of imaginary identifications, the child's self-consciousness is entirely dependent on a primal symbolic identification—that is, the ideal ego must be supplemented with the ego-ideal.) The unconscious is a symbolic structure and, as such, it is not inherited by the individual subject: quite the opposite, it is strictly dependent on the (resolution of the) Oedipus complex. If, on the one hand, by the time the child starts to formulate his first phonemes and to convey his demands with them, a certain repression has indubitably already taken place—what he demands is, by definition, alienated in language, that is, given the latter's non-bi-univocal nature, it is necessarily misinterpreted and thus always doomed to ever greater frustration—on the other, we can speak of an unconscious *stricto sensu* only after the Oedipus complex has taken place. Enabling the child to access the symbolic order as an individual, the resolution of the Oedipus complex retroactively structures both his pre-Oedipal language and his pre-Oedipal unconscious.

I have already pointed out how the big Other can be considered from three different standpoints: language, the unconscious, and the Symbolic. In Chapter 2, I was mostly concerned with an analysis of the relation between the Other as language and the Other as unconscious. In this chapter, by examining Lacan's notion of the Oedipus complex, my primary intention is to explore the relation between the Other as language and the Other as Symbolic (how does the child manage to properly symbolize the letter?). In the last section of the chapter I shall also investigate the relation between the Other as Symbolic and the Other as unconscious (why is the unconscious symbolic? How does it specifically become un-conscious?).

It should be clear by now that the key notion at work in Lacan's Oedipus complex is retroaction: "One has always to grasp that which, by intervening from outside at each stage, retroactively rearranges what had been outlined in the previous stage; this happens for the simple reason that the child is not alone."[3] In spite of this, my explanation will be chronological. It must be noted how Lacan's own most detailed accounts of the Oedipus complex (to be found in Seminars IV and V) are themselves chronological. He repeatedly felt obliged to justify his choice in two different ways: (a) a chronological approach is pedagogically more effective;[4] (b) despite not being chrono-logical, the logical stages (*temps*) on the basis of which the Oedipus complex is investigated can occur only in a "given succession."[5]

More precisely, I shall proceed as follows: first, I will discuss what is defined by most psychoanalytic schools as the "pre-Oedipus," showing how Lacan renders it a paradoxical notion while nevertheless acknowledging its importance. Secondly, I shall closely analyze the three stages into which, according to Lacan, the Oedipus complex can be divided. Finally, I will examine the intricate interactions between two notions which are consubstantial with Lacan's description of the Oedipus complex: the Name-of-the-Father and the phallus.

For the sake of clarity, it may be convenient at this preliminary stage to list briefly the main tenets of Lacan's reinterpretation of the Oedipus complex:

(1) the Oedipus complex provides the individual subject with the necessary key to enter the symbolic order understood as the Law of culture;

(2) this is possible only if, in parallel, the subject is sexuated: if he or she assumes his or her symbolic position as man or woman;

(3) the process through which the Oedipus complex is produced can be compared to a metaphor; by substituting itself for the signifier Desire-of-the-Mother, the signifier Name-of-the-Father (the symbolic father as the bearer of the Law) initiates phallic signification in the child. This complicated operation will later be explained in much greater detail. For now, it is enough to realize that Lacan rereads what is arguably the most well-known theory of psychoanalysis through linguistics;

(4) the child is introduced to the three logically sequential "stages" of the Oedipus complex through three different "crises."[6] Each crisis is based on the subject's assumption of a distinctive lack of a distinctive object. Frustration, defined as an imaginary lack of a real object, first and foremost the mother's breast, initiates the child to the first stage, that of the "pre-Oedipal" dual relation with the mother, which Lacan rethinks in terms of the triad child–mother– (imaginary) phallus. The child then accedes to the second stage as soon as he realizes that the mother is "deprived," that she lacks (in the Real) a symbolic object, the (symbolic) phallus; at this stage, which could easily be related to Freud's phallic phase,[7] the child is involved in an aggressively imaginary rivalry with the (imaginary) father in order to control the mother. This stage corresponds to the doxastic idea of what the Oedipus complex is: "loving" the mother and "hating" the father (for Lacan, both boys and girls love the mother). Lastly, the third stage is initiated by the (real) father who shows the child that he is the one who has what the mother lacks: the child realizes that he cannot compete with him. This is the child's castration proper, to be understood as a symbolic lack of an imaginary object, the imaginary phallus. The

Oedipus complex is completely resolved when the child, irrespective of sex, identifies symbolically with the father, and thus internalizes the Law.

3.2 THE MYTHICAL STATE BEFORE FRUSTRATION, AND PRIMORDIAL FRUSTRATION

In the first part of Seminar IV, Lacan begins his discussion of the pre-Oedipus by claiming that the relationship between the child and the mother can never be dual. This is essentially due to the fact that there is no actual phase in which "a perfect reciprocity between what the child demands from the mother and what the mother demands from the child" is established.[8] The mother is already an active part of the Symbolic and, being embedded in its differential structure, is always lacking something: she is a desiring being. Although the child finds himself in a similar position long before actively entering the Symbolic by way of the resolution of the Oedipus complex, Lacan postulates a mythical moment in which he does not lack anything.

Originally, the child is in a "direct relation"[9] with the object of his needs, the mother's breast. This object, according to Lacan, should be considered as "real" even though it is not yet perceived by the child as an object: the breast "begins to exert its influence on the subject's relations long before the latter can perceive it as an object. It is only as a function of a periodicity in which gaps and lacks appear that a certain [active] mode of relation on the subject's behalf will be established."[10] Lacan then distinguishes the "real" object from its "agent," the mother.[11] The latter does not initially appear as real—that is, according to another meaning of this term, as an object of everyday reality—but as symbolic. What does this mean? The symbolic mother as agent of the "real" object corresponds to the opposition between her presence and her absence, +/−, which the child masters with his cries: "The maternal object [the breast as distinct from the mother] is precisely asked for when it is absent and it is rejected when it is present."[12] At this mythical stage, the mother is supposed to be always present whenever the child needs to be fed and absent whenever he is satiated: in other words, the child has not yet been frustrated. Lacan believes that this scansion of the appeal/cry shows us the beginning of the child's entry into the symbolic order:[13] however, in order properly to access the Symbolic, the opposition +/− will successively have to form for the child "a sequence which is grouped as such."[14]

I believe there is one fundamental problem with this otherwise fascinating account of the mythical stage that precedes primordial frustration. Lacan fails to distinguish clearly between time 0, in which the child is in a protoanimalic absolutely "direct relation" with the object, from time 1, in which, although he is always satisfied by his mother, and thus unable to grasp the object as object,[15] he nevertheless experiences the alternating presence/absence of the mother as agent of the (virtual) object. In other words, despite logically preceding primordial frustration, the opposition +/− which characterizes the symbolic mother is inevitably dependent on an even more original "division," and therefore possibly on an earlier frustration.

Following the early Lacan of "Les complexes familiaux," one could argue that this earlier frustration is provided by (the trauma of) birth, by part(urit)ition. In other words, the relation child–object could be considered as fully "direct" only in an intrauterine state: the fact that, by being exposed to the opposition +/−, the child is already implicitly differentiating the symbolic mother from the—as yet virtual—object proves that every postnatal scenario should necessarily be considered in terms of some sort of "indirectness." The simpler version of the child–breast relation presented in "Les complexes familiaux" was, from this perspective, much more consistent: the state of helplessness in which the child is born and the consequent disorder of his Imaginary was deemed immediately to trap him in an alienating—that is, "indirect"—identification with the *imago* of the breast. Lacan's argument in Seminar IV would have been much stronger if he had clearly differentiated between *two* mythical stages: an intrauterine one in which frustration is, by definition, impossible and an extrauterine one in which frustration is possible but never occurs, since the child is always satisfied.

How do we move on from this mythical state in which the child's appeal is always answered by the mother? Lacan's explanation is extremely clear:

> What is the pivotal moment in which the relation mother–child is opened to other elements which will introduce what we can call a dialectic? I believe we can formulate it schematically by asking the following question: what happens if the symbolic agent, the essential term of the child's relation with the real object, the mother as such, does not answer . . . the subject's appeal? . . . She decays. From being inscribed in the symbolic order, which made her a present–absent object as a function of the appeal, *she now becomes real* . . . that is, a *power*.[16]

Some essential consequences should be drawn from this key passage:

(1) The becoming real of the mother is accompanied by an "overturning of the position of the object."[17] That is, conversely, *the object becomes symbolic*. Objects (first of all the breast) that up to this point were, for the child, simply (virtual) objects that satisfied a biological *need* are transformed into *gifts* that may or may not be donated by the real mother understood as a power. After the mother has neglected the child's appeal, she thus becomes omnipotent for him.

(2) The object can now be considered as an object of satisfaction in two different ways: as real, it satisfies the child's biological need; as symbolic, "it symbolizes a favorable power"[18] which dispenses gifts.

(3) It is only by becoming symbolic that the real object actualizes its earlier virtuality and turns into an object of everyday reality. "A real object acquires . . . its signification [only] as symbolic, as being part of the love object."[19] *The virtual Real precedes the Symbolic, but it can be actualized only by the Symbolic.*[20] The real object of the child's need can be perceived as such only after he has confronted himself with a *lack of object*, having realized that the object may *not* be donated; the relation subject–object is clearly based on the productivity of the lack.[21]

(4) Lacan calls this first form of the lack of an object frustration. More specifically, he defines frustration as the imaginary lack of a real object whose agent is symbolic. It should be clear by now in what sense the object is real and the agent symbolic. But why is the lack imaginary? Here it is sufficient to recall that, as we saw in Chapter 1, all relations that the subject establishes with objects in everyday reality are always filtered through imaginary introjections and projections: the Real *qua* objectified everyday reality is essentially imaginary. As a consequence, it is also the case that the child–object relationship inaugurated by primordial frustration should be considered as fundamentally narcissistic. This explains why Lacan thinks that frustration is lived by the child as "imaginary damage" ("What is not given to me, belongs to me and therefore has been stolen from me—I want it back!").[22]

3.3 THE DIALECTIC OF FRUSTRATION, OR, THE FIRST ("PRE-OEDIPAL") STAGE OF THE OEDIPUS COMPLEX

Primordial frustration establishes a productive dialectic between the child, the mother, and that which keeps her busy when she cannot answer the child's appeal. Lacan calls this phase both the "dialectic of frustration" (in Seminar IV) and the "first stage [*temps*] of the Oedipus complex" (in Seminar V). Since it concerns primarily the relationship between the child and the mother, this stage clearly overlaps with what was traditionally designated by psychoanalytic theory as the "pre-Oedipus." This does not, however, constitute a contradiction for Lacan, since, as we have seen, he affirms that the "pre-Oedipus" acquires its symbolic significance only retroactively, after the resolution of the Oedipus complex (in its third stage): Lacan acknowledges the existence of a specific triadic phase which is not yet explicitly Oedipal, yet he concedes that it is meaningless to consider it *per se*, independently of the Oedipus complex. "The triangle [child–mother–what prevents her from answering the child's appeal] is, as such, pre-Oedipal. Nevertheless, it is here isolated only by way of abstraction; it interests us only because it is successively resumed in the quartet which is constituted by the entry of the paternal function."[23]

The relation between the mother and the child that follows primordial frustration is said to be dialectical. Why? "The child expects something from the mother, he even gets something. . . . Let's say, by approximation, . . . that the child may believe himself to be loved for what he is."[24] Following the emergence of the symbolic object as gift, the child demands that the mother love him. His demand (to be distinguished from a mere appeal/cry relating to the satisfaction of biological needs) consists in an unconditional demand for love: up to a certain point, the child thinks he is loved by her. It is crucial, however, to distinguish between what happens from the child's perspective and what happens from the perspective of the mother: the dialectic that unites them is asymmetrical. For what does the mother expect from the child? Does she really love him? We should recall that the mother is already an active part of the symbolic order and, as such, a desiring being. Lacan reminds us that, according to Freudian theory, the privileged object of desire is the phallus. Two important specifications should immediately be made: first, the phallus is not the penis. "This object is defined as imaginary, and thus it is impossible to confound it with the penis in its reality, of which it is the proper form, that is, an erected image."[25] Secondly, the imaginary phallus "is more important for those members of humankind who lack its real correlate [the penis], that is, women."[26] Lacan believes that, from the mother's standpoint, a dialectic is established with the child insofar as the child can represent for her a substitute for the missing imaginary phallus: "If the woman finds a satisfaction in the child it is precisely for as long as she finds in him something that, to different degrees, calms her need of the phallus."[27] This is precisely where the asymmetry in the mother–child dialectic that follows frustration lies: on the one hand, the child may believe himself to be loved for what he is, but on the other, the mother only "calms" her search for the phallus through him. For the mother, there is never a complete equation between the phallus and the child: "Far from being harmonic, the relation of the mother to the child is redoubled . . . there is always something that remains irreducible in the mother."[28] Commentators usually fail to make this distinction between what happens from the child's perspective and what happens from the perspective of the mother, and thus wrongly claim that, in the first stage of the Oedipus complex, the child identifies with the imaginary phallus. Lacan is very clear on this point: "Is it in a spontaneous and direct way that the relation mother–phallus is given to the child? Does everything happen simply because he looks at the mother and realizes that she desires a phallus? It seems this is not the case."[29]

At this stage, therefore, one fundamental question should be asked: *when* does the child realize that "it is not he who is loved but a certain image [in/on him]"?[30] When does he understand that he is just the (imperfect) replacement of his mother's missing imaginary phallus? Lacan's answer is straightforward: this "fundamental disappointment"[31] can occur only after the child has grasped for the first time—and in an incomplete way—the difference between the sexes, during what Freud calls the "phallic phase." What is more, this phase is in the child strictly related to the emergence of infantile masturbation, the commencement of genital activity, both of the penis and of the vagina.[32] These two complementary experiences mark the child's passage from the first to the second stage of the Oedipus complex.

But *how* does the child effectively *begin* to grasp the difference between the sexes? How does he understand that he is not loved *per se*, and thus enter the second stage of the Oedipus complex? It is not surprising that, for Lacan, this stage is thought to be initiated by the intervention of the imaginary father who deprives the real mother of the child as phallus. In concomitance with this, the child enters into a narcissistic-aggressive relationship with the imaginary father to control the mother's desire, to *be* her phallus. The child aggressively competes with the father by carrying out an imaginary alienating identification with his body image; although Lacan is rather elusive on this point, the fact that the father is here considered as imaginary represents, I believe, a precise indicator that the child is relating to a *Gestalt*.[33] Unlike the mother's body image and the child's own body image, as perceived in siblings and the mirror,[34] that of the father is supplied with something supplementary that obtrudes: the phallic *Gestalt*.[35] To put it simply, this is how sexual difference is *initially* assumed by the child.[36] What is certain is that the child soon realizes, by way of comparison, the utter inadequacy of his own real correlate of the imaginary phallus: such an association between the image and the organ is facilitated by the fact that, meanwhile, the child's own genital drives have begun to manifest themselves in infantile masturbation. This sense of impotence also gives rise to anxiety before the Desire-of-the-Mother, which is now perceived as a threatening and engulfing force.

On this point, one common misunderstanding should be avoided: the mother considers the "totality" of the child as her imaginary phallus, "the child as a whole is involved";[37] it is *as if* she desires to devour him, but she does not want his penis, even after masturbation has begun. With the latter's emergence, nothing changes for the mother. It is clear that, for Lacan, anxiety is *not* provoked in the child by the mother's desire for his real phallus. On the contrary, in a sense, anxiety is caused precisely by the fact that the mother does not want his (inadequate) real phallus. All changes occur in the child: "Anxiety consists in the fact that he can measure all the existing difference between that for which he is loved [his whole body as a gigantic phallic *Gestalt*/image] and what he can give [his little real penis]."[38] It should by now be clear how the competition with the father (via alienating identification) in the second stage of the Oedipus complex represents a preliminary escape from the mother: it enables the child to keep her at bay, as it were, *by means of the father's imaginary phallus*—which, at this stage, the child literally *em-bodies/is*.

Let me add a brief preliminary definition of the phallic *Gestalt*. Safouan writes that "the phallic *Gestalt* provides human society with a signifier which serves to differentiate the two sexes as marked and unmarked."[39] The phallic *Gestalt* is therefore an *imaginary signifier* lying at the crossroads between the imaginary and the symbolic order. At the imaginary level, the phallus works as a *Gestalt* which promotes alienating identifications. As a signifier, it differentiates man and woman in the first symbolic couple +/− (undoubtedly, the minus does not count here as "less" than the plus; it is an oppositional element, not a deficiency in the Real *per se*). There are few places in which Lacan discusses this basic point; however, the following quotation seems to me to point uncompromisingly in the above direction: "The signifier avails itself of a series of elements which are linked . . . to the body. . . . There are a certain number of elements, given to experience as accidents of the body, which are resumed in the signifier and which, as it were, give it its novitiate. We are dealing here with things that are both elusive and irreducible, amongst which there is the phallic term, plain erection."[40]

Above all, it is imperative here to emphasize that the consolidation of the phallic image in the child during the passage between the first and the second stage of the Oedipus complex must correspond with the realization that "the mother *lacks* this phallus."[41] The child has not perceived the mother's lack any earlier than this. During the first stage of the Oedipus complex, due to primordial frustration, the mother is experienced as a desiring Other (the Desire-of-the-Mother), but this desiring Other is not thought to lack anything (the imaginary phallus). This distinction is central: at first, *the Desire-of-the-Mother is not associated with lack*. How else could we justify the fact that Lacan continuously maintains that the child considers his mother to be *omnipotent*? Conversely, it is exclusively by (retroactively) supposing that the mother is phallic that the child may believe that he is loved by her *per se*.[42] In other words, the child wrongly presumes that he is able to satisfy the Desire-of-the-Mother fully—although at no point does he consider this desire to be extinguished.[43] Why? Because he identifies himself with the various concrete objects of her imaginary desire, the same objects which are responsible for his own frustration: more specifically, the child carries out a *double* imaginary and alienating identification. We have already seen how, even simply at the imaginary level, desiring the other means, for Lacan, both desiring to be desired by the other—to be the object of his desire—and desiring the objects of his desire. The child temporarily manages to superimpose these two dimensions upon one another: he conjectures that he is the *exclusive* object of the Desire-of-the-Mother—that he is loved by her, love corresponding here to "having the Other to oneself"[44]—precisely insofar as his identification with her body image means that he desires what she desires while, at the same time, also identifying himself with these objects.[45]

We can therefore conclude that, at the end of the first stage of the Oedipus complex, the child realizes that the mother does not have the (imaginary) phallus, and thus that she desires it insofar as she lacks it: this superimposition of desire and lack necessarily terminates her omnipotence.[46] Moreover, the child retroactively realizes that he has been desired only as a partial stand-in for the imaginary phallus. To summarize: a "fundamental disappointment"[47] is produced in the child when he acknowledges that (a) "he is not the mother's unique object," because (b) "the interest of the mother . . . is the phallus," since (c) she is "deprived" of the latter, "she herself lacks this object."[48]

Before moving on to treat the second and third stages of the Oedipus complex, we should consider the dialectic of frustration more closely by focusing in particular on what the emergence of the symbolic object implies for the subject.

(1) After primordial frustration, what is at stake in the child's relation with the mother "is not really the object [the real object] but rather the love of the one who can give you this gift [the object *qua* symbolic object]."[49] In such a way, the child *actively* symbolizes his relation with the Other for the first time: however, in this protosymbolization "the gift is only associated with a certain gratuitousness. . . . That which is behind the other, the entire chain thanks to which the gift takes place, is not yet grasped."[50] In other words, the child does not yet realize that the mother wants something specific *in return*.

(2) As a consequence of protosymbolization, the child's demand (for love) is *always* unsatisfied. Even when a particular demand is satisfied, the child perceives the gift as somehow frustrating: demand "immediately projects itself onto something else," onto a "symbolic chain of gifts,"[51] in order to confirm the mother's unconditional dedication. It is in this context that Lacan formulates his well-known definitions of love for the first time: "What one loves in a being is beyond what she is, that is, in the end, what she lacks";[52] and, in parallel, "there is no bigger sign of love than donating what one does not have."[53] The first formula implicitly refers to the lover, the second to the beloved: we can infer that, during the dialectic of frustration, they indiscriminately apply to both the child and the mother. Theirs is a "love relation":[54] as lover, the child does not demand the object of satisfaction but "the [symbolic] object as grasped in what it lacks": Lacan also calls it "being,"[55] given that this object, "which is beyond, . . . is not nothing since it has

the property of being there symbolically";[56] furthermore, this "object *qua* lacking object [is] the phallus."[57] The same goes for the mother: she loves the child for what he lacks, or better, for what literally is in him more than himself, the phallic *Gestalt*. Conversely, as beloved, both child and mother give what they do not have: the child is the stand-in for the mother's missing phallus (without knowing it); similarly, the mother, who has not yet been perceived as deprived by the child, is considered as omnipotent and thus capable of satisfying *all* his demands. In this way, what both the child and the mother give without having is the phallus: a temporary superimposition of lacks is obtained. Such a result becomes even clearer if one recalls that, due to a double imaginary alienating identification, the object of the child's demand is nothing but the object of his mother's desire. However, we shall later need to clarify the distinction between the phallus as "universal object,"[58] the impossible object that the child pursues with his demand, and the phallus as phallic *Gestalt* which the mother provisionally identifies with the child taken as a whole.

(3) What happens when there is actual frustration? Lacan maintains that when demand is not satisfied, "the subject begins to make a claim [*entre dans la revendication*], insofar as the object is considered as demandable by right":[59] that is to say, the child enters into an imaginary narcissistic relation with the object. Consequently, whether demand is "satisfied" or not, the object as such (the real object) soon fades into the background. Focusing on the situation in which demand is not satisfied, Lacan then insists on distinguishing between the symbolic frustration of love and the real frustration of a need (despite the fact that they may be linked to the same lack of object). Only the former "generates reality."[60] In other words, the productivity of the imaginary narcissistic relation between the child and the object which is refused to him can only rely ultimately on symbolic frustration. Undoubtedly, (primordial) frustration is, by definition, the lack of a *real* object (of need), but "it is not simply because the child does not obtain the mother's breast that he fosters its image. . . . It is necessary that the image is taken in itself as an original [symbolic] dimension. It is not the breast that is essential here, but the breast's tip [the erected +/−], the nipple."[61]

(4) From the protosymbolic stance of the dialectic of frustration, what is the value of the real object insofar as it satisfies need? Lacan's answer is ingenious: "The satisfaction of need corresponds to a *compensation* for the frustration of love."[62] In this sense, the real object functions as an "alibi": I eat or drink (milk, sweets, chocolate, etc.) to compensate for the love I lack. . . . [63] Again, one can see how the virtual object becomes real only in the Symbolic, after primordial frustration, insofar as it compensates for the structural lack which goes together with the symbolic

the real object functing as on alibi – compensation for the love I lack

object/gift as an always insufficient sign of love. Furthermore, this newly conceived role of the real object allows Lacan to clearly differentiate (animal) need from (human) libido. It is doubtless the case that, for instance, oral libido "aims at the preservation of the individual," however, the libido is also inevitably influenced by the symbolic order. "Precisely insofar as it has entered into the dialectic for which satisfaction is substituted for the demand for love," the libido cannot be reduced to need: in other words, it has become an "eroticized activity."[64] To summarize: Lacan believes that *libido is nothing but the eroticization of need*, the noneliminable imprint that the demand of love leaves on man *qua* instinctual animal.

(5) With another brilliant move, Lacan uses his theory of "compensation" to propose a hypothesis regarding how the child learns to speak. "From the moment in which a real object that satisfies a real need has become an element of the symbolic object,"[65] it is possible for any other real object to take the place of the (lacking) symbolic object. This also applies to *words* which, as we have seen, indeed partake of both the symbolic dimension of speech (for the Other/Mother) and the real, "perfectly materialized," dimension of the letter (for the child). The symbolic speech of the mother is "devoured" by the child as a real material object which compensates him for the lack of love.[66]

Remaining at the level of language apprehension, it is important to underline how the moment of primordial frustration and the parallel emergence of the symbolic object also necessarily distinguish, from the child's perspective, the child's merely passive cries from the active articulation of his first signifiers/phonemes. It is clearly the case that the child is always-already immersed in the Symbolic and, for this reason, even his less articulated cries can never function as a bi-univocal sign (they are always openly interpreted by the mother);[67] however, if we postulate the existence of a mythical—and, as such, concretely inexistent—state in which everything that the child needs is perfectly satisfied, it also follows that, at this stage, he is not yet producing any signifier for himself.[68]

Despite the fact that Lacan never really developed this argument, I believe this to be a strictly necessary implication of his overall premises. Let us then clearly differentiate the *cry*, as a sign that precedes frustration and keeps the child in a state of complete passive helplessness with respect to the signifying universe, from *demand* as a signifier that follows frustration and which, by attempting to cope with the latter, initiates the child's active presence in the symbolic order while accompanying his permanent dissatisfaction. Let us also consider the *appeal* as indiscriminately applicable to both situations. As Lacan himself points out—but this statement seems to be contradicted elsewhere—there is a "position zero," the "opposition, the institution of the pure symbol plus or minus, presence or absence," that is, as we have seen, the presence/absence of the symbolic mother (or, more precisely, of her nipple) which already punctuates the mythical state of total satisfaction (modulated by the cry only from the mother's standpoint), and a "second time" which consists "in the fact that the declaration you make *saying even* or *odd* is a sort of demand which puts you in the position of being or not being gratified by the answer of the other."[69] In other words, at a purely abstract level, a cry becomes a demand when, in concomitance with primordial frustration, the child's cries start to be actively modulated in order to facilitate the attainment of the (symbolic) object which has by now been experienced as lacking or, more generally, to cope with (the mother's) absence. (To make things easier, we are here supposing that the child's "technical" mastery of language, his actual capacity to articulate the first basic phonemes of his parents' language—to say "o"/"a," "fort!"/"da!," "even"/"odd," "it belongs to me!". . .—is increased at the precise moment of frustration. But the same still holds if we presume, more realistically, that even after frustration the child can only cry; we would nevertheless be dealing with a *signifying* cry. . . .)

Lacan could therefore be said to have rethought the Freudian Fort!–Da! game through the dialectic of frustration. Freud's original discovery may be summarized as follows: a baby reacts to his mother's absence by throwing a cotton reel with a piece of string tied around it over the edge of his cot; while doing so, he utters "o-o-o-o!" and "*da!*" ("fort" and "*da*," the German words for "gone" and "there").[70] Freud understood this game as the "child's [first] great cultural achievement": [71] Lacan specifies this definition by equating the Fort!–Da! with the "birth of the symbol"[72]—or, better, of primordial symbolization—in the individual. What he already emphasized in his early account of the game in "Function and Field" is, once again, the fundamental role played in the child's early development by the productivity of lack. If, on the one hand, the Fort!–Da! marks the first assumption of absence (of the mother) in the child's universe (frustration), on the other, it contemporaneously entails a certain domination of surroundings through the uttering of some basic phonemes and, for the same reason, a partial symbolic overcoming of the initial state of helplessness (radical dependency on the mother). For Lacan, this very twofold character of the symbol is even experienced by the child when, in the Fort!–Da!, he is confronted by the first emergence of the idea of death: death is inextricable from the symbolic order, given that it is both passively encountered by the child when he is forced to acknowledge his finitude ("lack of being") due to frustration *and* actively imposed by him on the mother when he replaces her (absence) with a symbol, a phonetic oppositional couple (in this last sense, "the symbol manifests itself . . . as the murder of the thing").[73] To conclude, it should be noted that the *Fort!–Da!* game, the fact that "the signifier is introduced . . . in demand,"[74] also coincides, from the child's standpoint, with the mythical moment at which pure need is somehow repressed for the first time. I shall discuss this multifaceted point in the final section of this chapter.

3.4 THE SECOND AND THIRD STAGES OF THE OEDIPUS COMPLEX

Lacan clearly considers privation and castration to be two different kinds of lack of an object. Privation is defined as the real lack of a symbolic object, the symbolic phallus, and it applies exclusively to woman. Castration is defined as the symbolic lack of an imaginary object, the imaginary phallus, and it applies to both woman and man;[75] symbolic castration—which initiates the third stage of the Oedipus complex, its resolution—is the precondition of the subject's active entry into the symbolic order; without undergoing castration, no subject can truly individuate him- or herself through symbolic identification.

Let us start with privation, which, as we have seen, determines the passage from the first to the second stage of the Oedipus complex. First of all, what does it mean to lack a symbolic object in the Real? What does woman as such lack? Two notions of the Real are implicitly at stake here: in the Real to be understood as everyday reality, woman clearly "lacks" the penis (the real phallus); yet the vagina as a real organ is not *per se* a lack, it does not stand for that which one acquires when one is deprived of the penis. . . . In other words, it is clear that, according to a different definition of the Real—on the basis of our previous discussion of the real object, we could call it "the virtual Real" which precedes symbolization—woman does not lack anything. Privation as a real lack makes sense only when the lack of the penis is oppositionally related to the penis (or, better, to its *Gestalt*), when the object which is "really" lacking is symbolized $+/-$, that is, when the penis turns into the phallus. As Lacan clearly points out: "Everything that is [virtually] real is always and necessarily at its place. . . . The absence of something in the [actual] real is purely symbolic."[76] It is only insofar as we establish by some kind of law that something should be in a certain place that we can say that "an object is missing"; this expression is nothing more than an oxymoron when it is abstracted from a symbolic context.[77] Most importantly, privation as a real lack of a symbolic object means that, within a symbolic dialectic $+/-$, "what one does not have is as existent as the rest. Simply, it is marked by the minus sign."[78] Woman's lack of the symbolic phallus $(-)$, her state of privation, which is not to be confounded with the vagina as a real organ, is, even at the symbolic level, as existent as the symbolic phallus $(+)$.

If we return to the onset of the second stage of the Oedipus complex, it is once again important to remember how the child is able fully to assume privation, and therefore sexuation *tout court*, only when the complex is finally resolved: the initial emergence of sexual difference during the phallic phase is completely symbolized only in a retroactive way. Moreover, as in the case of the dialectic of frustration, it is vital here to take account of the fact that the second stage of the Oedipus complex is two-faced: by depriving the mother of the child *qua* phallus, the (imaginary) father also simultaneously dispels the child's mistaken belief that he is the only object of his mother's desire. For both the mother and the child, what is prohibited by the (imaginary) father is their incestuous relationship ("You will not sleep with your mother!"; "You will not reintegrate your offspring [*produit*]!").[79]

At this point, we should ask ourselves one basic question: when precisely does the (imaginary) father interrupt the dialectic of frustration, the child–mother love relationship? Why was it not considered incestuous from the very beginning? The exact moment at which the "No!" of the father—the voice of the Law—resonates for the first time is logically concomitant with the child's realization that the mother (and he himself) lacks the phallus and, as a consequence, with his attempt to *directly* identify with it, to be her phallus. During the dialectic of frustration the child does not know about the phallic *Gestalt*: this is why the father does not yet openly intervene. The child starts to compete aggressively with his (imaginary) father in order to be his mother's phallus only after the mother has actually been deprived (of him).

In a few pages of Seminar V, Lacan provides a particularly dense but lucid account of this key passage. As we have already seen, a double alienating movement allows the child to identify himself with a "multiplicity of elements . . . in reality,"[80] that is, with the imaginary objects of his mother's desire. The child has to "delude her desire,"[81] in order to preserve himself as the exclusive object of her desire (in order to delude himself). He identifies himself with the mother and, thanks to this identification, he identifies himself with what she desires. (For this same reason he is able to believe that she is a desiring being who does not lack anything.) Lacan points out how this series of identifications is not only imaginary, given that the child's demand for love, which here perfectly overlaps with what the mother desires, is already based on an experience of symbolic lack: through "all his successive identifications [the child] himself assumes the role of a series of signifiers, . . . of hieroglyphics . . . which punctuate his reality with a certain number of marks and makes it a reality filled with signifiers."[82] The objects of the mother's desire with which the child identifies himself (+) are given always against a background of lack (−). These double identifications are ended when the mother really desires the phallus/penis (of the father) and, as a consequence, the child attempts directly to identify with it: at this precise moment, the imaginary father intervenes to stop the incestuous relation. By prohibiting the child's direct identification with the phallus, the father "suddenly promotes the object of the mother's desire to a properly symbolic rank."[83] In other words, it is only the Law's designation of the phallus as a forbidden object that allows the child to group his previous oppositional signifying identifications (with the object of the mother's desire) +/− into an ordered sequence. I shall return to this point.

If we compare this account of privation with my previous description of it, we realize that the two are by no means incompatible: Lacan is simply drawing our attention to different aspects of privation. The first account emphasized the "natural" role of the phallic *Gestalt* in the child's initial assumption of sexual difference (the child realizes that the mother is deprived as a result of the fact that he is captivated by the phallic *Gestalt*). The second account underlines how this same realization can effectively be put into practice only insofar as the mother is already characterized as a deprived being by a preexisting symbolic Law. We could attempt to link these two accounts of privation by supposing that, for Lacan, the moment at which the child is captivated by the phallic *Gestalt* (first account) coincides with that at which he directly identifies with the phallus *qua* forbidden object of his mother's desire (second account).

We should emphasize that the prohibition of incest undoubtedly concerns both the use that the child makes of his penis and the circulation of the phallus/phallic *Gestalt* as an imaginary signifier. With regard to this issue, how is the second stage of the Oedipus complex experienced by its protagonists more specifically?

- After privation, *the child* offers himself to his mother as a gigantic phallic *Gestalt*/ imaginary phallus: he is now aware of her lack, which, from his standpoint, he had been able temporarily to avoid during the first stage. We must also remember, however, that the prohibitive "No!" which inaugurates the second stage is also logically concomitant with the genital drive's first emergence in the child—that is, infantile masturbation—and with the child's consequent awareness of the utter inadequacy of his real organ. The child understands that his mother desires him as an image but, at the same time, it is only at this stage that he would like to be desired for his by now awakened real phallus, which he therefore also offers to her. More generally, we should emphasize how, despite the fact that, according to Lacan, unlike most psychoanalytic theories, genitality can never be understood simply as the synthetic and harmonious achievement of psychosexual maturity—sexuality as such can never be harmonious—there undoubtedly exists a relationship between the Oedipus complex and genitalization.[84]

• *The mother* has always desired the child as a huge imaginary phallus (even before privation) and has never been completely satisfied by it—this is why she also consoled herself with the father's penis, which could be defined as a privileged embodiment of the phallus. Now, the child's offer of his own penis, which the Law prohibits, simultaneously makes her recollect that she must also renounce the child *qua* imaginary phallus. With reference to little Hans's case, Lacan says: "The mother's behavior with little Hans—whom she drags everywhere she goes, from the loo to her bed—clearly shows that the child is her indispensable appendix"; however, "when she has to get down to brass tacks and to put her finger on the little thing that the child has taken out and is asking her to touch, she is suddenly taken by a blue funk."[85]

• *The imaginary father* is not, by definition, a real person. The "No!" is not actually uttered by the real father: the Law is already internalized by the mother, since she is already actively involved in the symbolic order. Privation is therefore operated in "a mediated way by the mother"[86] herself. "The function of the father, the Name-of-the-Father, is linked to the prohibition of incest, but nobody has ever . . . believed that the father effectively promulgates the law of prohibition of incest. . . . The mother is herself able to show the child how that which he offers her is insufficient and to pronounce the prohibition to use the new instrument."[87] Because of all this, I think we could actually reread the aggressive competition between the child and the imaginary father for control of the mother as the mother's "inner fight" with herself: the child's—by now explicit—offer of himself as a phallic *Gestalt* is juxtaposed to the Father's prohibition of incest.

Some further points should be made with regard to the way in which the symbolic Law, the Name-of-the-Father, already functions in and through the mother:

(1) What specifically does it mean to say that the Law is "mediated" by the mother? How does the Law concretely enable the child to perceive that his mother is deprived? The acknowledgment of privation is triggered in the child not by the "personal relationships between father and mother"—"it is not about whether one plays footsie with the other or not"[88]—but by the way in which the mother relates to the father's *speech*.[89]

(2) The agency of the father is already present in a "veiled form"[90] during the first stage of the Oedipus complex. In other words, the dialectic of frustration is itself dependent on the symbolic Law insofar as "the question of the phallus is already posed somewhere in the mother,"[91] and it is a matter for the child to track it down. However, this very phase is ambiguously called by Lacan the "law of the mother":[92] with this definition he intends to emphasize the fact that, although the mother is

already being subjected to the paternal Law, by allegedly being omnipotent, she imposes on the child an "uncontrolled law."[93] As we have seen, her "articulated whims"[94] render the child an *assujet*: his demand is totally dependent on her desire. We shall later explore the paradoxes of this law understood as a signifier *sui generis*. For the time being, suffice it to underline how Lacan feels obliged clearly to distinguish the "veiled" form of the paternal Law in the first stage of the Oedipus complex from its "mediated" form in the second stage: in the first case, the Name-of-the-Father remains inaccessible to the child, he perceives only the discourse of the mother "in the wild state,"[95] the mother does what she wants with the father's speech; in the second, "the father's speech effectively intervenes in the discourse of the mother"[96] by promoting a "Do not!"

(3) The command "You will not reintegrate your offspring (*produit*)!" actually deprives the mother for a *second* time. She is now deprived *as mother*, having been deprived *as woman* when she was a little girl and underwent the Oedipus complex. In other words, one must distinguish between: (a) the first privation of woman as a speaking being whose sexuation is obtained by identifying symbolically with the "minus side" of the fundamental signifying couple +/− provided by the phallic *Gestalt*; (b) the second privation of woman *qua* mother who attempts to compensate for her symbolic lack, as well as for the imaginary lack generated by the differentiality of the symbolic opposition +/− as such,[97] by equating her child with the (symbolic and imaginary) phallus. I will return to this issue, as well as to the problematic way in which Lacan thematizes the little girl's initial privation, her sexuation, in due course.

How do we overcome the second stage of the Oedipus complex? One final crisis is needed, namely castration, which coincides with the intervention of the real father. Since "the [real] father is revealed as the one who *has* it,"[98] and he "neither exchanges nor gives it,"[99] the child realizes that it is useless to compete with him, to keep on attempting to *be* the phallus of the mother. We can speak of a resolution of the Oedipus complex in the third stage only insofar as, due to castration, the child identifies himself symbolically with the real father as the one who has it: this same identification marks the emergence of the ego-ideal.[100]

Here it is important to underline the fact that during the second stage of the complex the child is unable to understand that the father *has* the phallus/phallic *Gestalt*. And this despite the fact that the child (a) identifies aggressively with the image of the father as a rival, and (b) identifies with the phallic *Gestalt* as the object of the mother's desire; at this stage, the child *is* the imaginary phallus, his proto-ego equates with it. If the second stage negatively imposes on the child the fact that the imaginary father (the way in which the mother relates to his speech) deprives the mother of the phallus, it is only during the third stage that the child manages constructively to "symbolize, to render privation fully significant."[101] This can occur only if the real father demonstrates to the child that the "No!" which deprives the mother depends on him; if he can show that, as the sole agent of the Law, he can donate and withdraw the forbidden phallus at will.[102]

Lacan defines castration as the symbolic lack of an imaginary object: it might be helpful to analyze this rather obscure formula in more detail. Where symbolic lack is concerned, Lacan specifies that it should be understood in terms of debt. This can be interpreted in two overlapping ways. First, the child is indebted to the real father insofar as he saves him from the threat of being engulfed by the mother: "The subject is freed from the impossible and anxiety-provoking task of having to *be* the phallus by realizing that the father *has* it."[103] Secondly and more generally, by accepting that the phallus belongs to the real father alone, the child actively enters the domain of symbolic Law, of which the real father is the agent; as Freud had already envisaged in *Totem and Taboo*, the subject's very entry into the Law—the institution of the tyrannical agency of the superego—renders him always-already potentially liable to be persecuted, and consequently a priori guilty. Moving on to the nature of the castrated object, this is nothing but the imaginary phallus—it is clear that the very menace of castration, "If you use it one more time, I'll cut it off!," does not operate on the real organ. The fact that the child is castrated of the phallus actually means that he renounces *being* the imaginary phallus of his mother. During the passage from the second to the third stage of the Oedipus complex, "the question is: to be or not to be the phallus?"[104] Why does the child generally decide *not* to be the phallus anymore? Because the real father finally intervenes as the one who *has* the phallus. On the other hand, in the second stage, rivalry with the father relied on the fact that, in a certain sense, the imaginary father *was* himself the imaginary phallus.[105] We could suggest that the child was simultaneously identifying and competing with the same *Gestalt*, as always happens in narcissistic alienation: on the one hand, the rivalry with the paternal *Gestalt* was clearly based on the fact that the child compared the latter's completeness/perfection, due precisely to the presence of the phallus, with his own incompleteness. On the other, in order to be the phallus, the child was identifying with the same paternal *Gestalt qua* phallic *Gestalt*: but he was not identifying with the father *qua bearer* of the phallic *Gestalt*.

Having said this, one should not underestimate the importance of the competitive relation that the child establishes with the imaginary father during the second stage of the Oedipus complex: it is nothing less than the precondition of the symbolic identification which is achieved in the third stage. Lacan is extremely clear on this point: "The conquest of the Oedipal realisation . . . is carried out . . . by way of an aggressive relationship [with the father]. In other words, *it's by way of an imaginary conflict that symbolic integration takes place.*"[106] He goes so far as to draw a general equation between the paternal *imago/Gestalt* and what he calls the "*image* of the big Other":[107] the symbolic order possesses an imaginary dimension of its own. Two important specific points should be made to avoid possible confusion here:

(1) Imaginary identification with the father furthers symbolic identification with him, but this does not mean merely that he is introjected by the child as an ideal ego. Imaginary identification with the father is fundamental because it entails, for both boys and girls, the symbolic assumption of one's own sexuality "with respect to the function of the father," the Name-of-the-Father—the symbolic father, that is, whether the child *has or does not have the (symbolic) phallus.*[108] Here, we should briefly refer back to our discussion of the distinction between ideal ego and ego-ideal: Lacan is basically suggesting that the formation of the ego-ideal, which introduces the subject to an active participation in the symbolic order as a sexuated being, re- lies on an imaginary identification with the paternal *Gestalt* to be understood as the ideal ego. Simultaneously, it is thanks to "the ego-ideal [that] the imaginary ele- ments assume their stability in the symbolic":[109] it is only after the emergence of the ego-ideal *qua* symbolic identification that the subject is properly individuated at the level of the Imaginary, and his ego is consolidated. Thus the ego-ideal cor- responds to the way in which I (imaginarily) see others (symbolically) seeing myself: this double reflection provides a symbolic "form" to the way in which I see myself (the ideal ego).

(2) Imaginary identification is necessary but not sufficient to bring about symbolic identification with the father and the consequent emergence of the ego-ideal: as we have seen, the real father has to intervene. "It is on the path to imaginary crime [aggressive rivalry with the father] that [the child] enters the order of the law. However, he cannot really enter this order of the law if, at least for a moment, he has not met a real partner [the real father]."[110] In order to enter the Law, passing through the imaginary rivalry with the father, the child has to relate to the real father insofar as he transcends the protosymbolic +/− that links the child to the mother, insofar as he anchors, or "groups" the oppositional sequence +/− by somehow *embodying* the +, by showing that he has the symbolic phallus. Neverthe- less, it is vital to observe that if, on the one hand, the Law needs to be embodied in a concrete figure for the child to be able to access it, on the other, this very embodi- ment can never be complete. In other words, the distinction between real father and symbolic father ultimately consists of the fact that the symbolic father as the ab- stract "paternal function" (the Name-of-the-Father, the Law of the +/−) "is strictly speaking unthinkable,"[111] that nobody has ever fully occupied the paternal func- tion.[112] Consequently, being a father as the bearer of the phallus means being a "real person covered by a symbol";[113] the real father is not the so-called biological or

genetic father, but the person who partially embodies the symbolic father (as function) for the child in reality—and who might, but need not necessarily, correspond to the so-called biological father.[114] On a closer inspection, the very notion
of a real father as biological or genetic father is absurd: the Real (father) can make
sense only from the standpoint of the Symbolic—one then understands why
Lacan sarcastically observes that "there is only one ['genetic'] real father: the
spermatozoon."[115]

Such a discrepancy between the paternal function and its embodiment also explains another fundamental distinction: although we are compelled to assume that
what the real father concretely has and "shows" at the moment of castration is the
penis, his possession of the latter is important only inasmuch as it represents the—
always partial—embodiment of the phallus. As Lacan puts it in a particularly intricate passage from Seminar IV, during the third stage of the Oedipus complex,
everything "is about knowing where [the phallus qua real penis] really is": on the
contrary, up to that moment "the phallus was never there where one found it."[116]
In other words, in the first two stages of the Oedipus complex the phallus should
be equated with the imaginary "absolute object" that the child attempted to be for
the desire of the mother: such an imaginary object could originate only within
the dialectic of a symbolic object +/− which was "contemporaneously present
and absent."[117] The symbolic object emerged as absent precisely when it was present (as gift) in the guise of some contingent imaginary object, and as present
when it was absent, that is, it was precisely the fact that no contingent imaginary
object (of demand) was ever sufficient to represent the symbolic object fully, it was
such an inadequacy, that rendered the latter present. (The "absolute object," the
imaginary phallus, would then be nothing but the—by definition—impossible
representation of the sole + "pole" of the symbolic object +/−.) Therefore, the
child undergoes castration only when there is an "*equalization between a sort of absolute
object, the phallus, and its being put to the test in the real* [the penis]";[118] as a consequence of
this operation, it is no longer for the child a matter of "all or nothing" (+ as "all,"
− as "nothing"),[119] "the object is no longer the [*absolute*] imaginary object thanks
to which the subject can lure [the desire of the mother], but the [*partial*] object
which the Other [father] can always show the subject that s/he does not have [girl]
or has in an insufficient way [boy]."[120]

3.5 SEXUATION AND THE FEMININE OEDIPUS COMPLEX

As Lacan clearly points out in Seminar III, there is, in the end, one basic principle
on which Freudianism relies: "The subject's sexual position is . . . tied to the symbolic apparatus."[121] Therefore, if the (resolution of the) Oedipus complex corre-

sponds for the child to his active entry into the symbolic order, then the Oedipus complex will also entail the fact that "the subject finds his place in a preformed symbolic apparatus that institutes the *law in sexuality*."[122] This Law (in sexuality) coincides with the existence of the Name-of-the-Father, which we should here interpret in a literal way as the superindividual surname that allows the constitution of a lineage. With regard to castration, it is then easy to see that the child's realization that the father has the phallus and that, as agent of the Law—as the one who prohibits incest—he can either donate it or withdraw it, marks both the child's sexuation—through an identification with the father as the bearer of the phallus—and his assumption of a surname, the fact that "he is called Mr. So-and-so" (which "has nothing to do with his living existence").[123]

But why is sexuality necessarily related to the Symbolic for human beings? "The symbolic order has to be conceived as something superimposed, without which no animal life . . . [nor] the most natural of relations, that between male and female . . . would be possible for . . . man."[124] Lacan's continual claim that the Oedipus complex has a *normalizing* and *normative* function with respect to sexuality should be interpreted within this framework:[125] first and foremost, the Oedipus complex is needed not to keep man from the "excesses" of animal life, but to find a remedy for his "natural" deficiencies. To cut a long story short, Lacan believes that the symbolic Law ("in sexuality") is essential for the survival of the human species: the end of symbolic sexuation would not confine man to mere animal copulation, but would lead to the extinction of the species. Commentators usually underline how, according to Lacan, the Symbolic is responsible for the fact that "there is no sexual relationship"; as Evans succinctly puts it, this means that "there is no reciprocity or symmetry between the male and the female positions because the symbolic order is fundamentally asymmetrical," that is, the phallus is the only signifier that governs the relations between the sexes.[126] What is, on the contrary, almost unanimously overlooked is the fact that *the Symbolic constitutes the structural condition of possibility for any sort of (reproductive) human sexual relationship to occur.*

As we saw in Chapter 1, the "natural" helplessness of man as "disadapted" animal is logically prior to the emergence of the Symbolic. Lacan believes that, already at the imaginary level, "there is no sexual relationship," propagation of the species is impossible: because of the prematurity of birth and the ensuing narcissistic alienation in the other's body image, unlike animal *Gestalten*, man's "disordered imagination" is unable to fulfill the basic sexual/reproductive requirements of the species. Without a symbolic "superimposition" on the realm of animal sexual instincts, the human Imaginary and the ego-libido would inevitably reduce us to aggressive self-destruction: the incestuous relationship mother/child is sterile, and "doomed to conflict and ruin."[127] Unlike the humanist leitmotiv of the misleading Lacanian doxa according to which the Imaginary is the domain of (man's) animal life and the Symbolic is what radically distinguishes man from animal life, Lacan is fully aware of "the *paradox* that results from certain functional interweavings between the two planes of the symbolic and the imaginary."[128] In more detail: if, on an initial level, it seems that the Symbolic is what renders our "world system" specifically human ("it's because man has words that he has knowledge of things"), and that the Imaginary is unequivocally linked to ethology ("the sexual relation implies capture by the other's image"), on a second level everything becomes more complex given that (a) it is only insofar as "the function of man and woman is symbolized . . . literally uprooted from the domain of the imaginary . . . that any normal, completed sexual relationship is realized"; and (b) the realm of knowledge is dependent on imaginary identifications thanks to which "the object is realized as an object of competition."[129]

This analysis provides us with a general explanation of the symbolic character of human sexuality. Two broad overlapping issues, however, remain to be tackled. First, we need to analyze the consequences of the fact that sexuation is asymmetrical for man and woman: in order to be properly sexuated, man needs only to be castrated, whereas woman undergoes both castration and privation. Secondly, it is necessary to examine closely the role of the phallus in sexuation; as we have seen, the phallic *Gestalt* is an imaginary signifier, and consequently it always partakes of both the Imaginary and the Symbolic. Yet, if during the first two stages of the Oedipus complex the imaginary aspect of the phallus is prominent (the child attempts to be the *imaginary* phallus of the mother), in the third stage it is the symbolic aspect of the phallus that acquires more importance.

Castration is a prerequisite for the child (boy or girl) to be able to identify symbolically with the father as the bearer of the *symbolic* phallus:[130] the result of such an identification is the subject's assumption of his or her sexual position (masculine or feminine). On the one hand, renouncing being the imaginary phallus of the mother, the girl assumes her sexuality insofar as she realizes that she *does not have* the (father's) symbolic phallus; this not-having, her being deprived, is itself a symbolic form of having. On the other hand, the renunciation of being the imaginary phallus entails for the boy the assumption that he *has* the symbolic phallus, albeit for the time being through the intermediary of the father: the symbolic debt to the father is for him also a pact, the promise that he will effectively dispose of the symbolic phallus once he reaches puberty. For the boy, having the symbolic phallus means above all that "he will one day be able to access the problematic and paradoxical position of being a father," partially embodying the Law.[131]

The girl's castration, and her consequent identification with the father as the bearer of the symbolic phallus, presupposes that she also undergoes privation. In other words, the sexuation of man and woman is asymmetrical insofar as "there is no symbolization of woman's sex as such"; this is due to the fact that, in the case of the female sex, "the imaginary furnishes only an absence where elsewhere there is a highly prevalent symbol . . . the phallic *Gestalt*."[132] In other words, this asymmetry means that the girl is not able to identify symbolically with the mother,[133] and that she has "to take the image of the other sex as the basis for her [symbolic] identification."[134] She cannot assume her sex at the symbolic level in a direct way; her "minus" cannot be acquired from another (maternal) "minus": she is sexuated only with respect to the father's phallic "plus."

Two points should be made here: (1) The fact that the vagina as a real organ cannot be directly symbolized—due to the fact that in the woman's case "the symbolic lacks the material"[135]—does not exclude the possibility that "the little girl herself feels something in her womb and that her experience is without doubt different from that of the little boy from the beginning."[136] The important issue lies, rather, in the fact that in order to symbolize her sexual organ—and as we have seen, it is meaningless to talk about a nonsymbolic sexuality in the case of human beings—the girl has to relate herself to the phallus, which she does not have.[137] (2) As I have repeatedly pointed out, "not having the phallus symbolically also means participating in it out of absence and therefore, in a way, having it."[138] Insofar as woman is deprived, at the imaginary level she nostalgically desires the phallus, but at the same time the phallus as imaginary *signifier* is also functioning in and through her at the symbolic level; "Given that she is taken up into the intersubjective relation, there is for man, beyond her, the phallus that she does not have, the symbolic phallus, which exists here as an absence. This is entirely independent of the inferiority that she might feel at the imaginary level."[139] To put it simply, *man, who is also symbolically castrated, does not have woman's not-having as a form of symbolic having*: his desire depends on such a lack. This is one way in which to explain why: (a) "the biggest desire is lack";[140] (b) what one loves (as a man) in a being is what the beloved (woman) lacks.[141] One should not, however, overlook the fact that such a love of what woman as such lacks in the end paradoxically coincides with the most radical quest for the *whole*. Woman's missing phallus is the *pendent* of man's "plus" as a *castrated* being: man is castrated since he symbolically lacks the lack (*qua* imaginary object).

How does the girl relate to her father more specifically? Here Lacan takes up Freud's idea that the girl attempts to compensate for her privation by asking her father for a baby as a substitute for the missing phallus. If the symbolic identification boy–father relies on the promise that he will have the phallus, the symbolic identification girl–father relies on the girl's expectation that she will have the baby (*qua* phallus). The girl's sexuation as "minus" is consequently reinforced inasmuch as the father fails to provide her with the baby she desires: she then waits "until the father is finally substituted with the one who will adopt exactly the same role, the role of the father, and will effectively give her a baby."[142]

More importantly, when a woman becomes a mother, the child functions both as a symbolic substitute for her symbolic lack of an imaginary object (castration), as an imaginary phallus, and as an imaginary substitute for her real lack of a symbolic object (privation), as a symbolic phallus. This detail is of fundamental importance if one is to understand the entire dynamics of sexuation and the overall role of the symbolic order as such. Through her child, the mother attempts both to have the symbolic phallus—that is, to overcome her privation and to symbolically *be a man qua* "plus" in the "plus/minus" dialectic of sexual difference—and, beyond man, who is himself castrated, to have the imaginary phallus, that is, to suspend castration, to *become whole*. Consequently, when the imaginary father deprives the mother in the passage from the first to the second stage of the Oedipus complex, he actually deprives her of (the child as) both the imaginary and the symbolic phallus. It is in this context that we can appreciate most appropriately what the prohibition of incest as the imposition of the Law (of sexuality) aims at: far from applying to the avoidance of incestuous "animal" mating—which is strictly speaking impossible for human beings—the proscription of the mother's "reintegration" (+) of her child must be interpreted as the preservation of symbolic difference +/− and therefore of the order of the Symbolic *tout court*. Mythically, woman enters culture and allows its propagation when she exchanges her child for her symbolic designation as "minus":[143] in this way, she also furthers the preservation of the species. Conversely, her temporary revocation of castration/privation risks pulling her out of culture and endangering the preservation of the species.

Despite overcoming Freud's misogynous psychological explanation of woman's "inferiority" and consequent "penis envy" by explaining this phenomenon through the superimposition of the logic of the signifier and *Gestalt* theory— to cut a long story short, for Lacan, the problem with the vagina is simply that it does not "stick out"[144]—in his discussion of the feminine Oedipus complex in Seminars IV and V, Lacan *never* really departs from the father of psychoanalysis. Given that in these seminars he often openly disagrees with Freud on other issues, we must assume that he believed the Freudian account to be substantially reliable. A more radical rethinking of woman's symbolization will be offered only in the 1970s with the so-called "formulas of sexuation" after the discovery of a specifically feminine dimension "beyond the phallus."[145]

It is often argued that Lacan's explanation of the feminine Oedipus complex is radically different from Freud's, since according to Lacan, (a) both boy and girl "love" the mother; (b) both resolve the complex by identifying with the father. One could object that although it is evident that Freud initially believed that the

girl's Oedipus complex worked in a perfectly symmetrical fashion to the boy's—
love for the father and hatred for the mother—he himself later came to acknowledge the existence of a "pre-Oedipal" indiscriminate attachment to the mother.[146]
And as we know, the first stage of the Lacanian Oedipus complex, in which both
sexes love the mother, is nothing but a rethinking of the "pre-Oedipus." The same
ambiguity also applies to the resolution of the complex: unlike Lacan, Freud
thought that the girl's sexuation implied an identification with the mother, but at
the same time he also assumed that a privileged relationship was established between the girl and the father (from whom the girl wants a child). The hypothesis
of a proximity between Freud's and Lacan's ideas concerning the final identification of the Oedipus complex is reinforced by Lacan's own hesitations, if not contradictions, on two specific points. First, if on the one hand, in Seminar III, Lacan
explicitly affirms that the girl resolves the Oedipus complex by symbolically identifying with the father's image,[147] on the other, in Seminar V, he explicitly denies
that the girl identifies with him in such a way.[148] I believe that the only way to resolve this deadlock is to assume that Lacan is here implying that the girl assumes
her sexuality by "negatively" confronting herself with what he elsewhere names
the "paternal object"—the symbolic phallus—as the object of her desire, not with
the paternal *Gestalt stricto sensu*. Such a distinction nevertheless remains partly unclear.
Secondly, Lacan does not even seem to be sure whether the girl ever leaves the Oedipus complex: thus he seems to share Freud's view according to which for her, unlike the boy, the castration complex is the point of *entry* into the Oedipus complex
(she loves the father from whom she expects a baby).[149]

In one specific passage of Seminar IV, things are interestingly rendered even
more complicated: "Castration is the essential crisis through which *every subject* . . .
qualifies to be . . . *fully oedipized.*"[150] Lacan seems to suggest that if the child appropriately carries out symbolization, regardless of his or her sex, he or she *never*
leaves the Oedipus complex. Here Oedipal attachment is clearly synonymous with
successful heterosexual symbolic sexuation, and should not be identified with a
sterile incestuous relationship with the mother. In the end, it is not only woman
who tends to re-create with men her primordial relationship with the father;[151]
man equally tends to re-create with women his original relationship with the
mother.[152] Does this mean that we eventually recover some sort of symmetry between the sexes? Not at all. Lacan believes that woman's phantasmatic "model" of
sexual relationship is *monogamous*, precisely because it is always founded on her link
with the father: in her case, there is an "identification between the [symbolic] love
object [the phallus that she lacks] and the [imaginary/real] object which gives
satisfaction";[153] in other words, all she really wants is "the [paternal] phallus all for
herself."[154] On the other hand, man is *bigamous* "insofar as the normative and legal

union is always marked by castration," the renunciation of the child–mother love relationship: in other words, man undergoes a "division, a split" between woman as legal object of satisfaction authorized by the Law of the father and the forbidden/inaccessible woman as maternal object of love. Man pursues the latter precisely for what he symbolically lacks—that is, the phallus that she lacks.[155]

3.6 THE PATERNAL METAPHOR, THE NAME-OF-THE-FATHER, AND THE PHALLUS

As I have repeatedly pointed out, the phallic Gestalt partakes of both the imaginary and the symbolic order. The phallus is an imaginary signifier. Despite referring to one and the same notion, Lacan often distinguishes the imaginary phallus (φ) from the symbolic phallus (Φ). We have also already analyzed how φ and Φ are interrelated as a result of asymmetrical sexuation in man and woman. On this point, everything could in the end be reduced to the fact that the phallus is, as symbolic object $+/-$ par excellence, always an object that lacks (something). Even possessing it $(+)$ actually always means lacking the oppositional $-$ on which the $+$ depends. In other words, man can partially embody (Φ as $+$) the symbolic phallus (Φ as the transcendent Law of the $+/-$) only after being castrated. Castration is in fact expressed in Lacanian algebra as $-\varphi$, the symbolic lack of the imaginary phallus. The differentiality proper to the signifier creates the space of symbolic lack which is equally valid for woman, who locates/sexuates herself on the $-$ pole of the signifier, and man, who locates/sexuates himself on the $+$ pole of the signifier.

The asymmetrical fashion in which sexuation is achieved, however, obliges us to treat φ as the unachievable "universal object" that emerges as a consequence of castration $(-\varphi)$ independently of φ as the imaginary aspect of the phallic Gestalt $+/-$. The former does not directly refer to the image of the penis: it would be appropriate to suggest that it is that which lurks in the background of the (always different/renewed) concrete[156] object that both man's and woman's unstoppable demand for love perpetually request. This explains why Lacan also defines this first acceptation of φ as a "metonymic object":[157] the space of symbolic lack opened by castration $(-\varphi)$ is strewn with an imaginary sliding of objects that can never attain the status of "universal object." On the other hand, the second acceptation of φ undoubtedly is the image of the penis:[158] if, on the one hand, such an image has a certain importance for the child regardless of his or her sex during the passage from the first to the second stage of the Oedipus complex, on the other, after sexuation, it becomes the privileged object only of woman's desire. This noticeably entails that, in the case of woman, the pursuit of the universal object which, as a consequence of $-\varphi$, is always missing, overlaps with the pursuit of the + of the phallic *Gestalt* of which she has been deprived.

Two important points should be made with regard to this matter: (1) Whenever woman is granted temporary access to the + of phallic *Gestalt*, in the guise of the baby in the "pre-Oedipal" relation or in the guise of the penis during sexual intercourse, she is not completely saturated by it. In other words, insofar as she dwells in the symbolic order, φ as the unachievable "universal object" always remains for her beyond φ as the imaginary aspect of the phallic *Gestalt* $+/-$. (2) Woman's simultaneous search for φ as the unachievable "universal object" and the + of the phallic *Gestalt* is obviously also superimposed upon and facilitates her (reproductive) relation to the *real* penis.[159]

The question now arises concerning how to reinterpret the distinction and interrelation between the imaginary and the symbolic phalluses on the basis of the linguistic distinction between signifier and signified. Lacan in fact believes that the entire dynamics of the Oedipus complex and its resolution could be interpreted in terms of a paternal metaphor: "The [symbolic] father is a metaphor."[160] As we have seen, a metaphor can be defined as the substitution of one signifier for another which gives rise to an effect of signification: "It is in the relation between a signifier and another that a certain relation *signifier over signified* will be generated."[161] This can be expressed as shown in schema 3.1:[162]

$$\frac{S}{S'} \rightarrow \frac{S}{s}$$

Schema 3.1

The Oedipus complex is itself resolved after castration thanks to the metaphorical substitution of the signifier Name-of-the-Father for the signifier Desire-of-the-Mother: all subsequent metaphors—and consequently signification *tout court*—rely on such a primordial paternal metaphor. As Lacan clearly states, "the father is a signifier which is substituted for another signifier . . . the first signifier introduced in symbolization, the maternal signifier . . . that is the mother who comes and goes."[163] He then proposes schema 3.2:[164]

$$\frac{\text{Father}}{\text{Mother}} \cdot \frac{\text{Mother}}{x}$$

Schema 3.2

"The father comes in the place of the mother, S in the place of S', S' being the mother insofar as she is already linked to something which was x, that is the signified in the [child's] relation to the mother."[165] During the Oedipus complex, the child's relation to his mother is marked by a basic question: "What does her desire want (so that I can be it)?"; the signified of the mother's desire—which is the signified of what the child desires, since he desires what she desires—is an enigmatic x, an unknown signification. This question can be answered only when the Name-of-the-Father, the Law of the +/− which allows sexuation, comes into play: at this stage, it becomes clear for the child that "the signified of the mother's coming and going is the phallus."[166] By substituting itself for the Desire-of-the-Mother, the Name-of-the-Father actualizes for the child the phallus φ as the object or signified of the former:

$$\frac{S}{S'} \cdot \frac{S'}{x} \rightarrow S\left(\frac{1}{s'}\right)$$

Schema 3.3

that is:[167]

$$\frac{\text{Name-of-the-Father}}{\text{Desire-of-the-Mother}} \cdot \frac{\text{Desire-of-the-Mother}}{\text{Signified for the subject}} \rightarrow \text{Name-of-the-Father}\left(\frac{\text{Other}}{\text{Phallus}}\right)$$

Schema 3.4

What can invariably be deduced from both schema 3.4 and Lacan's statement quoted above is that, as a result of the paternal metaphor, the phallus finds itself in the position of a signified. The phallus here is the imaginary φ, the signified of the signifier Desire-of-the-Mother which has contemporaneously been substituted. In a sense, the paternal metaphor causes the substituted signifier (Desire-of-the-Mother) to "fall" to the level of the signified (the imaginary phallus): in parallel, the substituting signifier (Name-of-the-Father) could be said to signify the original substituted signifier (Desire-of-the-Mother). As we will see later in more detail, this is a specific feature of the paternal metaphor; in general, in metaphor, the substituting signifier does *not* signify the substituted signifier, the signifying effect is created by the substitution itself—in between the two signifiers—and not by the substituting signifier. Three further points should be made apropos the imaginary phallus as the signified of the Desire-of-the-Mother:

(1) The right-hand side of schema 3.4 shows that φ is nothing but the signified of the Other as such; in other words, *signification* (in the big Other) *can only be phallic*. The fact that the signifier Desire-of-the-Mother—as the inscrutable m-Other—is substituted by the signifier Name-of-the-Father allows the child actually to relate to a *signifying* Other for the first time: the utter impenetrability of the signifier Desire-of-the-m-Other prevented it from being experienced as an actual signifier.

(2) Consequently, we can understand why, in the schema of the paternal metaphor (schema 3.4), the signifying Other corresponds to what Lacan had designated as "1" in the general schema of the metaphor (schema 3.3). The intervention of the Name-of-the-Father and the ensuing emergence of phallic signification makes the Other become One for the child. Lacan's underestimated false tautology from Seminar V "*Un Autre, c'est un Autre,*"[168] could adequately be rendered in English as "*An Other is one Other.*"

(3) This phallic oneness of the Other is simultaneously constituted as differential. φ is the signified of the Desire-of-the-Mother but, at the same time, the phallus is also an oppositional imaginary *signifier*. The fact that the Name-of-the-Father is a substitute for the impenetrable Desire-of-the-Mother, and institutes the latter as φ, *also* means that the desire-of- φ is symbolically instituted as a "rebellious lack"[169] which can never fully be satisfied. From this it follows that phallic oneness is perfectly compatible with the fact that the phallus is the "*signifier* of lack," "the signifier of the impossibility or of the vanity of the demand to be whole."[170]

More generally, one should realize that, in and around Seminar V, Lacan thinks the phallus as *both* a signified *and* a signifier: his most frequently repeated definition of the phallus is that it is a "privileged *signifier*."[171] These apparent contradictions have misled many a commentator. Even Safouan, in his otherwise impeccable summary of Seminar V, is not able to reconcile these different definitions: indeed, when he wrongly concludes that the phallus is a "signifier and not an object or a signified" he is, from what we have just seen, unknowingly contradicting Lacan in the most blatant way.[172]

How precisely should we understand the phallus as both a signified and a signifier? The phallus is an imaginary signified (φ) with respect to the Name-of-the-Father. At the same time and for the same reason, it is a symbolic signifier (Φ) with respect to the "signified as such." Signification as such is in fact phallic for Lacan; the phallus is therefore also defined as "the signifier of the signified in general," hence its "privileged" character.[173] In other words, the fact that the phallus partakes of both the signified and the signifier can rightly be grasped only if one realizes that, despite being strictly related to each other, the Name-of-the-Father and the phallus are *not* the same thing. The former is understood by Lacan in Seminar V as the "signifier of signifiers,"[174] as "the Other of the Other":[175] this means that signifiers are somehow *signified* by the Name-of-the-Father. The phallus as a privileged signifier, signifier of the signified as such, is obviously no exception. In other words, if the Name-of-the-Father is the signifier of signifiers and the (embodied) symbolic phallus (Φ) is the signifier of the signified as such, then the Name-of-the-Father will also be the signifier of the symbolic phallus (Φ) understood as the imaginary phallus (φ) which emerges as the signified of the paternal metaphor.

To use Lacan's formulas: (1) "The phallus is in the signified that which results from the existence of the signifier":[176] the imaginary phallus φ is the signified which results from the mere fact that the signifier Name-of-the-Father signifies signifiers, and thus makes them exist; (2) The symbolic phallus Φ is "the last/ultimate [privileged] signifier in the relation between signifier and signified";[177] this is why Φ can never fully unveil that which, as signifier, it signifies: the latter is in fact nothing but φ itself, the universal object. The fact that the phallus is the signifier of the signified as such ultimately means that Φ is the signifier of itself *qua* φ (the signified as such).

The distinction between the Name-of-the-Father and the phallus can more easily be grasped if we refer to another of Lacan's schemas in Seminar V:[178]

$$S$$

$$\overline{\text{S S S S S S S}}$$

$$\text{S S S S S S S S S}$$

Schema 3.5

He comments on this by saying that "the [name-of-the-] father [the upper S] is, in the Other, the signifier that *represents* the existence of the place of the signifying chain [S/s] as law."[179] Here Lacan is advocating the absolute *transcendence* of the signifier Name-of-the-Father with respect to the Other *qua* signifying chain (S/s); as he unequivocally maintains: "The Other itself has *beyond* itself an Other which is able to found the law."[180] In order properly to exercise its function as Other, the Other as the "deposit" or "treasury of signifiers" has to be anchored in the "signifier of the Other *qua* Other."[181] The Name-of-the-Father articulates the order of the signifier, it groups the signifying oppositional couples that the child had already experienced in the protosymbolic relation with the Desire-of-the-m-Other: such an articulation amounts to the promulgation of the phallic Law (of sexuation +/−), the founding of the fact that the Other is lawful. Moreover, the dimension of the Name-of-the-Father must then be "embodied in those people [the real fathers] who support its authority":[182] the Law of the +/− is embodied in a specific +, the paternal symbolic phallus Φ. On the basis of Lacan's schema, one could perhaps picture the relation between the Name-of-the-Father, the phallus, and the signified as in Schema 3.6:

$$\frac{\frac{\text{Name-of-the-Father}}{\text{Phallus}}}{\text{signified}}$$

Schema 3.6

We can also break this schema down into its two components:

(a) $\dfrac{\text{Name-of-the-Father}}{\varphi}$ (b) $\dfrac{\Phi}{\text{signified}}$

Schema 3.7

One should not underestimate what structurally distinguishes the signifying function of the Name-of-the-Father from that of the phallus. The latter is, as signifier of the signified as such, the most important oppositional signifying couple +/−; on the contrary, the former is, as signifier of signifiers, definitely not a signifying couple: the Name-of-the-Father as the imposition of the Law of the +/− functions bi-univocally in relation to the Desire-of-the-Mother which it replaces. In this sense, one could argue that the phallus is a privileged signifier to be understood as the fundamental signifying couple that is introduced by the signifier Name-of-the-Father as the "natural" sign or index of the Law; again, the Name-of-the-Father, through the production of phallic signification, retroactively "legalizes" or groups the signifying oppositional couples that the child had already confusedly experienced in the protosymbolic relation with the Desire-of-the-m-Other. More precisely, the Name-of-the-Father should be understood as a shifter, a signifier which also works as a bi-univocal index/sign. The Name-of-the-Father as *signifier* signifies "the Other *qua* Other," the existence of the differential signifying chain as such; for the same reason, it is precisely, as *name* (of the Other), a "rigid designator," it always designates the same thing, that is, φ *qua* object of the Desire-of-the-m-Other. For Lacan, this bi-univocal relation is typical of indexes/natural signs and not of signifiers which are never bi-univocally related to one given signified. In other words, by signifying always one and the same signified (φ, the Other *qua* Other) the Name-of-the-Father is actually meaningless: it is both that which allows the emergence of (phallic) signification as such in the signifying chain—by anchoring it—and, *per se*, meaningless. On the contrary, as we know, all signifiers in the signifying chain both signify in various—non-bi-univocal—ways, and do not signify anything specific; this is of course valid, first and foremost, for the privileged relation signifier over signified given by Φ over φ.

Having described the relationship between signifier and signified in the signifying chain as non-bi-univocal, Lacan faces the problem of explaining how, despite the incessant slippage of the signified under the signifier, the chain actually holds together, how and where "the signified and the signifier are knotted together."[183] In Seminar III, he names these places "quilting points" (*points de capiton*). Where the diachronic horizontal dimension of language is concerned, the notion of quilting point can easily be explained through the idea of retroactive punctuation: "It is only when the sentence is completed that the sense of the first words is determined retroactively."[184] In simple terms, punctuation corresponds to the overall effectiveness of grammar in a given language: for instance, if one does not know the grammar of a foreign language well enough, one cannot appropriately punctuate a given sentence, and the signifying chain simply falls apart; in this case, signifiers cease to have meaning—or signify too many things at the same time—even if we actually know the "meaning" of a given signifier (hence we ask questions such as "what does that word mean in this context?"). On the other hand, where the synchronic vertical—unconscious—dimension of language is concerned, Lacan thinks that quilting points should be identified with metaphors.[185] In Seminar III, before the explicit formulation of the paternal metaphor, he indicates that "the notion of father . . . gives the most palpable element in experience of what I've called the [vertical] quilting point between the signifier and the signified,"[186] hence, implicitly, how the (Name-of-the-)Father, by linking a signifier and a signified in a bi-univocal way, functions as a *sign*. In other words, as we have seen, the (Name-of-the-)Father knots together the paternal imago as signified with the phallic symbolic Law as signifier.[187] Two years later, in a brief passage from Seminar V, Lacan—strangely—seems to contradict the equation between metaphor and quilting point: he considers the latter to be a "mythical matter, since nobody has ever been able to stick a signification to a signifier";[188] on the other hand, it is possible to "stick a signifier to a signifier" in order to produce a metaphor. The fact is that, at this stage, Lacan is primarily interested in explaining the notion of the (Name-of-the-)Father in terms of a paternal metaphor, and detaching it from the simpler idea of quilting point. However, he does not seem to fully acknowledge that the Father as a metaphor is no less a sign than the Father as quilting point. This is clear from schema 3.5, which he himself contradictorily provides straight after the above quotation: one can easily glean from it the fact that the signifying chain S/s is nothing but the bi-univocal signified of the signifier (of signifiers) Name-of-the-Father.

Should we consequently understand all (unconscious) metaphoric substitutions as signs, or is this the prerogative of the paternal metaphor as the metaphor on which all other metaphors rely? On one level, it is possible to propose that all metaphors function as signs insofar as they all entail a bi-univocal relation between the substitution of one signifier for another and the effect of signification that such a substitution causes; it is only in this precise sense that Lacan can claim that metaphors correspond to vertical quilting points. One must, however, emphasize the fact that the paternal metaphor as primordial metaphor is at the same time different from all others: the signifier Name-of-the-Father generates (phallic) signification by replacing the signifier Desire-of-the-Mother, but, unlike all other signifiers, the Name-of-the-Father is the "signifier of signifiers"—and, in the first instance, of the Desire-of-the-Mother as the anomalous signifier that precedes it. The signifier Name-of-the-Father directly signifies the (substituted signifier) Desire-of-the-Mother, while in all other metaphors it is the substitutive operation *between two signifiers* that bi-univocally signifies a certain effect of signification: it is only in this last sense that all metaphoric substitutions correspond to vertical quilting points.

Lacan repeatedly suggests that the Desire-of-the-Mother is a signifier:[189] indeed, one can generally admit that the child first enters symbolization precisely by confronting the mother's presence and absence as an alternating +/−. Given the ultimate impenetrability of this "coming and going," however, the Desire-of-the-Mother fully becomes a signifier only retroactively, after it has been replaced by the Name-of-the-Father. In other words, in the paternal metaphor, the Name-of-the-Father bi-univocally signifies an enigmatic "What does she want?," the Real of a trauma which the child had not thus far been able to symbolize (completely): as we have seen, despite attempting to satisfy the Desire-of-the-Mother by identifying with its various concrete objects, the overall signified of such a signifier remains an inscrutable x for him. For this reason, the paternal metaphor is not only the point at which the dimension of the signifier inextricably overlaps with that of the sign: it is also the locus where the Symbolic and the Imaginary are themselves linked to the Real. With regard to this last point, I should mention one final detail: all metaphoric substitutions that follow the paternal metaphor also differ from it because, in their case, one signifier substitutes itself for another *proper* signifier; the substitutive operation is *not* in direct contact with any traumatic Real.[190] In parallel, this is also what distinguishes primal repression—of a Real—in the paternal metaphor from secondary repressions—of a signifier—which are brought about by successive metaphoric substitutions, and which all presuppose the paternal metaphor.[191]

3.7 THE OEDIPUS COMPLEX AND THE BIRTH OF THE UNCONSCIOUS

Both Freud and Lacan are extremely reluctant to discuss openly the notion of primal repression—that is to say, precisely how the unconscious first arises. As Laplanche and Pontalis point out, however, it is clear that Freud believed that primal repression was the consequence of a "very intense archaic experience."[192] For this very reason, I think that this notion should be related to that of "primal scene" understood as an (at least partly) actual traumatic event—corresponding to the witnessing of parental coitus—which is only later retroactively signified by the fundamental fantasy, the basic structure of the unconscious. Having thoroughly explained Lacan's Oedipus complex and the way in which it can be understood linguistically in terms of a metaphor, in this final section I put forward the hypothesis that Lacan endorses and expands such an interpretation of Freudian primal repression through his notion of primordial frustration. This corresponds in fact to an archaic traumatic event generated by the absence of the mother and, as such, should be considered as the logical cause of primal repression. After all, frustration occurs because the mother is (sexually) busy with the father. . . . The child cannot make sense of what he either materially sees or infers from other clues (the primal scene), hence he does not know what his mother's desire wants (from him).

In order to corroborate this speculative parallelism between Freud and Lacan, we should focus on two interrelated sets of questions: (1) Does Lacan, at the time of his reelaboration of the Oedipus complex in Seminars IV and V, implicitly rely on Freud's theory of the "ideational representative" (*Vorstellungsrepräsentanz*), which is key for the notion of primal repression? If so, is such a theory compatible with Lacan's basic tenet according to which the unconscious is made up of signifiers?[193] (2) At which stage of the Oedipus complex does the fundamental fantasy emerge for Lacan and, more importantly, how does it impose itself as the basic structure of the unconscious?[194] We can certainly answer affirmatively to the first set of questions. For Freud, ideational representatives are "delegates of the instinct in the sphere of ideas."[195] The instinct as soma does not *per se* leave any trace on the psyche: it is only through the ideational representatives that the instinct is fixed to the psyche—hence their role as proxies. Consequently, it is these and not the instincts that are repressed in the unconscious. In addition to representing the content of the unconscious, being that which is repressed in secondary repression, ideational representatives also *set up* the unconscious *tout court*, which means that they are responsible for primal repression. The latter should thus be understood as the *fixation* of an instinct to an idea that is not allowed to enter consciousness: "The representative in question persists unaltered from then onwards and the instinct remains attached to it."[196] As Laplanche and Pontalis correctly observe, Freud also understands such a fixation in terms of a *registration* (*Niederschrift*) in the unconscious of the ideational representative *qua sign* (*Zeich*). At this point, it is relatively straightforward to see how this scenario could be translated into Lacanese. First, fixation corresponds to the bond between an image and a need: as we have repeatedly seen, Lacan understands the sign as a connection between the Imaginary and the Real. Secondly, the idea of the registration of these imaginary–real signs entails the formation of a *series* of signs (the repressed ideational representatives) in the unconscious. At the outset, however, this sequence is not yet adequately grouped: in this way it is possible to relate it to the range of protosymbolic signifiers that are created during the dialectic of frustration between the child and the mother. For Lacan, the protosignifier Desire-of-the-Mother is indeed properly symbolized only after it has been replaced by the Name-of-the-Father at the end of the Oedipus complex.

This brings us back to the second set of questions concerning the fundamental fantasy. What is certain is that, for Lacan, the retroactive character of pre-Oedipal symbolic processes is equally valid for pre-Oedipal unconscious life. The unconscious is structured symbolically, hence it will also be formed retroactively: consequently, one could correctly speak of a "proto-unconscious" which becomes unconscious *stricto sensu* only later. Freud had already envisaged the retroactive character of the trauma—of its repression—yet he repeatedly seemed to fall back into a linear understanding of the emergence of the unconscious. For instance, as we have just seen, he thought of primal repression as the original moment at which an ideational representative was denied entry by *consciousness*: according to Freud, consciousness as self-consciousness is already fully formed when primal repression occurs. Lacan firmly disagrees on this point: the emergence of self-consciousness and the unconscious must be strictly contemporaneous. If the unconscious should be thought retroactively, the same applies to self-consciousness. Pre-Oedipal unconscious life is, at the same time, pre-Oedipal conscious life: no clear distinction has yet been drawn between the two psychic agencies. In other words, proper repression requires proper individuation, and the unconscious can properly be so named only with the emergence of self-consciousness: this is achieved only with the formation of the ego-ideal at the end of the Oedipus complex.

In the end, we have to admit that Lacan is providing us with two different notions of primal repression: generally speaking, primal repression is the consequence of primordial frustration at the beginning of the first stage of the Oedipus complex. "Primal repression corresponds to the alienation of desire when need is articulated in demand."[197] For the sake of clarity, we could call this kind of primal repression inscription. On the other hand, primal repression *stricto sensu* will correspond to the retroactive shaping of the unconscious—in concomitance with the consolidation of a conscious ego—enacted by the paternal metaphor at the end of the third stage of the Oedipus complex; in this sense, primal repression corresponds to the repression of the traumatic proto-signifier Desire-of-the-Mother, and to the parallel formation of a fundamental fantasy. In other words, the primal scene is finally "legalized" by the fundamental fantasy: the father has the right to have the mother; his apparently violent conduct during coitus finally makes sense, and the "What does she want?" finds an answer in the phallus.

With specific regard to the fundamental fantasy, an apparent contradiction needs to be resolved immediately: the fundamental fantasy provides the structure of the (unconscious) subject but, at the same time, contains "signifiers in their pure state . . . emptied of their subject";[198] the symbolic order here is desubjectivized. All things considered, this simply means that the fundamental fantasy retroactively structures the trauma (Desire-of-the-Mother) and, for this very reason, the subject can never consciously assume it: in the phallic fundamental fantasy, the Name-of-the-Father works retroactively as a sign with respect to the trauma. Since the unconscious is ultimately held together by the fundamental fantasy, accessing it, exposing the trauma, is ultimately the same as undoing self-consciousness itself. This also explains why the paternal metaphor as the imposition of a phallic fundamental fantasy is itself necessarily repressed:[199] it is so since, by substituting itself for the Desire-of-the-Mother, the signifier Name-of-the-Father is directly linked to the Real of a trauma.

In Seminar III, Lacan suggests that there are two fundamental sets of questions that the symbolic order, due to its differentiality, cannot answer. The first concerns the subject's singular existence, his individuation: "Why do I live and die?"; "How was I born and how will I die?" The second concerns, for both men and women, the "minus" of female sexuality when considered independently of the phallic "plus": "What is it to be a woman?"; "What does a woman want?"[200] The (primal) repression of these questions is a prerequisite for the subject's active entry into the symbolic order, as well as for his concomitant sexuation. In this context, fundamental fantasies are nothing but (unconscious) palliative answers to these questions. It is only by covering the lack inherent to the Symbolic that the child can enter it as an individual at the end of the Oedipus complex. At this stage of his work, however, Lacan thinks that the phallic answer provided by the Name-of-the-Father is an entirely successful panacea: there is an Other of the Other; the differentiality of the Other is contained/encircled by the oneness of a transcendent Law.[201] In other words, Lacan believes that the paternal metaphor efficaciously freezes the "intense archaic experience"—witnessing parental coitus, but also, for instance, being "seduced" by the mother—in which the child is compelled to ask himself questions that the Symbolic cannot answer ("Why is Daddy 'violent' with Mummy?"; "What does Mummy want from me?"); the trauma is thus retroactively organized in a (phallic) fundamental fantasy. Again, the latter is therefore nothing but a defense against these questions. One should at the same time, however, underline how it is only with the formation of the fantasy that the trauma—which had thus far been "inactive"—becomes operative in a retroactive way. Certainly, we should not understand these questions as being literally asked by the child: in a sense, it is the Symbolic as such that asks itself these questions through the child at the moment when the latter is undergoing an "intense archaic experience." Strictly speaking, their traumatic value for the child is only caused/actualized by the answers that will have been given to them in the fantasy: "Woman wants the phallus," therefore "what is feminine sexuality *beyond the phallus?*" (scene/trauma of seduction); "The father's phallus generated me," therefore "how was I really born?" (scene/trauma of parental coitus).

To conclude, it is important to emphasize how the retroactive nature of the process through which both the subject's access to symbolization and the emergence of his unconscious are achieved obliges us to acknowledge that Lacan is tacitly presupposing the existence of four different kinds of signifier: (1) the Desire-of-the-Mother; (2) the Name-of-the-Father; (3) the phallus; (4) all other signifiers involved in the life of a subject who has successfully resolved the Oedipus complex. As for this last category, in Chapter 2, we considered how signifiers (S2) operate both in consciousness and the unconscious according to the laws of metaphors and metonymy. In the early 1960s, Lacan will move on to elaborate his formula according to which signifiers (S2) represent the—unconscious—subject for a Master-Signifier (S1): in the context of the first formulation of the paternal metaphor, the Name-of-the-Father, the signifier that fixes the primal scene in a fundamental fantasy, functions as a precursor of such an S1. In addition to this, we have also already analyzed the relation between the Name-of-the-Father as the signifier of signifiers and the phallus as the signifier of the signified as such. Against the background of our attempt to read Freud's notions of primal repression and primal scene together with Lacan's notion of primordial frustration, we should now finally focus on the exact nature of the signifying function of the Desire-of-the-Mother.

(1) Desire-of-the-Mother is, for Lacan, a *general* designation for the protosymbolic relation child–mother as a whole—or, better, for the protosymbolic "signifiers" that constitute and are constituted in such a relation.

(2) Desire-of-the-Mother is a flow of oppositional "signifiers" which have not yet been organized or grouped.

(3) More precisely, these "signifiers" correspond to the (ever-changing contingent stand-in for the) metonymic object of the mother's desire: as Lacan says, "the subject identifies imaginarily with it in an absolutely radical way."[202] Consequently, they can be understood as *oppositional* insofar as any object that temporarily occupies the place of the metonymic object is given—precisely because it is already experienced as a symbolic object—against a background of absence. In parallel, they can be said to represent a *flow* since, despite not being grouped, they nevertheless form a metonymic chain: such a flow is sustained by the perpetual dissatisfaction of demand. Grouping will then be brought about by the primordial paternal metaphor.

(4) Primordial signifiers are, first and foremost, *imaginary* signifiers and, as such, *signs*. If, on the one hand, their oppositional aspect—accompanied by vocalizations such as the *Fort!–Da!*—is what allows us to consider them as "signifiers," on the other, they are also signs (*Zeichen*) precisely in the sense of Freud's ideational representatives. Primordial signifiers that compose the Desire-of-the-Mother are, according to Lacan, nothing but representatives of (the child's) need in the domain of images. For the same reason, these imaginary signifiers/signs equally mark the moment of primal repression as inscription: insofar as the child articulates his need in demand, and demand creates imaginary signifiers, he undergoes repression. From this, we can conclude that for Lacan, unlike Freud, *all* ideational representatives are, as such, necessarily repressed/inscribed in the proto-unconscious. Once the unconscious is properly distinguished from self-consciousness by the action of the paternal metaphor, such an incessant inscription of ideational representatives will continue: this is why we can state that, for Lacan, after primal repression

proper has taken place, all signifiers are *doubly inscribed* (in the conscious diachronic chain and in the unconscious synchronic chains).

The complex signifying function of the Desire-of-the-Mother necessarily has important repercussions for the status of the Name-of-the-Father: insofar as both are considered to be signifiers, the substitutive operation between the two can rightly be named a (paternal) metaphor. On the other hand, given that the Desire-of-the-Mother is, at the same time, only a protosignifier, a nonorganized flow of ideational representatives whose imaginary–symbolic signifying elements are still somehow in direct contact with the Real of a trauma, the Name-of-the-Father can also be seen as a sign. As we have previously concluded from a slightly different perspective, by promoting phallic signification, the Name-of-the-Father biunivocally signifies an enigmatic "What does she want?" which the child has not thus far been able to symbolize (completely). It is precisely in this sense that the phallus should in its turn be regarded as the Master-Signifier (S1) of the unconscious of those subjects who have successfully entered and resolved the Oedipus complex. To use one of Lacan's most effective expressions from Seminar V, the phallus is in the end a *"signe constituant."* Interestingly enough, at this stage, Lacan seems to apply such an expression only to those signs / imaginary signifiers (such as the whip, the stick, etc.) which, in "abnormal" Oedipal relations, help the child to actively enter the symbolic order in an "alternative" way (which will be marked by masochistic perversion).[203] *"Signes constituants"* are here qualified as that "through which the creation of value [of other signs] is ensured," as well as that "through which this real something that is involved . . . is hit by a ball which makes it a sign."[204] These "alternative" Master-Signifiers are needed as substitutes whenever a disturbance in the dialectic of frustration between the child and the mother prevents the emergence of the phallic *Gestalt*.[205]

More generally, we should emphasize that, as long as the transcendence of the paternal Law grants the self-sufficiency of the symbolic Other, Lacan does *not* explicitly recognize the existence of a *standard* phallic fantasy which corresponds to a successful implementation of the Oedipus complex. Fantasy is secluded in the domain of perversions, and the inevitable overlapping of the "normalization/normativation" of appropriate sexuation with masochism is disregarded. Things will change as soon as Lacan arrives at the conclusion that "there is no Other of the Other": this simply means that there is no transcendent Law, and that the Symbolic is thus *per se*—independently of psychotic and perverse pathologies—an order that is structurally lacking. At that point, despite remaining responsible for correct sexuation/Oedipal resolution, the Name-of-the-Father will be: (a) perfectly identified with the symbolic phallus; (b) qualitatively "lowered" to the level of any other (perverse) Master-Signifier (S1). In other words, the Name-of-the-Father/ symbolic phallus as S1 will in any case be considered as the *most standard* phantas-matic compensation or defense against the lack in the Symbolic, but no structural difference will distinguish it from "perverse" Master-Signifiers. The Name-of-the-Father will no longer "encircle" the Other; it will simply suture it by "veiling" its lack. Consequently, *all* S1s will be defined as equally privileged signifiers on which their respective signifiers S2 depend. Such a dependence will, however, be con-fined to the level of signification: the fact that signifiers S2 depend on a given S1— represent or signify an unconscious subject for his S1—will no longer imply that that S1 signifies its S2s. There will no longer be any signifier of *signifiers*, only a mu-tually exclusive—though potentially infinite—plurality of signifiers S1 that sig-nify the *signified* as such by fixing the subject's unconscious in a fundamental fantasy. With regard to the algebraic formula of fantasy $\$\Diamond a$—to be read as "the castrated subject in (retroactive) relation to the Real of the primordial trauma"—S1 will be precisely that which keeps the two elements bound.

S1 as phallus covers gap in the Symbolic-
authority? "why? Because I say so"

PART III

THE SUBJECT OF THE REAL (OTHER)

"What have you done?" one of them said to me,
"what need did you have to invent this little object *a?*"
Lacan, Seminar XIV

CHAPTER 4

THERE IS NO OTHER OF THE OTHER

In Chapters 4 and 5 I propose to explore Lacan's late theory of the subject, centered as it is on the notion of the Real. In this chapter, I initially intend to analyze fully the meaning of the formula "There is no Other of the Other" and its paradigmatic function in summarizing Lacan's work of the 1960s and 1970s. What does the Other stand for here? How is this formula related to the decline of the hegemony of the symbolic Other—the Other of the paternal Law, the "signifier of signifiers"—and to the simultaneous emergence of the "absolute Other of the subject"?[1] And, last but not least, why does Lacan superimpose this notion of "absolute otherness" with what he calls "the Real"?

Secondly, I aim to show how the explicit thematization of the Real and its complex relationships with the Imaginary and the Symbolic directly imply a thorough reconsideration of the field and function of the subject. The Real "subverts" Lacan's previous notions of subjectivity insofar as it obliges him to reconsider the precise role of the signifying structure that founds the subject of the unconscious. Undoubtedly, the main focus of Lacan's late research is still directed at the subject of the unconscious, but the unconscious is now to be conceived as not being completely exhausted by the presence of signifiers: there is something real in it which escapes the Symbolic, something which renders the symbolic Other "not-all" and, for the same reason, makes it possible precisely as a differential symbolic structure.

As Lacan himself clearly states in Seminar VII (1959–1960), "the subject is not simply the subject subjected to the mediation of the signifier," but is also a "middle term between the real and the signifier."[2] Such a qualification of the subject of the unconscious should immediately strike the reader for its incongruity with what Lacan had repeatedly expressed in his earlier work, most noticeably in his article "The Freudian Thing" (1955): at that stage, the unconscious was fully reducible to the signifier and, indeed, straightforwardly defined as the "rational" Thing that speaks. On the other hand, by the time of Seminar VII, the unconscious is somehow bound to a real Thing whose main characteristic is—rather surprisingly—its "dumbness,"[3] its being "outside-of-the-signified."[4] As we shall later see in more detail, although Lacan's claim that in these two instances he is, after all, delineating exactly the same notion of the unconscious is unconvincing, it is nevertheless the case that we are not simply being presented with two opposed theories of the subject. In other words, it is important to insist on the fact that, despite some substantial changes, it is yet again the subject of the unconscious structured like a language that finds a new elucidation through the notion of the subject of the Real.[5]

In addition to this, it is essential to emphasize that the order of the Real does not exclusively appear in the margins of the subject's symbolic functions: it is at the same time that which lurks beneath the subject's imaginary dimension. In Chapter 5 I shall also be concerned with the exploration of this issue: this will give me an opportunity to show that, by the early 1960s, Lacan arrives at a thorough reworking of the theories I have discussed in the opening part of this book. Simply put, in Lacan's late work, the specular nature of the imaginary order is ultimately dependent upon a real element which cannot be specularized. As he himself states in Seminar VII, "man . . . as image is interesting for the hollow the image leaves empty."[6] At this point, the subject is deemed to be especially "interesting" for what is in the image (of his body) more than the (specular) image itself: this is what Lacan names "object a," a nonspecularizable remainder, a void ("hollow") that resides at the frontier between the Imaginary and the Real.

It must be noted that this frontier itself borders on the domain of the Symbolic. The notion that lies at the junction of the three orders—and will be dealt with meticulously in three long sections of Chapter 5—is the notion of the fundamental fantasy. As we have already seen, the formula of the fundamental fantasy is in fact precisely $\$\Diamond a$ which should be read as: the subject barred by the symbolic effect of the signifier in relation to the real object a. It is under the apparently trivial phrase "in relation to" and its many possible readings that Lacan groups two of the most significant concepts of his theory of the subject: desire and the drive. I will follow his analyses in an attempt to demonstrate how desire—which Lacan, like Spinoza, considers to be "the very essence of man"[7]—and the drive—which, for the time being, is simply to be understood as that which partially satisfies desire—can adequately be interpreted only if they are located within the framework of the fundamental fantasy.

At this preliminary stage, it is sufficient to introduce the fundamental fantasy by roughly outlining its increasing importance in Lacan's thought. If in its first articulated appearance, in Seminars IV and V, it is deemed exclusively to characterize the (unconscious) psychic economy of perverse masochists,[8] in the second phase of its elaboration, beginning with Seminar VI, Lacan is progressively obliged to assume it as a universal structure that provides the basis for the unconscious of all subjects (apart from psychotics, who do not have an unconscious). As I argued in Chapter 3, the "standard," phallic version of the fundamental fantasy is in point of fact already implicitly presupposed by Lacan's reading of the Oedipus complex in terms of a paternal metaphor that guarantees the subject in the Symbolic thanks to a transcendent "Other of the Other," the paternal Law. On the other hand, the subsequent conclusion that all fundamental fantasies—and not only (pathologically) perverse fantasies—ultimately participate in a psychic economy whose nature is fundamentally masochistic will be one of the consequences of the recognition that "there is no Other of the Other," that the Real "holes" the Symbolic.[9] This last juncture necessarily raises the question of *jouissance*, of a "pleasure in pain" that regulates the unconscious life of the subject and is intimately linked to the order of the Real. For this reason, I devote the final two sections of Chapter 5 to a discussion of *jouissance*.[10]

4.2 FROM "THERE IS AN OTHER OF THE OTHER" . . .

In the 1960s and 1970s, Lacanian theory seems to be firmly relying on the presupposition that "there is no Other of the Other" (which is algebraically rendered as A barred). Given that this phase of Lacan's thought is preceded by one in which he provides us with often contrasting statements on this matter, it is difficult to identify clearly the specific moment at which this essential conclusion was fully assumed for the first time. Seminar V (1957–1958) unequivocally introduces the functioning of the paternal metaphor as being based on the assumption that there *is* an Other of the Other; as Lacan puts it, "[analytic] experience shows us the indispensability of the background [*arrière-plan*] provided by the Other with respect to the Other, without which the universe of language could not articulate itself."[11] Less than a year later, Seminar VI unhesitatingly proclaims that "there is no Other of the Other . . . no signifier exists which might guarantee the concrete consequence of any manifestation of the signifier."[12]

How should we treat these apparently irreconcilable quotations? I suggest that the hasty singling out of a fundamental *Kehre* in the time between Seminars V and VI would probably overlook the multifaceted and nonlinear evolution of Lacan's thought. Nevertheless, it is certain that during the prolific years between 1958 and 1963 Lacanian theory rapidly moves beyond the prevalence it had given in the mid-1950s to the notion of "structure," a notion for which "there *is* an Other of the Other" should be considered the implicit motto. Let us briefly recapitulate what this formula means.

The fact that there is a (symbolic) Other of the (symbolic) Other indicates that the Other as the order of signifiers is guaranteed by another transcendent Other, namely the paternal Law. The Other as Law, the Other of the Other, corresponds to the Name-of-the-Father: this is precisely what allows the resolution of the Oedipus complex, and consequently the detachment of the subject from the disquieting relation he entertained with the mother. The subject is thus enabled actively to enter the intersubjective symbolic field. I refer at this point to graph 4.1, which shows the relationship that exists between the barred subject ($), the Other of the signifiers (S2), the Master-Signifier (S1), and the Other of the Other *qua* Name-of-the-Father. Insofar as the subject is barred as a consequence of the *Spaltung* induced by language, he is to be regarded as that which one signifier (any signifier S2 in the

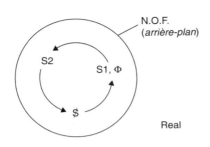

Graph 4.1

unconscious signifying chains) represents for another (privileged) signifier (S1); in the case of the standard phallic fantasy, the Master-Signifier is identifiable with the symbolic phallus Φ that embodies the transcendent Law of the Name-of-the-Father. Graph 4.1 is primarily meant to represent topographically the transcendence of the Name-of-the-Father with respect to all other signifiers (including Φ), the fact that its function of "*arrière-plan*," its being the "signifier of signifiers" singles it out. It is precisely because the Name-of-the-Father encircles all other signifiers that, at this stage, Lacanian theory seems to posit the existence of a self-enclosed and fully independent symbolic Other: "All language implies a metalanguage."[13] As a result of this, the order of the Real is entirely separated from the Symbolic. The Real can be defined only negatively as that which the Symbolic is not.

It is not by chance, then, that, in this context, Lacan defines psychosis as a fore-closure, a radical rejection of the Name-of-the-Father due to which the subject finds himself in direct contact with the Real. The psychotic subject lacks the Other of the Other. This is why, in "A Question Preliminary to Any Possible Treatment of Psychosis" (1957–1958), Lacan suggests that psychosis does not correspond to an absence of the Other *tout court* but, rather, to the effect of the lack of the Name-of-the-Father (as signifier of signifiers). "To the point at which the Name-of-the-Father is called may correspond in *the Other*, then, a mere hole, which by the inadequacy of the metaphoric effect will provoke a corresponding hole at the place of the phallic signification."[14] In other words, the psychotic is far from lacking a relation to language, he is indeed immersed in a linguistic Other which is not "phallically" organized by the paternal metaphor. Insofar as, in his case, the Other of the signifiers (S2) is not regulated by the Other of the Law, the psychotic remains a victim of language; he is "spoken" by it. This is what I schematize in graph 4.2. The Other of the symbolic Other prevents the subject from being invaded by the Real. Such an invasion occurs, with disastrous consequences, in the case of psychosis.

Real

Graph 4.2

Lacan is convinced that the psychotic's psychic life is fully determined by signifiers. He also seems to believe that the psychotic can produce imaginary significations—as a matter of fact, a psychosis is often latent. Conversely, delusions are thought to be "partial" even in the most serious cases.[15] What the psychotic cannot do—lacking the Name-of-the-Father, and consequently the Master-Signifier (S1)—is order the significations he produces in a consistent discourse. In other words, the psychotic's psychic life does not merely consist of an endless metonymic slide from signifier to signifier: metaphoric processes are also possible; Lacan indeed speaks of "delusional metaphors" in which "signifier and signified are [temporarily] stabilised."[16] There is a certain degree of symbolic articulation thanks to which various signifying chains overlap and signification is produced—"these patients speak to us in the same language as ourselves"[17]—yet these chains are not more broadly ordered by the signifier of signifiers.[18]

The most important conclusion to be drawn here is that, however serious and persistent a delusion is, the psychotic is never confined to a mythical domain beyond language, a pure, primordial Real. To avoid such a frequent misunderstanding, it is necessary carefully to reassess one of Lacan's most famous formulations about psychosis; I take "what is foreclosed from the Symbolic returns in the Real"[19] to mean primarily: if the Name-of-the-Father as external guarantor of the Symbolic is foreclosed, then delusions may arise in which everyday reality turns into the Real-of-language. In psychotic delusions, the ordinary perception of external reality—which, in order to function properly, necessitates a symbolic articulation ultimately rooted in the Name-of-the-Father—is indeed replaced by phenomena such as auditory hallucinations whose "verbal" nature is a matter of fact. The unconscious as Real-of-language—as unmediated, unsymbolized letter—appears in reality. As I have already observed in Chapter 2, in these instances the unconscious is "out in the open":[20] for the same reason, given that we are dealing with an "unconscious without a subject,"[21] there is, strictly speaking, no more unconscious, and subjectivity collapses due to a lack of distinction between the ego and the unconscious.[22]

If what characterizes the psychotic's psychic life is his unmediated relation with the Real-*of-language*—the letter or, to put it with one of Lacan's definitions of psychosis in Seminar III, "the signifier in its dimension as a pure signifier"[23]—then we are also obliged to specify graphs 4. 1 and 4.2 above. They should in fact also take into account the distinction between the individual dimension of the Symbolic (that of speech) and the universal dimension of the Symbolic (that of language), the way in which the former structurally depends on the latter.

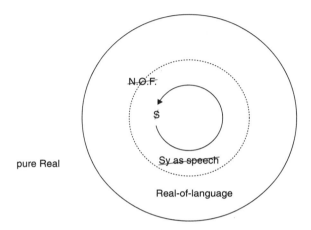

Graph 4.3

Graph 4.3 indicates how, in psychosis, there is no Name-of-the-Father to delimit the field of the subject's speech. In other words, the foreclosure of the primordial signifier makes the barrier between speech and language collapse.[24] Hence, the universal dimension of the Symbolic into which the psychotic is not able to actively introduce himself is to be regarded as that which "inhabits" and "possesses" him[25] in the guise of the Real-of-language. On the other hand, in nonpsychotic subjects, signifying chains are ordered in speech by the Name-of-the-Father. This is what I schematize in graph 4.4. The Name-of-the-Father encircles individual speech, and thus allows the active entrance of the subject into the universal dimension of the Symbolic. There still remain signifying chains— "portions" of the universal Symbolic—that are not directly symbolized by the individual Symbolic of the subject but *could* nevertheless potentially be symbolized by him. It is in this context that one should take up the transindividual notion of the unconscious as that which is "outside," and hence allows all letters to "arrive

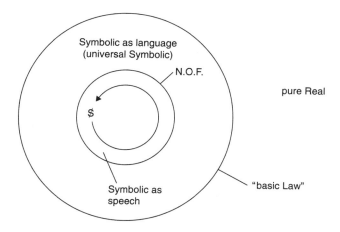

Graph 4.4

at their destination" independently of whether the addressee receives them (and opens them). At this stage, for Lacan, "the unconscious . . . this symbolic construction, covers all human lived experience like a web . . . it's always there, more or less latent":[26] despite his limited vital resources, a subject who has successfully resolved the Oedipus complex is able potentially to proceed to an all-encompassing process of symbolization.

Two further topographical issues stand out from graphs 4.3 and 4.4: (1) The Real-of-language that invades the psychotic and the universal Symbolic as that in which the nonpsychotic successfully introduces himself are simply two sides of the same coin.[27] Furthermore, as we saw in Chapter 2, the Real-of-language as letter remains the fundamental agency of the (nonpsychotic) subject's unconscious. (2) Positing that "there is an Other of the Other" logically entails presupposing the existence of a pure Real which is simply definable as that which the Symbolic is not. One should indicate, however, that such a pure Real is what stands outside of the *universal* symbolic Other: despite the fact that psychotics are never in a pure Real, there is a pure Real which should be located beyond the universal dimension of the Law/Name-of-the-Father. Lacan talks about this other level of the Name-of-the-Father on several occasions,[28] most noticeably in Seminar III, where he defines it as the ultimate "non-deceptive element" and as the "unique principle at the foundation . . . of the law."[29] As we have seen, the Name-of-the-Father is, as Other of the Law, the Other of the Other *qua* Other of the signifiers: when we are confronted with the "principle of the law," we are thus dealing directly with the very foundation of the universal Name-of-the-Father.

Let us analyze more closely the meaning of this basic Law of the Symbolic as such. In Seminar III, Lacan draws one fundamental conclusion from his commentary on Schreber's memoirs: for the deluding psychotic, the Other as universal locus of the signifiers—Schreber's God—is a deceiver who enacts "a permanent exercise of deception which tends to subvert any order whatsoever."[30] The psychotic is *certain* about that.[31] This is the inevitable consequence of what I have been explaining so far: when there is no Other of the Other, the Other of the signifiers—which, because of its differential structure, is deceptive by definition—is not guaranteed by an external nondeceptive element. On the contrary, nonpsychotic subjects know they "are in the presence of a subject insofar as what he says and does can be *supposed* to have been said and done to deceive [them]."[32] Such a supposition of deceit goes hand in hand with a "non-deceptive element" to which nonpsychotic subjects secure symbolic truths as well as objects of everyday reality insofar as these are always symbolically mediated. "The dialectical correlate of the basic structure which makes of the speech of subject to subject speech that may deceive is that there is also something that does not deceive."[33] By securing the Other's (potentially deceiving) discourse to "something that does not deceive," we move from the plane of the mere feint—at which the psychotic is stuck—to that of fictions. This is why Lacan suggests that "the fictitious is not, in its essence, that which deceives, but is precisely what I call the symbolic" and, conversely, "every [symbolic] truth has the structure of a fiction."[34] The dimension of "true lies" or "lying truths"—to which all (symbolic) truths as fictions ultimately belong—together with the related dimension of doubt can thus provide us with a minimal definition of a symbolic order that functions properly; this is well captured by Freud's famous Jewish joke, endlessly recounted by Lacan: "Why are you telling me you are going to Cracow if you really are going to Cracow?"[35] While it is possible to find instinctively deceptive behaviors—based on the Imaginary—in nature, man as being of language is definitely the only animal who has the ability to *pretend to lie.*

Lacan suggests that, because of the deceptive nature of the Other of the signifiers, man as being of language has always needed to guarantee the objects of everyday reality by means of "something non-deceptive."[36] This function, however, "is fulfilled in various ways according to the cultural region,"[37] and, above all, history. For instance, Aristotelian science assured itself of the "truthfulness of the Other"[38] by means of a direct reference to nature, to incorruptible celestial spheres: the fact that celestial bodies seemed to follow a regular spherical trajectory in the sky, and thus "always returned to the same place," offered the ancients a basic Law of nondeception. Lacan seems to propose that in Aristotle's universe it is still nature *qua* unmediated Real that ultimately assures its own symbolically mediated forms in everyday reality as well as the inherently deceptive dimension of the symbolic Other; in Aristotle's universe, the Other of the Other still corresponds to the (primordial) Real.

On the other hand, for Lacan, modern science relies on an anomalous Judeo–Christian tradition which is no longer preoccupied with what goes on in the celestial domain but, rather, secures the Other to a nondeceptive a priori which is itself symbolic. This is nothing but Descartes's nondeceiving God. "The notion that the real [everyday reality] is unable to play tricks on us," which is so "essential to the constitution of the world of [modern] science"—and still influences "the mentality of people like us"[39]—ultimately depends on "Descartes' meditation about God as incapable of deceiving us."[40] In other words, for modern science, the Other of the Other is symbolic: this presupposes "an act of faith."[41] Modern science relies on a "unique principle at the foundation, not only of the universe [objects as perceived in everyday reality], but of the law."[42] The Law is thus created ex nihilo. The reason why Lacan believes that science took such a step ("which was not obvious")[43] at a specific moment of its development will be analyzed in Chapter 5. In Seminar III, Lacan does not offer any explanation of the transition from Aristotelian to modern science: however, further hypotheses can be obtained by juxtaposing this passage from Seminar III to a series of challenging passages that he dedicates to the birth of modern science in Seminar VII.

For the time being, let us limit ourselves to the delineation of the differences and similarities between Aristotelian and modern "non-deceptive elements." To recapitulate: at this stage of his thought, Lacan believes that all symbolic systems necessitate a "non-deceptive element," a basic Law that functions as the universal Other of the Other in a given epoch of history, yet he also deems modernity to be special insofar as it founds itself on a symbolic Other of the Other. Having said this, one should not overlook the fact that the precise functioning of premodern symbolic systems is irremediably lost to us—and this independently of whether we still have faith in the Judeo–Christian God. Despite his own endeavor to sketch the foundation of Aristotelian science "from the inside," Lacan believes that we inevitably end up retroactively reinterpreting the Aristotelian (and pre-Aristotelian) universe as being based on a symbolic Other of the Other: this is the only way in which we can formulate any truth (as fiction) about it. Consequently, it should not surprise us that: (1) in the same passage from Seminar III, Lacan speaks of a (nonlinear) "evolution of human thought" that—one presumes—would link Aristotelian science to modern science;[44] (2) in these years, he often attempts to apply the "principle of the law" qua (Judeo–Christian) universal Name-of-the-Father to the most disparate historical epochs, and consider its consequences at various levels of man's libidinal economy throughout history.[45] How can he do this?

One could propose that, for Lacan, all different "non-deceptive elements" tacitly presuppose the universal Name-of-the-Father insofar as this ultimately stands for the Law of sexuation that prohibits incest and, in so doing, distinguishes *any* culture—the Symbolic as such—from nature. The basic Law of the prohibition of incest is what one discovers at the root of any historically determined Other of the Other.

From a slightly different angle, we could suggest that, for Lacan, the first mythical emergence of the *universal* Other of the Other—the birth of the Symbolic as such—should be regarded as being homologous with what we now know happens at the *individual* level of the child who resolves the Oedipus complex thanks to the Law of the Name-of-the-Father. The first basic Law of/in history, the beginning of history itself, should thus be associated with the conclusion of an explicitly phallic prehistorical period (the universal correlate of the phallic phase). Lacan certainly hints at this in Seminar IV, when he describes the importance of the phallic *Gestalten* at the level of the subject's individual entrance into the Symbolic together with the importance of "erected stones" (taken as gigantic phallic *Gestalten*) at the dawn of history.[46] We are therefore entitled to infer that successive basic Laws presuppose this first basic Law in the same way as the child's increasing ability to symbolize (or "learn") presupposes the presence and effectiveness of the Name-of-the-Father. I do not think I am forcing Lacan's own words in suggesting that the individual child's symbolic apprenticeship somehow makes him go through the phases of the universal "evolution of human thought." At this stage, one should also be able to demonstrate that Lacan's theory of the Symbolic is characterized by the interplay of three levels of retroaction: (1) the level of the sentence uttered by individuals: the first word of a sentence acquires a signification only retroactively, after the sentence is completed; (2) the level of the subject's individual (active) entrance into the universal Symbolic: pre-Oedipal life is retroactively signifierized by the resolution of the Oedipus complex; (3) the level of the first establishment of a universal symbolic Law thanks to which prehistory is retroactively posited from the standpoint of history. As I have just suggested, this first basic Law *qua* universal Name-of-the-Father is, by definition, at the same time the Law that prohibits incest and thus retroactively symbolizes (on the universal level) all the protosymbolic activities of the species that preceded this moment—in simply terms, the allegedly phallic culture of menhirs.[47]

This having been said, in Seminar XVII Lacan candidly admits that the Oedipus complex is, after all, simply Freud's "dream," his own myth.[48] On similar lines, we might suggest that the Name-of-the-Father is simply Lacan's own mythical reinterpretation of Freud's own discoveries filtered through the tradition of modern philosophy and the history of science. It must, however, be stressed that, in Lacan's view the mythical origin of many of the axioms of psychoanalytic theory does not by any means diminish their epistemological validity. The quotation from Seminar XVII is widely known, but commentators do not pay sufficient attention to a similar quotation from Seminar VII which, I believe, reveals the hidden motivation behind the former: "Freud contributes what some call the discovery and others the affirmation, and what I believe is the *affirmation of the discovery*, that the fundamental or *primordial law*, the one where culture begins in opposition to nature, is the law of the prohibition of incest."[49] A scientific discovery is not merely "discovered" but must also be "affirmed"; it ultimately entails—as modern Cartesian science demonstrates—an "act of faith." In other words, we are facing here an irreducible tension between the conviction of the scientific "objectivity" of the theory of the Oedipus complex/Name-of-the-Father throughout human history, and the admission of the historical contingency of its universal validity as a specific (post) modern episteme—one which is nevertheless also applied transhistorically in a retroactive way. . . . Lacan often closely associates the notion of retroaction with that of the myth. First and foremost, he deems the origin of the Law (of the Symbolic) to be mythical insofar as it is retroactive. In discussing the fact that, according to Freud's *Totem and Taboo*, the symbolic Law originates from the killing of the primordial (real) father, Lacan states that such a notion is mythical—that is, it implies a "categorization of a form of the impossible"—given that the primordial father's basic trait is that "he will have been killed.". . . [50] And yet, as I have just illustrated, Lacan assumes that all science—as the gem of the Symbolic—is, by definition, retroactive. . . . A detailed investigation of these difficult issues would, first of all, entail an accurate examination of the multiple links that, for Lacan, exist between science, history, and the myth—an examination which, unfortunately, I am not able to carry out in this book.[51]

4.3 . . . TO "THERE IS NO OTHER OF THE OTHER"

If one were to select a specific text in which Lacan finally assumes the fact that "there is no Other of the Other," and manages to provide an elaborate explanation of such a formula, I believe it should definitely be "The Subversion of the Subject and the Dialectic of Desire in the Freudian Unconscious" (1960). This reinterprets one of the most important conclusions of Seminars III, IV, and V. In this article, it is indeed clear that, despite preserving its key role in the resolution of the Oedipus complex, the Name-of-the-Father can no longer be considered an "external" metaguarantor of the Other of the signifiers. In Lacan's own words: "Let us set out from the conception of the Other as the locus of the signifier. Any statement of authority has no other guarantee than its very enunciation, and it is pointless for it to seek it in *another signifier, which could not appear outside this locus in any way.* Which is what I mean when I say that no metalanguage can be spoken, or, more aphoristically, that there is no Other of the Other."[52] By contrast, in Seminar IV, Lacan clearly maintained that "the symbolic father [the paternal Law/Name-of-the-Father] is a necessity of the symbolic construction which we can only locate in a *beyond*, I would dare to say a *transcendence*."[53] I am firmly convinced that even a superficial comparison of passages like these leaves little room for doubt that, in the late 1950s, Lacan's conceptualization of the symbolic order underwent a fundamental change.

More specifically, according to "Subversion of the Subject," the Name-of-the-Father is still what renders the subject's entrance into the proper functioning of the Symbolic possible. Nevertheless, it can be said to work only as an "organizer" which is now, so to speak, "internal" to the Other of the signifiers. It still exercises a fundamental role, and is still a "privileged" signifier, but can no longer be accounted for as the "signifier of signifiers" in a strictly structural sense. Consequently, the necessarily differential signifying structure which the Name-of-the-Father was itself sustaining, by way of "enclosing" it, becomes an open structure, which is directly exposed to the Real; in the case of nonpsychotics, the paternal metaphor can suture this structure only in a time which is—at least from a logical standpoint—secondary and contingent (see graph 4.5).

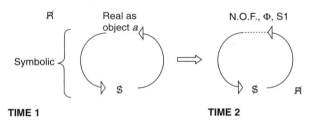

Graph 4.5

The same is obviously valid with regard to the universal basic Law (the universal Name-of-the-Father): the symbolic structure is by now open and in contact with the Real on both the particular and the universal level. To be more precise, the fact that there is no Other of the Other also necessarily entails the impossibility of distinguishing between these two levels of the structure. When there is an Other of the Other, the individual subject's Symbolic is a particular "part" of the universal symbolic structure by which it is ultimately sustained and contained; when there is no Other of the Other, the Symbolic of individual subjects itself sustains the universal structure in a particular (phallic) way. Adopting the terms Lacan used in Seminar V, and interpreting them in a new manner, one could argue that, after A is barred, the universal symbolic father—who has by now lost his transcendence—exists only through the particular instantiations of the symbolic Law in the real father.

In parallel, this amounts to saying that the nondeceptive element that guarantees the symbolic order as such—in a phallic way—eventually relies upon the successful unfolding of the Oedipus complex of the (majority of the) subject(s), and that such a success obviates a potentially generalized psychotic condition. The openness or crack that earlier characterized the "deficit" of psychosis is now seen as structural: madness is a structural possibility for all beings of language that can only subsequently be obviated. It is in this shift that the passage from "there is an Other of the Other" to "there is no Other of the Other" essentially consists. In other words, at this stage, the Name-of-the-Father can suture the symbolic order only as a "cork" (bouchon):[54] such a cork fills in the gap of a real hole which, as we shall see later in more detail, somehow remains present in spite of being corked. At the same time, and for the same reason, Lacan relativizes the function of the Name-of-the-Father and, from the early 1960s, speaks of the Names-of-the-Father in the plural.[55] The real hole in the Symbolic can now be corked in many different ways. The Name-of-the-Father represents the standard way in which this is achieved; however, it does not follow that the Name-of-the-Father is more structural than any other (perverse) Master-Signifier: indeed, these are now deemed equally efficient in (phallically) suturing the open structure. This contradicts those parts of Seminar V in which the formation of the ego-ideal through an identification with the symbolic father—that is, as an effect of the instauration of the Name-of-the-Father—was structurally opposed to the formation of "pathological" Master-Signifiers in the case of perverts.[56]

As I anticipated in Chapter 3, another strictly related consequence of the barring of the Other is the perfect superimposition of the Name-of-the-Father with the symbolic phallus Φ, two notions which Lacan had made every effort to differentiate in 1958. This can again be demonstrated by comparing two particularly dense passages from Seminar V with one taken from "Subversion of the Subject." From different perspectives, they all attempt to elucidate the algebraic notation S (A barred), which should be read as "the signifier of the lack in the Other." Here is the first quotation from Seminar V:

> Just as we have defined the paternal signifier as the signifier which, in the locus of the Other, poses and authorizes the game of the signifiers, so there is another privileged signifier which has as an effect the constitution in the Other of what follows, [namely something] which changes its nature—this is why the symbol of the Other is here barred: [the Other] is not purely and simply the locus of speech but,

like the subject, it is also implicated in a dialectic situated on the phenomenal plane of the reflection in relation to the little other.[57]

I take these words to be unequivocal on a number of noteworthy issues. Lacan is clearly stating that there are definitely two "privileged signifiers" which have distinct functions: on the one hand, there is "the paternal signifier," the Name-of-the-Father, which "authorizes the game of the signifiers" by working as the nonbarred legal Other (A) of the linguistic (and thus differential by definition) Other of the signifiers, the locus of speech (A barred). On the other hand, there is "another privileged signifier," the symbolic phallus Φ, that "institutes" in the Other as the "locus of speech"—ultimately guaranteed by the Name-of-the-Father, and thus turned into a nonbarred Other—something which "changes [the Other's] nature." This can only mean that the phallus signifierizes the level on which the Other is barred. The level on which the Other is barred—"like the subject" $—and signifierized as such by Φ is the level on which the Other "is implicated" in the imaginary dialectic ("of reflection") with the imaginary ("little") other. The fact that Φ and S (A barred) should here be regarded as strictly linked—and thus equally distinguished from the Name-of-the-Father—is confirmed on the same page of Seminar V where Lacan states that "Φ, the phallus, is this signifier through which the relationship [of the subject] with a, the small [imaginary] other, is introduced in the Other as locus of speech."[58] Φ is therefore what makes possible the superimposition of the imaginary relationship between the subject and the image of the other with the subject's relation to the symbolic Other: the imaginary relationship must be introduced in the symbolic Other so that "something may be established for the subject between the big Other qua locus of speech and the phenomenon of [the subject's] desire."[59]

The second quotation from Seminar V helps to confirm what I have just inferred:

> Besides speech and super-speech [sur-parole]—the law of the father, whichever way one decides to denominate it—something else is necessary. It is for this reason that the phallus, this elective signifier introduces itself. . . . This is what in my little formulas I have named for you S (A barred), the signifier of A barred. This is all about what I have just defined as being the function of the signifier phallus, that of marking what the Other desires insofar as [the Other] is marked by the signifier, that is, is barred.[60]

Here again, the Law of the father as metalanguage is clearly distinguished from Φ as S (A barred). Interestingly enough, the function of the latter is on this occasion primarily associated with the desire of the Other, not with that of the subject. The fact that the Other is barred can only mean that insofar as the dimension of the

Other is "marked by the [differential and thus lacking logic of the] signifier," it should itself be related to the dimension of desire; the phallus therefore signi-fierizes the lack caused in the Other as desiring Other by the very nature of the signifier. If we refer these observations back to the first quotation, we can con-clude that in order for the *subject's* own desire to be able to emerge, a superimpo-sition of his relation with both the imaginary and the symbolic Other has to occur; this is brought about by the symbolic phallus insofar as it manages to mark—sig-nifierize—the Other as a lacking, desiring Other. This extremely complicated process has already been explained from a slightly different angle in Chapter 3, where I discussed the way in which the sexuation of the subject is made possible only when the desire of the (m)Other is retroactively signifierized by the phallic signifier: it will later be analyzed in more depth when we examine the funda-mental fantasy.

For the time being, what should concern us the most is that both quotations en-tail that, in Seminar V, Φ as the signifier of the "signified as such" is also the signi-fier of the lack in the Other, S (A barred), and thus has to be distinguished from the Name-of-the-Father, the "signifier of signifiers" whose nature as a transcen-dent sign excludes any irreducible lack. To cut a long story short, at this stage, there still is an Other of the Other. It is important, however, to emphasize that in Semi-nar V the Other of the Other is, for Lacan, by no means irreconcilable with S (A barred). In other words, at this stage, the symbolic phallus Φ to be understood as that which "carries out" ("*réalise*") S (A barred)[61] is still "encircled" by the Name-of-the-Father. This is definitely not the case in "Subversion of the Subject," where Lacan makes it clear that there is no Other of the Other, nothing standing outside of S (A barred).

Consequently, the most important effect of the passage from "there is an Other of the Other" (A) to "there is no Other of the Other" (A barred) is that the lack in the Other—the fact that, because of the differential logic of the signifying struc-ture, a signifier is always missing from the battery of signifiers—is no longer in-trasymbolic but should be considered as *real*, as a presence of the Real in the open structure of the Symbolic. Whenever Lacan refers now to the Name(s)-of-the-Father, he is speaking of something which is perfectly identifiable with Φ and S (A barred). In Seminar V, the Name-of-the-Father could be written as S (S/s), which is, after all, the same as S (A). In "Subversion of the Subject," when there is no Other of the Other, the Name-of-the-Father is S (A barred); the statement "the father [*qua* law] is a dead father"[62] finds its true implication here. In other words, this means: the Master-Signifier S1 relies on A barred; there *is* a Father or Master-Signifier, but it cannot be detached from S (A barred). As Lacan writes: "If we are to expect . . . an effect from the unconscious enunciation it is to be found here

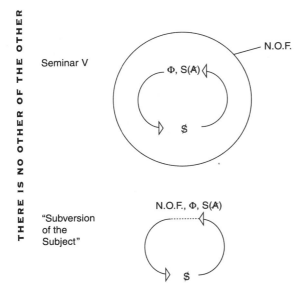

Seminar V

N.O.F.

Φ, S(Ⱥ)

$

"Subversion
of the
Subject"

N.O.F., Φ, S(Ⱥ)

$

Graph 4.6

in the S (A barred) and read as: signifier of a lack in the Other, *inherent in* [that is immanent to] *its very function* as the treasury of the signifier";[63] the signifier of the lack in the Other is at the same time the signifier that, as S1, allows any "effect" of signification to follow "from the unconscious enunciation." Lacan then adds that the "lack referred to here is that which I've already formulated: that there is no Other of the Other." If we compare these quotations with another passage from the same article in which Lacan argues that S (A barred) must be distinguished from other signifiers but *not separated* from them,[64] we can conclude that the "inherency" in the function of the Other as the "treasury of the signifier" should be attributed to both the lack and its signifier.

What precisely does Lacan imply when he claims that S (A barred) is to be *distinguished* from while not being separated from the signifiers S2? I believe this can be explained by emphasizing how Lacan also mathematically qualifies S (A barred) as −1. Given that there is always a signifier missing from the Other, A is ultimately A barred. S (A barred) is −1 in the sense that the missing signifier is itself signifierized as missing, and hence as −1. We could equally argue that Φ is the signifier that, due to castration and the resolution of the Oedipus complex, signifierizes itself as missing (−φ). Although the real lack in the Symbolic is never canceled, it is precisely by becoming −1 that it is phallically "organized": such an "organization" of lack is nothing less than what allows the functioning of the symbolic order *tout court* by means of a sublation of lack. To return to our original question: S (A barred) is both different from other signifiers S2 insofar as it represents the missing signifier, and not separated from them insofar as this missing signifier is counted *within* the set of signifiers as −1. As Muller and Richardson correctly remark, S (A barred) "must be somehow *inside* the universal set and conceived of as a lack (−1) within it. In this sense it is the complement of the universal set, i.e. an 'empty,' or 'null' set."[65]

But this is not the whole story. If, with respect to the signifiers S2, the missing signifier can be counted phallically as the "one-less," with respect to the Real this same lack can be counted phallically as the "one-more." Although this point remains implicit in "Subversion of the Subject," it is clear that Lacan, having assumed that there is no Other of the Other, considers S (A barred) as both −1 *and* +1. The empty set which is complementary to the universal set is *empty*, yet it *is* still a *set*. Let us analyze this more closely.

Φ, S (A barred) is not only the signifier of the real lack in the symbolic Other (−1), it is also the signifier of the fact that this lack *is* real (+1) or, even better, that it is the Real *tout court*. In other words, S (A barred) as +1 is the signifier of the fact that the Real as lack is nothing but the consequence of the fact that the signifier as such originally holed the primordial Real, that language "killed the Thing," and that before the advent of the signifier such a Thing was exactly no-thing. While the phallus as −1 is the signifier of the fact that the Real holes the Symbolic, the phallus as +1 is the signifier of the fact that the Real as 0 was primordially holed by the Symbolic, and that this 0 is now retroactively postulated as an absolute 1. This last point, a cornerstone of the Lacanian logic of the signifier, was elucidated by Miller in his seminal article "Suture" as early as 1966; S (A barred) is nothing but the suture of the Symbolic. "There is 0, and 0 counts for 1 [*compte pour 1*]. . . . That which in the real is pure and simple absence finds itself . . . noted as 0 and counted as 1 [*compté pour 1*]."[66]

It is now important to distinguish between the retroactive *mirage* of a primordial 1 created by the disruptive emergence of the signifier out of a homeostatic zero (the primordial Real) from the *actual* fact that such an emergence is necessarily associated with a +1. In other words, one has to distinguish the mythical 0 which the symbolic order makes us deceptively perceive as a Whole, as a lost 1, from the concrete presence of what *remains* of that 0 in the domain of signifiers in the guise of a +1 (as lack). This is nothing but the difference between the primordial Real (the mythical 1) and its remainder, which Lacan calls object *a* (+1). To be perfectly clear, however, it should be emphasized that, strictly speaking, object *a* is *not* +1: rather, it is the real lack in the symbolic Other (A barred), which logically, if not chronologically, precedes its quantification as +1 by means of the signifying action of the phallus S (A barred). The signifier primordially holes the Real; such a hole transforms the "neutrality" of the Real into a lack which is then inextricable from the Symbolic as such; it cannot be "filled in," despite the fact that the phallus manages to "organize"/mark it.

Let us now take a step back and recapitulate all this in simplified terms. Since there is no Other of the Other, it follows that the symbolic Other is in contact with the radical otherness of the Real. The Real stands for that which cannot be symbolized: but now this impossibility is inherent to the Symbolic—that is, the Symbolic as Symbolic is inherently prevented from fully symbolizing itself. More precisely, the Real with which the symbolic Other is now in direct contact is a leftover, a remainder of the primordial Real: Lacan defines it as object *a*, the "*peu de réel*"[67] which is left to us. There is just a little piece of Real, since the primordial Real is that which was eliminated by the emergence of the signifier: this "murder" occurred in a mythical but logically necessary time; it is retrospectively indispensable to postulate it. In parallel, by being the remainder of the Real, object *a* will also be its *reminder*, that which reminds us of the loss of an always already-lost Unity.

Here, one point should be made absolutely clear: the reminder actually reminds us of something which ultimately *never* existed. Indeed, there is/was/will be no possibility of having the whole Real since, strictly speaking, there is no Real beyond the symbolic order. Lacan invites us to acknowledge that not only is it possible to posit the primordial Real solely from the standpoint of the Symbolic, in a retroactive way, but that it is precisely because this homeostatic 0, this no-Thing, was holed that the Real (as lack of the Symbolic) was created. Thus *all of the Real is nothing but the Real-of-the-Symbolic*. Nonetheless, as we have just seen, this Real-of-the-Symbolic resists the Symbolic which consequently cannot be whole: a whole Symbolic would in fact correspond to a *real*-ized Symbolic, a mythical return to the primordial Real (as 0) by means of a "saturation" of the Symbolic.

In the end, all this amounts to saying that the dictum "There is no Other of the Other" entails at least three different, though strictly interrelated, conclusions:

(1) There is no Name-of-the-Father as a supreme, "external" guarantor of the symbolic order. This spells the end of Lacan's conciliatory, "structuralist" moment.

(2) There is a real "absolute" otherness that enters into contact with the symbolic Other. Consequently, from this standpoint, the fact that "there is no (symbolic) Other of the (symbolic) Other" implies that there is a "new" (real) Other of the (symbolic) Other. The relativization of the Name-of-the-Father entails the formation of a necessary relationship between the Other of the signifiers and the Real of the object *a*. The notion of the phallus and the related theory of the fundamental

fantasy attempt to formalize such a relationship while at the same time showing how it intersects with the imaginary order.

(3) From yet another complementary perspective, the fact that real otherness enters into contact with the symbolic Other entails that there is no such Thing as a "pure" real otherness, that absolute otherness is, after all, not absolute. . . . Point (3) actually represents a supplement of point (2). Point (3) means that there is no "purely" real Other of the symbolic Other. In other words, the fact that the object *a* holes the Symbolic means that there is no whole Real. In this sense, the statement "There is no Other of the Other" can be read in two different but perfectly compatible and complementary ways. It can indicate both that there is no self-contained Symbolic *and* that there is no purely external, whole Real which surrounds it. There is no Symbolic without the Real, and no Real without the Symbolic. The Name-of-the-Father which guaranteed symbolic self-sufficiency was at the same time preserving intact the mirage of a Real "outside."

If the Symbolic is symbolic only insofar as there is a Real-in-the-Symbolic, and the Real is real only insofar as it is the Real-of-the-Symbolic,[68] how should we understand that which lies outside the interpenetration of these two orders? I suggest that we call it the "undead." Such a definition is derived from Lacan's own recurrent references to the notion of the "closed world" of the animal as that which is always "already dead" from the perspective of the individual and "immortal" from that of the species or nature.[69] I take the undead to correspond to both the "pure" Real and the "real-ized" Symbolic; the undead is a "not-One," a Real which was and will be barred *in itself* before and after the presence of the signifier. Here I am tempted to introduce a new algebraic sign: the R barred.[70] This of course, does not exclude the possibility that the undead could be regarded as—in Lacan's parlance—having "no fissure." The undead, however, is not some-thing that is substituted for the positivity of the pure Real that the Other of the Other implicitly presupposed, a notion of a negatively substantial Real: it is, rather, the pure Real to be considered as purely barred in itself. More precisely, the undead corresponds to both the mythical extrasymbolic not-One which is deceivingly postulated from the standpoint of the symbolic order as being the One *par excellence*, and what actually preceded and will succeed the interpenetration of the Real and the Symbolic, namely, the opposite of history. It is therefore extremely important to distinguish the Real(-of-the-Symbolic), the object *a*, from the undead: the former is some-thing as lack, the latter is no-thing. In other words, the Real-of-the-Symbolic is not "a piece" of the undead: although we perceive the object *a* as "the piece of the Real" that is left to us, this partial remainder actually amounts to *all* the Real that there ever was, is, and will be.

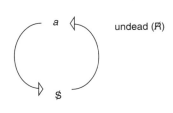

Graph 4.7

In concluding this section, I should attempt to answer the following broad question: how does Lacan arrive at the conclusion that "there is no Other of the Other"? I suggest that there are basically two answers to be given. From a practical, clinical point of view, the formula "There is no Other of the Other" is the result of the impossibility of accounting fully for the dynamics of neurosis on a purely "structuralist" basis. Lacan realized that something in the symptom inevitably continues to resist symbolization however far one carries psychoanalytic treatment. In brief, one might say that the completeness of the symbolic Other did not explain the dimension of *jouissance*, an unconscious pleasure in pain which could no longer be relegated to the sphere of pathological perversions, and demanded an urgent reassessment of the Freudian notions of repetition and death drive (which Lacan had earlier attempted to describe in intrasymbolic terms).

These clinical observations regarding *jouissance* revealed themselves to Lacan in the late 1950s, a time at which he also faced considerable theoretical difficulties with regard to the notion of the Real. In Seminar IV, for instance, Lacan was clearly aware that he had not yet provided his audience with a consistent analysis of the order of the Real, despite continually referring to it.[71] One could argue that, from a theoretical standpoint, the holing of the symbolic Other results from, among other things, the necessity finally to thematize the Real in a more direct and convincing way. As we have seen, the existence of the Other of the Other logically entailed a purely external Real; despite many oscillations—there are in fact passages in Seminar V which seem to put forward such a notion of a "pure" Real[72]—Lacan never explicitly maintained this. On the contrary, as I shall demonstrate in Section 4.4, there are places in his work of the mid-1950s in which he obviously adopts the opposite stance, and thus unintentionally criticizes his own theory of the Other of the Other. . . . This clearly constituted an overall contradiction in his general theory of the three orders. We could finally propose that, during his "structuralist" phase, Lacan seems to believe in a "pure" Real only insofar as he confronts this notion as an inevitable consequence of his major preoccupations apropos the self-sufficiency of the Symbolic; yet he finds it hard to assert it on the rare occasions when he attempts to question the Real directly. As soon as the Real is more openly tackled, the idea of a pure Real soon becomes manifestly untenable and, as a result, the notion of a transcendent Name-of-the-Father is itself dismantled. In parallel, such an explicit thematization of the Real brings Lacan inextricably to intertwine this notion with that of *jouissance*.

4.4 WHAT IS THE "REAL"?

I have already pointed out how the passage from "There is an Other of the Other" to "There is no Other of the Other" should be regarded as a gradual one in Lacanian theory. Although only a very short span of time separates these two formulas in the Seminars, it would be wrong to assume that there is an abrupt break between them. Lacan clearly preserves some notions that are consistent with the idea of a transcendent Other even after he begins to maintain that there is no Other of the Other; similarly, one can detect the anticipation of some of the notions that derive from the barring of the Other right at the heart of Lacan's most "structuralist" period. For instance, the introduction of the notion of *jouissance* in Seminar V already implicitly involves the universal validity of the fundamental fantasy as a basic anchor of the unconscious that lies at the crossroads of the Symbolic, the Imaginary, and the Real, and thus negates the self-sufficiency of the Symbolic—to obviate this potential contradiction, Lacan has naïvely to relegate *jouissance* and the fundamental fantasy to the domain of the perversions. On the other hand, it is also the case that in Seminar VII the real hole in the Symbolic is at the same time contradictorily considered to be some-thing in itself—a patent legacy of the Other of the Other. . . .

With regard to these issues, it is my intention in this section to focus on the way in which Lacan engages in a thorough, and often tortuous, reassessment of his notion of the Real. Of particular importance in this context is Seminar VII (1959–1960) which, according to many commentators, represents the most tangible proof of a turning point in Lacanian theory; although I do not disagree with such a pronouncement, I nevertheless prefer to highlight the fact that, despite being undoubtedly the first Seminar in which Lacan openly tackles the notion of the Real, Seminar VII at the same time presents clear evidence in favor of the gradual nature of the passage from "There is an Other of the Other" to "There is no Other of the Other." Why is this the case? We have seen that the Other of the Other is what allows a neat demarcation between the Real and the Symbolic; conversely, the barring of the Other causes their mutual dependency—that is, there is no "pure" Real any longer, and all we are left with is the Real-of-the-Symbolic and a mythical extrasymbolic "undead." I will attempt to demonstrate that, in Seminar VII, while defending the idea of a Real-of-the-Symbolic, Lacan also unintentionally falls back into a quasi-mystical understanding of the pure Real by promoting the notion of a transcendent real "Thing" understood as a positive absence. If my argument is correct, then Lacan is holding a profoundly contradictory view here, since the barring of the Other should categorically exclude any transcendence whatsoever.

Before embarking on an analysis of the status of the Real in Seminar VII, let us now take a step back and briefly examine the various meanings that were assigned to this notion up to the mid-1950s—when there was still an Other of the Other. In his early work, Lacan associates the Real with both (1) objects as they are given to us in everyday reality; and (2) a rather vague notion of undifferentiated matter as it is in itself before the advent of the Symbolic—or beyond the latter's domain.[73] This inevitably gives rise to blatant contradictions insofar as the superimposition of the Symbolic onto the Imaginary is, according to Lacan, precisely what accounts for the filtering of our perception of everyday reality. Furthermore, as we saw in our investigation of Lacan's description of psychosis, the term "Real" is also understood in a third sense as a nonsymbolized Symbolic which should be located within language.

Although such a terminological confusion will persist even in later years—it still complicates any accurate discussion of the Real in Seminar VII—it is nevertheless the case that around 1955 Lacan commences sporadically to clarify several different acceptations of the Real. One might well argue that his efforts are indeed oriented toward distinguishing the Real from objects of everyday reality as well as from primordial matter. As early as Seminar III, Lacan claims that "the real in question [in psychoanalysis] is no doubt not to be taken in the sense in which we normally understand it, which implies objectivity."[74] Both Seminar IV and Seminar VI dedicate some significant pages to this issue, and both conclude that a better evaluation of the Real might entail the formulation of a number of different concepts. It is only by closely examining these passages that we shall then be able to grasp appropriately the subtle distinctions of Seminar VII.

In Seminar IV, Lacan opens by clearly stating that "the real has more than one sense."[75] The Real that psychoanalysis deals with is to be located "at the limits of our experience," at the limits of reality. Why? Because our perception of everyday reality is filtered through a "screen" which makes its "conditions very artificial."[76] As a consequence, "we can refer to the real only by theorizing." More specifically, the Real should be understood as the "whole of what effectively happens," that which "involves in itself any possibility of effect": this "function," this "effectivity" of the Real, can better be "distinguished in [everyday] reality" by the German term *Wirklichkeit*.[77] I believe that Lacan proposes here to distinguish *Wirklichkeit* from reality in order to emphasize that there are things which "effectively happen," "effects" (Wirkungen), that are irreducible to what normally happens in "reality": for instance, the loss of reality caused by anxiety, the manifest unreality of dreams, the undecidable (psychosomatic) reality of symptoms and, more generally, all the formations of the unconscious. Wirklichkeit is meant to give voice to "the [unconscious] mechanism in its entirety,"[78] to those effects of the interplay between the three orders which are marginalized by the superimposition of the Symbolic and the Imaginary determining our (self-conscious) everyday reality. As I pointed out in Chapter 2, symptoms, the return of the repressed, go hand in hand with the process of metaphorization (as repression) that creates new signification; Wirklichkeit is the Real-of-the-Symbolic which, despite being "at the limits of experience," is nevertheless absolutely necessary for the functioning of the Symbolic as such. Indeed, Lacan later specifies that he is referring to a "symbolic Wirklichkeit"[79]—a Real-of-the-Symbolic—which is usually misrecognized.[80]

The Real that psychoanalysis deals with is the Real-of-the-Symbolic, which is not to be confused with everyday reality and should also be clearly differentiated from what Lacan calls "the primitive Stoff,"[81] matter unmediated by the Symbolic. This last distinction is meant to uncover the naïve materialism of the majority of psychoanalysts, whose "reference to the organic foundations is dictated by nothing but a need to be reassured."[82] Lacan replaces this organic vision of the Real, which always surreptitiously entails a reference to a transcendent "ultimate reality,"[83] with an "energetic perspective," that of effectivity. He explains his point by way of a long example in which he compares the functioning of a hydroelectric power plant with that of the unconscious. "What is accumulated in the machine is first of all strictly related to the machine": the Real (energy) is to be thought in relation to the Symbolic (the machine). "To say that energy [the Real] was already there, in a virtual state, in the current of the river . . . does not mean anything at all since energy . . . begins to interest us only from the moment it begins to be accumulated, and it is accumulated only from the moment the machines have started to work."[84] It is certain that the machines are activated by a propulsion that comes from the river, but "believing that the current of the river is the primitive order of energy,"[85] "confusing the Stoff, primitive matter . . . or instincts" with symbolic Wirklichkeit, is as much a mistake as taking energy for a notion like that of mana or "the sprite of the current."[86]

Lacan needs the example of the power plant in Seminar IV to point out plainly that the Freudian notion of the libido—a psychosexual energy which he will later reconceptualize in terms of jouissance—should be located on the level of the Real-of-the-Symbolic and, conversely, that no libido precedes the Symbolic. The libido is "an abstract notion, like that of energy," and "there is nothing less dependent on a material support than the notion of libido."[87] But what about the material support of the unconscious power plant? According to Lacan, the primitive *Stoff* is definitely not interesting for psychoanalysis insofar as the Real as energy necessarily involves a symbolic operation—"energy comes into play only when you measure it"[88]—but is the current of the river, matter *per se*, some-thing? Is Lacan here already considering the presymbolic Real as an "undead," a "not-One," or is he granting it some kind of minimal consistency, as he will contradictorily do in Seminar VII? He is rather evasive on this point: I think it is impossible to give a definitive answer. However, when the audience pressures him to elucidate further what seemed to be an omission in his account of the concept of potential energy, Lacan comes up with another definition of the Real which should focus "on that which is there at first,"[89] before the symbolic functioning has started. While it does not clarify the status of the presymbolic Real—the Real (or the undead) from its own standpoint—this new explanatory detour allows us to identify a "third perspective"[90] on the Real: the Real as that which is there at first, before the Symbolic starts to function, from the standpoint of the *Symbolic* itself. Here we are at the level of the power plant *after* it has been constructed but *before* it has been put to work (before it starts to produce energy, to have *Wirkungen*). This Real is nothing but the *Es*, the unconscious as it is in itself, says Lacan. I suggest that we are dealing here with the level of the letter, of "pure" signifiers. My supposition is confirmed by the way in which Lacan further develops his simile: "What is the *Es*? What does the introduction of the notion of the power plant allow us to compare it with? . . . With the power plant itself . . . as it presents itself to somebody who does not know anything about the way in which it functions";[91] even though Lacan does not spell it out, the latter subject may be identified with the psychotic subject.[92] He then accounts for this comparison by reminding us that "the *Es* is not a raw reality," since it "is already organized, articulated, like . . . the signifier."[93] We should finally observe that this apparently trivial definition of the unconscious is, ultimately, what obliges Lacan to openly contradict what he had said a few minutes before: the *Es* "is *not* simply what is there at first"[94] (hence we are left to assume that there is something else which "is there at first," and that Lacan parried his students' question about the precise status of the primordial *Stoff* . . .).

To recapitulate: the example of the power plant allows Lacan to distinguish four different kinds of Real: (1) the primordial *Stoff*, which is not of interest for psychoanalysis and whose status cannot be specified more precisely; (2) the Real-of-the-Symbolic, the symbolic *Wirklichkeit*, which is the main concern of psychoanalysis and should be understood in energetic, nonmaterial terms; (3) the Real-of-language, the letter, which, strictly speaking, is not the same as the Real-of-the-Symbolic; (4) everyday reality, which is itself the domain of a series of very "effective" (perhaps the most effective) *Wirkungen*. At this stage, one might well object that Lacan did not consider for an instant what is obviously the main issue at stake here: how was the power plant built in the first place? In fact he does give an answer, a provocative one, which we shall be able to explore in due course: the power plant was built by the Holy Spirit; creation should always be regarded as creation *ex nihilo*.[95]

Toward the end of Seminar VI—a seminar principally devoted to the discussion of unconscious desire and the way in which it is organized in the fundamental fantasy—Lacan returns on various occasions to a classification of the distinct forms of the Real. The strict coherence of the development that links these passages with Seminar IV, however, is obfuscated by the use of an altogether different terminology. First of all, Lacan talks about a "twofold reality,"[96] indicating that there is "another dimension" of reality (that of the object *a*, the Real-of-the-Symbolic) which must be separated from everyday reality; the latter is merely that which "could be inscribed in a behaviorist experience" whereas the former represents "eruptions in the behavior of the subject."[97] This other dimension of reality should also not be identified with "primitive reality."

Consequently, we are actually dealing with three realities: (1) everyday "behaviorist" reality; (2) "primitive reality"; (3) a dimension of reality that differs from the first two and is given two basic attributes: first, it locates itself in a "beyond" with respect to everyday reality; secondly, it has been there "from the beginning" (as we shall soon see, this beginning should be identified with primordial frustration).[98] Although Lacan does not explicitly affirm this here, contrary to what one might suppose, "primitive reality" was not concretely there at the "beginning," since it was always-already lost—this issue will be developed in Seminar VII, where Lacan will show how everyday reality and the Real which "erupts" in it are both the consequences of the *loss* of "primitive reality."

For the time being, Lacan focuses on the fact that psychoanalysis must extract the Real from everyday reality in order to avoid confusing two different kinds of objects: the (imaginary) object of knowledge (*connaissance*) and the (real) object of desire. The first notion of the object, that of scientific objectivity, "has been the fruit of the elaboration of centuries of philosophical research," and proposes "a relationship of the object to the subject by means of which knowing involves a profound identification, . . . a connaturality through which any grasp of the object manifests something of a fundamental harmony."[99] The tacit superimposition of this notion of the object, the object of knowledge—which is, after all, "historically definable"[100]—onto the second notion of the object, the object of desire, is what leads many psychoanalysts mistakenly to promote the idea that the maturation of the subject's desire—and of his sense of reality—logically entails a maturation of the object of desire beyond the polymorphous sexuality that characterizes infancy. Against this stance, which considers genitality to be the harmoniously preestablished goal of psychosexual development, Lacan argues that "nothing seems to confirm that there is . . . an exact correlation between the perfect achievement of a world so well kept in hand in the ordering of all its activities, and a perfect harmony in relationships with one's counterpart."[101]

Lacan examines the status of the Real of the object of desire (the object of psychoanalysis) vis-à-vis the object of (scientific) knowledge more closely in two successive lessons of Seminar VI. We could summarize his conclusions in the following six points:

(1) The objects of everyday reality are secured for us by the hold modern science has on the world. In paradoxical opposition to the enormous development of technology, however, not only is the "objectivity," the "disinterested perspective," of science historically determined but, in our epoch, it also clearly reveals itself to be highly disappointing according to its own (philosophical) criteria: indeed, "we have less than ever the feeling of attaining . . . the end of knowledge, namely the identification by thought of the subject . . . to the object of his contemplation."[102]

(2) Freudian psychoanalysis is an answer to such a "crisis of the theory of knowledge"; its most revolutionary message consists in suggesting that "the real of the subject is not to be conceived of as a correlative to a knowledge,"[103] that "the real as real" should thus be opposed to the objects of everyday reality insofar as the latter are nothing but objects of knowledge.

(3) Although the "real as real . . . is not situated with respect to the subject of knowledge because something in the subject is articulated which is beyond his possible knowledge," it is nevertheless the case that this "real as real . . . is already the subject . . . who recognizes himself in the fact that he is the subject of an articulated chain."[104] What does this mean specifically? As Lacan suggests, the Real as real is "a real which has taken its place in the symbolic, and which has taken its place beyond the subject of knowledge."[105] The Real as real obliges us to postulate a Real which is, at the same time, within the Symbolic, a Real-of-the-Symbolic, and beyond (symbolic) knowledge; the Real as real is a beyond within the unconscious. . . .[106]

(4) The Real as real, the real object of the subject's desire, is the subject, or, more precisely, the Real-of-the-Symbolic is "the elective point of the relationship of the subject to what we can call his pure being as subject."[107]

(5) The "real object"—the object of the subject's desire that coincides with his being—is an object which is "in a close relationship to . . . the subject" only insofar as it is "detached from him."[108] In other words, the real object is what is cut from

the subject of desire, it is precisely what is missing from him.[109] Hence one must conclude that the Real-of-the-Symbolic (as being of the subject) is a lack: however, we shall now have to see how this lack profoundly differs from that of the "primitive reality," the "primordial Stoff," that is always-already lost.

(6) The real object as lack is an "object which can support fantasies."[110]

These dense formulas from the concluding lessons of Seminar VI prepare us for the discussion of the Real in Seminar VII. It is now my intention to demonstrate how Seminar VII could be located "in between" two Lacans, the transcendent Lacan for which "there is an Other of the Other" and the Lacan of the Other barred by the Real. I think my hypothesis can initially be supported by one straightforward piece of evidence: the notion of the real "Thing," around which the entirety of Seminar VII revolves, disappears almost completely from later Seminars. Conversely, the "dumb" Thing of Seminar VII differs by definition from the Thing "that speaks" in earlier essays: this is why I believe that Lacan's explicit attempt to consider them as interchangeable notions is far from convincing.[111] While the Thing "that speaks" in the mid-1950s is *completely* identifiable with the unconscious as a fully symbolic locus structured like a language, the dumb Thing of Seminar VII is related to the unconscious structured like a language only in an *indirect* way. Here the Thing corresponds to the mythical primordial object that was always-already lost for the subject, whereas the unconscious is regarded as a *consequence* of this loss. In other words, the unconscious as such, its phantasmatic structure $\$\lozenge a$ is supported by the object a which is related to the Thing but also differs from it.[112] Seminar VII is probably the only place where Lacan founds his examination of the Real on a neat distinction between the "real object" (the object a) and the real Thing—as he repeatedly states with various formulations, the object a "is a thing that is not the Thing."[113] In contrast, the detailed analysis of the object a carried out in the late 1960s and 1970s leaves no doubt that the "real object" is at this later point the only Real.

Let us now look closely at three quotations which are crucial for my interpretation of Seminar VII. Lacan states that: (1) The Thing is a "void at the centre of the real";[114] (2) "*The Thing is that which in the primordial real* [ce qui du réel primordial], *suffers from the signifier*—and you should understand that it [primordial real] is a real that we do not yet have to limit, the *real in its totality*, both the real of the subject and the real he has to deal with as exterior to him";[115] (3) "There is an identity between the fashioning of the signifier and the introduction of a gap, of a hole in the real."[116] By superimposing these three sentences, we are forced to deduce that Lacan is here assuming that, before the advent of the signifier, there was a mythical Real with *no* hole. . . . The "primordial real" (always-already) *was* something. The Thing *qua* hole is the primordial Real insofar as it has "suffered" or been holed by the signifier; hence the Thing is a *transcendent* "inaccessible"[117] hole. This is precisely what differentiates Seminar VII from Lacan's later assumption of what is logically involved by the barring of the Other—namely, that the primordial Real, "nature," is in itself *not-One*:[118] on the contrary, here the presymbolic Real is plainly said to constitute a "totality," a One.

We can now grasp why the distinction between the Thing and the object *a* holds only in Seminar VII: at this stage, the object *a* is the hole from the standpoint of the symbolic order, it is the hole of the Symbolic, whereas the Thing *qua* transcendent hole is somehow independent of the Symbolic (see graph 4.8). The Thing should be regarded as the reified negation of the primordial Real effected by the emergence of the signifier. In other words, we are dealing with the presence of an absence that exists *per se*; as Lacan puts it: "The Thing is not nothing, but literally *is not*."[119] It is a minus that negates a mythical plus (nature that was some-thing *per se*). If, on the one hand, the Thing *qua* hole is clearly caused by the signifier, it is a retroactive creation of the signifier; on the other, despite being its consequence, it is also independent of the signifier inasmuch as it is the minus of a mythical presignifying plus that is not caused by the signifier. From this contradictory standpoint, object *a* is not the Thing, since the Thing *qua* hole is what has been canceled by the signifier. In other words, the object *a* is considered in Seminar VII to be a *derivative* lack.

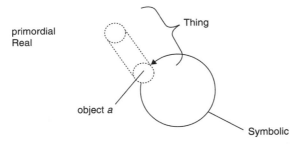

Graph 4.8

This last point allows us to suggest that we should understand the object *a* (the "real object" of Seminar VI) as the lost object which is, strictly speaking, different from the primordial object that was lost. Indeed, Lacan seems to postulate the existence of: (1) a *primordial object* which, in the end, is not an object, the "union" between the mother and the child that precedes primordial frustration. We are dealing here with a mythical undifferentiated whole—an "unlimited totality" in which there is no distinction between interiority and exteriority—in which any subject-to-come is initially located; (2) the Thing (the mother) as a transcendent lack which is the primordial object as *always*-already *lost* for the subject; one realizes that one "had" the primordial object only after one has lost it;[120] (3) the object *a* which is, for the subject, the lost *object*, an immanent lack that is accessible to the Symbolic. In Seminar VII, object *a* is considered only as a -1 or $+1$, as a lack-of-the-Symbolic. The problem with this seminar is therefore that, in creating the notion of the Thing, it associates the real lack as it is in itself, before being counted symbolically in the fantasy $\$\Diamond a$, with the transcendent "back" of the primordial Real. Against this stance, Seminar X will show that the real lack is in itself always immanent to the Symbolic, since there is no-thing presymbolic that could be holed; or that object *a* is to be situated on two inextricable levels—that of the real lack "in itself" and that of the lack-of-the-Symbolic.

Despite its mistaken, transcendent approach, Seminar VII lays the foundations of Lacan's theory of the subject of the Real in a number of different ways:

(1) The real object, the object *a*, is always-already a lost object. If in Seminar IV Lacan had already proposed that the subject's relation to the object had to be thought in terms of a relation to the lack of the object, in Seminar VII he reassesses this issue by problematizing the status of the Freudian notion of *das Ding* (the Thing), which for the father of psychoanalysis indicated precisely the primordial object of a mythical primitive satisfaction that was lost. Freud insisted on the fact that the subject can find the objects of reality only insofar as he is actually engaged in a search for the primordial object that was lost (the Mother). In other words, all objects—which are never fully satisfying—are found through a *repetitive* movement relying on a fundamental discordance: that which is found in repetition is not the object for which the subject is looking and which could never be refound. Repetition is therefore nothing but the impossibility of repetition, the consequence of a necessarily failed attempt to repeat a primordial experience.

(2) Lacan follows Freud in maintaining that the entirety of man's representative activity as a desiring being of language, and consequently the constitution of conscious and unconscious subjectivity *tout court*, revolves around the primordial extraneousness of *das Ding*, its being "alien."[121] The primordial object that was lost has thus a *causally* determinative value[122] with respect to the structurally insatiable nature of the subject's desire: this is what we shall be looking at closely in Chapter 5. As for the effects caused by the loss of the primordial object on the level of representations, Lacan unambiguously states that what one has found at the place of the object that cannot be refound is "precisely the object that one refinds always in reality . . . the world of modern physics."[123] In addition to this, the self-conscious

representation of objects in everyday reality is concomitant with the emergence of an unconscious Real-of-the-Symbolic (the object *a*) which Seminar VII primarily associates with the superegoic *jouissance* of the commandment. What one finds in the place of the object that cannot be refound is not only everyday reality, since "in the same place . . . something [else] substitutes itself for that dumb reality which is *das* Ding—that is to say, the reality that commands and regulates."[124] In other words, if on the one hand it is only by means of the law, "the moral command"—the prohibition of incest that resolves the Oedipus complex—that "the real [everyday reality] is actualized" for the subject in our symbolically structured experience,[125] on the other hand it is equally the case that "something in this very regulation is paradoxical . . . intemperate"[126]—that superegoic *jouissance* constitutes the other side of the symbolic law.

(3) Topologically speaking, the subject and his representations emerge in relation to what Lacan calls the "*extimité*" of the Thing.[127] As Miller observes: "*Extimité* is not the contrary of *intimité*. *Extimité* says that the *intime* is Other—like a foreign body, a parasite."[128] The Thing is thought as something that lies "at the centre [of the subject] only in the sense that it is excluded";[129] it is that around which the subject of the unconscious (and, in parallel, his self-consciousness) is organized in signifying—representative—relationships. More specifically, Lacan says that the Thing is "something *entfremdet* [alienated] . . . that on the level of the unconscious only a representation can represent."[130] What does this mean precisely? Here Lacan is referring to the Freudian notion of *Vorstellungrepräsentanz*: the profoundly different ways in which this term is translated into French ("*représentant-représentation*") and English ("ideational representative") makes Lacan's point sound more enigmatic than it really is. In Chapter 3, I explained how, in addition to representing the—signifying—content of the unconscious (which is repressed in secondary repression), the ideational representative—to be understood as a sign—also *sets up* the unconscious *tout court*, since it is responsible for primal repression. In Lacan's own language, this means that the unconscious is initially structured in a fundamental fantasy $\$\lozenge a$ when the loss (alienation) of the Thing—which occurred in concomitance with the traumatic irruption of the Desire-of-the-Mother after primordial frustration—is retroactively signifierized (represented) in the object *a* qua lost object (by means of a primitive phallic *Vorstellung* which allows lack to be counted as −1 or +1). As Safouan insightfully observes, the object *a* is thus here "a 'representation' that designates itself in the impossibility of the representation of a void that remains outside of all representations [the Thing] even though it determines their gravitation."[131]

(4) An accurate topological understanding of the precise coordinates of the relationship between $ (the subject barred by the Other of the signifiers), the object *a*, and the Thing paves the way for a proper grasp of Lacan's concept of sublimation. He famously defines sublimation as the "elevation of an object to the dignity of the Thing";[132] such an elevation is what takes place in the fundamental fantasy, "the form on which the subject's desire rests."[133] Hence the object *a* is here "the imaginary element of the fantasy"—imaginary in the sense of an unconscious *Vorstellung*[134]—that "is superimposed onto the subject [$] to lure him at the very point of *das Ding*."[135] We should now be able to understand why Lacan says that "the Thing is essentially the Other thing":[136] the Thing (*la Chose*) which is forever lost can be "refound" only in another thing (*autre chose*), object *a*, the sublime object that represents it (its lack) at the foundations of the unconscious.[137] Given that the subject's desire aims at the impossible repetition of what has structurally been subtracted by the intervention of the law (the always-already lost "union" with the Mother *qua* Thing), desire—or, better, its drive—can only partially satisfy itself through sublimation. As Di Ciaccia and Recalcati rightly observe: "If the Thing can only be found by means of a deferment in another thing . . . this indicates that sublimation [is] not merely one of the possible destinies of the drive but its ultimate structure."[138] In other words, human sexuality *always* entails sublimation, and sublimation can only be sexual: this is basically why human sexuality differs from animal sexuality. While the aim of animal instincts can never be changed, sublimation offers the human drive a satisfaction which is different from its ultimate aim (the Thing); this is "what reveals the true nature of the *Trieb* [drive] insofar as it is not simply instinct, but has a [indirect] relationship with the Thing insofar as it is distinct from the object."[139] The same point can further be clarified by referring once again to the notion of extimacy: the Thing is extimate with respect to the (unconscious of the) subject, it is *excluded* inside him; in this sense, it cannot coincide with the aim (*Ziel*) of the drive but is, rather, "surrounded"[140] and thus "defined" by the object *a*—the object of sublimation in $◇*a*—to be understood as the (derivative) aim of the drive.

Lacan's approach to the function of sublimation causes him to depart from Freud on two important issues: first, sublimation should not simply be related to apparently nonsexual activities such as artistic creation and intellectual work. On the contrary, from what we have just seen, all these activities are nothing but specific ways in which the subject as desiring being of language comes to terms with sexuality as sublimation. "Culture" *tout court*, as distinct from nature, is, after all, nothing but the consequence of the loss of the primordial object.[141] Secondly, despite Lacan's following Freud in considering the (implicitly *and* explicitly sexual) objects of sublimation as objects or activities in which the libido of the drive can be channeled in a socially acceptable way, unlike Freud, he also thinks that these objects are not acceptable just because they are useful to society. They are also acceptable because, on the level of "collective" fantasies (ideology and its superegoic *jouissance*) that are "historically and socially specified," they allow the subject to "colonise the [useless and even harmful] field of *das Ding*"[142] in a "domesticated"[143] manner. In other words, the structural necessity of sublimation as considered by Lacan is intimately related to a dimension beyond the pleasure principle which, although it is "domesticated," would definitely not be regarded as "sublimated" according to Freud's criteria.

(5) Lacan reminds us that the notion of sublimation is usually understood, even in everyday language, in terms of creation.[144] But what, more precisely, is creation? He believes that authentic creation can only be *symbolic* creation *ex nihilo*. What is again at stake here is the issue of the simultaneity between the initial "fashioning of the signifier" and the introduction of a void, a *nihil* (the Thing) in the primordial Real. With the introduction of the first signifier, "one has already the entire notion of creation *ex nihilo*" which is itself "coextensive with . . . the Thing":[145] the *nihil* must clearly be associated with the void/hole of the Thing whose emergence is concomitant with that of the signifier, not with the primordial Real for which the notions of fullness and emptiness have as yet no sense.[146] This, after all, is what sublimation is all about. Every successful sublimation—first and foremost that which allows the formation of the fundamental fantasy after castration has resolved the Oedipus complex—will ultimately correspond to a reinstatement, on the individual level, of the mythical birth of the first (Master-)Signifier that founded the universal order of the Symbolic and, at the same time, lost the Thing. Lacan thus claims that he is showing us "the *necessity* of a point of creation *ex nihilo* from which originates what is historic [on the individual and universal level] in the drive":[147] in other words, the "point" of creation *ex nihilo* is the mythical point at which man's animal instincts are sublimated into the subject's drive.

In Chapter 5, we shall look at how the drive should always be understood as a *death* drive: the "point" of creation inevitably coincides with that of the fall. For the time being, I limit myself to observing that the notion of creation *ex nihilo* as the extraction of the symbolic signifier which simultaneously annihilates the real Thing offers the most conclusive explanation of Lacan's recurrent reference to the opening line of St. John's Gospel: "In the beginning was the Word."[148] The word that was in the beginning—the Holy Spirit that created the unconscious power plant in Seminar IV—is nothing but "the entrance of the signifier into the world."[149] Here one might well be tempted to ask: is there any more need to confirm that Lacan's "system" is marked by what Derrida calls the "ideality of the signifier"?[150] From what we have seen so far, it is certainly difficult to deny that the phallic signifier has a *transcendental* role with regard to the constitution of the Symbolic as such— one which, however, also entails the production of an irreducible real remainder. Derrida is thus correct when he states that the phallus is a transcendental insofar as a transcendental position designates "the *privilege* of one term within a series of terms that it makes possible and by which it is presupposed";[151] he is incorrect insofar as he fails to acknowledge that the series of terms that is made possible by the phallus, the phallic set, somehow remains an *open* set, a nonset, despite all privileges. . . .

Contrary to what Lacan's provocative formulas often seem to suggest, his creationism does not presuppose any *transcendent* principle. Indeed, "it is paradoxically only from a creationist point of view that one can envisage the elimination of the always recurring notion of creative intention" which is tacitly "omnipresent" in evolutionism.[152] Evolutionism relies on a divine creative intention in that "the ascending movement which reaches the summit of consciousness and thought" is deduced from a "*continuous* process."[153] In other words, evolutionism is teleological and theological by definition, and derives human thought from an evolution of matter that ultimately depends on the transcendent consciousness of God. In contrast, for Lacan, the creation *ex nihilo* of the signifier on which human thought depends is truly materialistic; Lacan's creationism is a form of antihumanist immanentism, since it is grounded on the assumption that the Symbolic is un-natural,[154] not super-natural, the contingent product of man's successful dis-adaptation to nature. Such an unnatural dis-adaptation, which obviously dominates and perverts nature, can nevertheless originate only immanently from what we call "nature," and thus contradicts the alleged continuity of any (transcendently) "natural" process of evolution. Matter does not evolve. As Lacan will explicitly recognize in later years, matter is in fact only retroactively "materialized" by the contingent appearance of the signifier *ex nihilo*.

"The necessity of a point of creation *ex nihilo*" is the necessity of a point at which the Symbolic emerges as an immanent consequence of the primordial Real. Yet the point of creation *ex nihilo* is also the point of infinity: what precedes it can only be thought as impossible (to think)—one cannot think the primordial Real, or the point of creation. As Lacan puts it, the Symbolic "has been functioning as far back in time as [man's unconscious] memory extends. Literally, you cannot remember beyond it, I'm talking about the history of mankind as a whole."[155] The Symbolic started at a specific moment that *will have been* its (immanent) "absolute beginning."[156] This is also to say that the Symbolic should be regarded as an asymptotic curve that is both limited in time *and* equal to the infinity of man as being of language (*parlêtre*); for the *parlêtre* there is nothing beyond the *parlêtre*. Hence the calculation of the duration or length of the asymptotic curve does not make sense: no *parlêtre* witnessed the passage from the ape to the *parlêtre*, and no *parlêtre* will be able to count the precise day, month, and year when the last atomic bomb explodes. As Lacan observes, the points of creation and destruction (of history) are a strict logical "necessity," but they can be posited only through either retroactive or anticipatory mythical speculations. This is how the finitude of man as *parlêtre* engendered by creation *ex nihilo* opens a "limited" space of infinity, the "absoluteness of desire,"[157] that must be opposed to the eternal immortality of the undead—that is to say, the primordial Real, pre- or postsymbolic "nature" as not-One.

CHAPTER 5

THE SUBJECT OF THE FANTASY . . . AND BEYOND

The reformulation of the Oedipus complex through the theory of the paternal metaphor and the related notion of the Name-of-the-Father allows Lacan to put forward a series of definitions which emphasizes the key function of the signifier in the emergence of subjectivity. Continuing a critique that had already characterized his research in the sphere of the Imaginary, Lacan refuses to conceive the subject in terms of a mere "individual reality which is in front of you when you say *the subject*,"[1] especially if one were to relate such an individual reality to the primordial mythical condition of the baby's pure instinctual need ("need is not yet a subject").[2] As we saw in detail in Chapters 2 and 3, the subject is a subject only insofar as he is a "speaking subject" and, as such, his "position" is constituted by the big Other.[3] Yet, at the same time, this dependency on the symbolic order paradoxically "structures the subject [only] through a decomposition of himself,"[4] it divides the subject between self-consciousness (the ego) and the unconscious while rendering these two scenes unable to account for him except by relating to each other. Indeed, if, on the one hand, "there is no subject if there is no signifier that founds him,"[5] on the other hand, relying on the differentiality proper to the logic of the signifier and the process of repression to which it gives rise, Lacan is also adamant that the subject is not *signified* (in self-consciousness) by any given signifier, nor is it to be identified with a particular (unconscious) *signifier*.[6]

Are we then to infer that Lacan is proposing here a notion of a "quasi absent subject, a sort of support that would only serve to send back [*renvoyer*] the ball of the signifier"?[7] The answer to this question can only be negative, even if one refers to the period in which Lacan, somehow contradictorily, believes in the self-guaranteed autonomy of the symbolic order. It is doubtless the case, however, that in his later theoretical elaborations, especially after the notion of the Real acquires preeminence, he perceives the necessity to explain in more detail his claims in favor of a substanceless subject which is nevertheless not fully comprised of signifiers. As Lacan himself openly acknowledges in Seminar X, "the problem is now that of the entry of the signifier into the real and to see how from this the subject is born."[8] The function of the subject is to be located in between the idealizing effects of the signifying function and the Real of the drive.[9]

I suggest that the well-known formula according to which "the signifier is that which represents a subject for another signifier"[10] should itself be related to this kind of programmatic statement. It is definitely not a "structuralist" formula but one which gives full expression to the subject of the Real, or, more precisely, to the subject of the fantasy as the subject of the Real. In "Subversion of the Subject" (1960)—which is, significantly, the first article in which the formula appears— Lacan clearly says that the signifier (S1, the Master-Signifier) for which all other signifiers (S2) represent the subject is nothing but the phallic signifier, S (A barred).[11] As I explained above, Φ is precisely the signifier that brings about the formation of the fundamental fantasy $\$\lozenge a$,—which in its turn is responsible for the foundation of the unconscious and, in parallel, self-consciousness—and, what is more, it does so only by entering into contact with and "domesticating" the real lack of the object a. Lacan's formula is not simply telling us that the fading subject $\$$ is continuously represented in the diachronic dimension of conscious discourse, that of demand, by any signifier that, in place of the unconscious subject of the enunciation, the "speaking I," relates to other signifiers—the latter being conscious signifiers in the sentence as well as unconscious signifiers located in various synchronic signifying chains, as a result of double inscription. What is really at stake is that the unconscious subject of enunciation is himself represented in the unconscious by all signifiers S2 only if the S2s represent him for the phallic signifier S (A barred): "In the absence of this signifier, all the other signifiers represent nothing," there is no subject (of the unconscious).[12] S1 and S (A barred) are then one and the same thing; however, strictly speaking, they are not to be identified with the subject.[13] A similar argument is valid with regard to the fundamental fantasy: although S1 is that which links $\$$ and a in the fundamental fantasy, the latter begins to function retroactively only when it becomes the stage on which any signifier S2 represents the subject for S1.

How are we to understand the fundamental fantasy as the locus in which the subject emerges as a consequence of the knotting together of the three orders of the Symbolic, the Imaginary, and the Real? First of all, the fundamental fantasy should be regarded as a "compromise formation" *par excellence*: indeed, it is both the consequence of and a reaction (a defense) against the fact that the symbolic Other of the signifiers is a structurally lacking order.

In other words, the fantasy has two basic interconnected functions: it both relates the barred subject to the real lack in the Symbolic, that of the real object a, and, at the same time, "veils" this lack in the unconscious through the imaginary dimension of the object a. Two points must immediately be elucidated: (1) the Real of the object a is only retroactively actualized for the subject of the unconscious by the imaginarization of the object a; (2) the Real of the object a must itself be understood at two different, though inextricable, levels: the object a as real hole in the Other is both the hole as the *presence* of a residual Real—and, as we shall later examine, of a related residual *jouissance*—and that same hole as the *absence* of the whole Real, the mythical primordial zero which is retroactively counted as One—which is then to say that the object *a* simultaneously stands for the *absence of jouissance*. This is a preliminary distinction of fundamental importance if we are to understand Lacan's notion of the subject of the Real. In other words, in the fantasy $\$\Diamond a$, the real dimension of the object *a* as absence of *jouissance*, castration, is that to which the subject of unconscious *desire* and its infinite conatus is ultimately related; while, at the same time, the real dimension of the object *a* as the presence of a residual *jouissance* is that to which the subject of the *drive* is related. Although these complex definitions will become clearer only toward the end of this chapter, at this early stage one should already be able to grasp that, due to their mutual dependence, the subject of desire and the subject of the drive are one and the same.

It is now important to emphasize that, for Lacan, *every* drive should ultimately be regarded as a *death* drive.[14] What does this mean? The death drive contains the purest essence of the drive inasmuch as it corresponds to a subtractive element which emerges in concomitance with the mythical birth of the Symbolic *ex nihilo*—that is, with the formulation of the first signifier that transforms the primordial undead Real into the void of the Thing (or, more precisely, of the object *a*).[15] The *ex nihilo* is therefore nothing but the *ex nihilo* of the death drive. The death drive is thus a name for the irrevocable antisynthetic trait that forever separates the mythical undead (which is "killed" by the signifier) from its symbolic designation. As a consequence, the symbolic order as such relies on the conservation of difference provided by the death drive as a subtractive drive. For the sake of clarity, we should therefore logically distinguish:

(1) the death drive as *the subtraction from the primordial "One"* qua *absolute zero* (and from its alleged *jouissance*). This first movement, which is never repeated, corresponds to the instauration of the Symbolic,[16] and should be regarded as retroactive; in other words, it is possible here to consider the death drive as an "anti-synthetic" element only after the (supposed) primitive "synthesis" of the primordial Real has been broken by a contingent "material" change that is immanent to it. This point must be made clear once again in order to avoid the risk of surreptitiously identifying the death drive as initial antisynthetic element with any sort of transcendent "will";[17]

(2) the death drive as *the repetitive subtraction from that which has become a One* sui generis, or more precisely, as Lacan specifies, from the "distinctive unity,"[18] the "oneness as *pas-un*"[19] of the Symbolic *qua* differential order of the big Other. This is the death drive *stricto sensu*. It is only on the basis of such an abstract (and mainly pedagogical) distinction between these two movements or "phases" of the death drive that one can account for the difficulty Lacan apparently experienced in deciding

whether to assign it to the Symbolic, as he did especially in the early to mid-1950s, or to the Real, a more common choice in his later work. Indeed, the death drive is both that which retroactively transforms the primordial undead Real into the Symbolic as the order characterized by death and, given its subtractive nature, that which tends to transform the Symbolic into the undead "inorganic" Real—it is only in the latter sense that Lacan can claim that the drives tend toward the Thing.[20]

One important point should be made completely unambiguous: during its second phase, the subtractive antisynthetic principle of the death drive is necessarily—albeit paradoxically—turned into a *conservative* principle. This is why the drives tend toward the Thing without reaching it—and, what is more, are forced to *repeat* this tension. The death drive *stricto sensu* is a conservative drive precisely in that it is antisynthetic. More specifically, if, on the one hand, the subtraction from the primordial "One" as absolute zero causes the formation of a "distinctive unity" that is better understood as a (big) Other, on the other hand, the subtraction from this Other will obligatorily entail a tendency toward a return to the zero that *cannot* be fulfilled. Indeed, a complete subtraction from the symbolic Other, which would mean a mythical return to the undead "One" (as zero), is impossible insofar as the subtractive element is antisynthetic (anti-One) by definition. Thus the primordial subtractivity of the death drive turns into the repetitive conservation of this same subtractivity.[21]

At this stage, we should thus be able to isolate four basic consequences of this process (which I also illustrate below by means of graphs 5.1 and 5.2):

(1) The death drive aims at the lost object while, at the same time and for the same reason, it is forced to "circle around it"[22] without ever reaching it—the drive thus de-limits the lack as some-thing (satisfying).

(2) This same movement opens up the field of the "bad" infinity of a continuously unsatisfied desire that, if dissociated from the drive, would ultimately aim precisely at plunging itself into this lack. Yet, as long as the drive and desire remain associated in their relation to the real lack, they perpetuate the subject of the fantasy who veils this lack.

(3) In being an inherently thwarted tendency, which is as such compulsively repeated, the *jouissance* of the drive[23] as the partial satisfaction of desire through dissatisfaction should be related to a basic form of psychic masochism of the subject.

(4) The masochism of the drive is never simply identifiable with a "death wish," a will to commit suicide, even though the latter corresponds to the radical possibility occasioned by the paradoxical situation of the former.

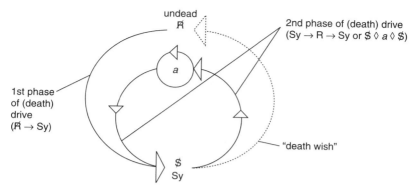

Graph 5.1

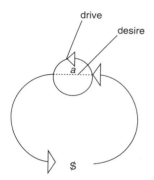

Graph 5.2

It should now be clear how Lacan's recourse to the "creationism" of the signifier solves many of the impasses in Freud's discussion of the death instinct. It does so precisely by problematizing Freud's understanding of the death instinct as that which is *beyond* the pleasure principle. Freud initially formulated the death instinct as a principle that was directly opposed to the pleasure principle—as life instinct that aims exclusively at avoiding unpleasure—in order to explain phenomena of masochistic *repetition*. This connection, however, was blatantly contradicted by the fact that the death instinct was concurrently regarded as a mere tendency to return to the *stasis* of the inorganic state—which was deemed to be equally operative in all living beings, from bacteria to humans. In addition, Freud also surprisingly conceded that "the pleasure principle seems actually to serve the death instinct":[24] the latter was therefore inconsistently located beyond the former while, at the same time, including it. As Laplanche and Pontalis observe, the only way out of this impasse for Freud was to implicitly presuppose two kinds of pleasure principle: the pleasure principle *stricto sensu*, which would be in charge of maintaining a constant level of libido understood as "life instinct," and the so-called Nirvana principle, which would instead work "towards the reduction of tensions to nil,"[25] thus serving the death instinct as the "essence of the instinctual."[26]

Despite the fact that he does not openly confront Freud on this point,[27] Lacan definitely refuses to consider the Nirvana principle in terms of the death drive. Adamant that they must be distinguished, he claims that there is a fundamental "*division between the Nirvana or annihilation principle and the death drive* [insofar as] the former concerns a relationship to a fundamental law which might be identified with that which energetics theorizes as the tendency to return to a state, if not of absolute rest, then at least of universal equilibrium"; that is to say, entropy.[28] By contrast, the death drive "has to be *beyond* the instinct to return to the state of equilibrium of the inanimate sphere,"[29] and this for three strictly interrelated reasons. First, it entails a historical dimension insofar as "it is articulated at a level that can only be defined as a function of the signifying chain." In other words, the death drive can be applied only to human beings and not to other living beings; the death drive is not a death instinct.[30] Secondly, such a historical articulation of the death drive presents itself in the guise of the repetitive "insistence"[31] of the fundamental fantasy—in Lacan's own intricate words, "of something memorable because it was remembered [*mémorisé*]."[32] Thirdly, this insistence as principle of conservation should at the same time be linked to a subtractive element that, for the reasons expounded above, must be differentiated from any sort of transcendent Schopenhauerian *Wille*: Lacan defines it as a "will to destruction," and later specifies that it should, rather, be understood as a destructive "will for something Other [*une volonté de quelque chose d'Autre*]," "a will to begin all over again," *ex nihilo*.[33]

To cut a long story short, the death drive could thus be said to be beyond the pleasure principle only insofar as we take the latter to express the Nirvana principle understood as the (alleged) tendency to return to an inorganic state. But if one considers the pleasure principle as "nothing other than the dominance of the signifier,"[34] it is clearly the case that the death drive—on which the differentiality of the symbolic Other of the signifiers ultimately relies—is *not* beyond the pleasure principle. This despite the fact that it involves a (domesticated) masochistic *jouissance*, which itself aims at the "inorganic" undead. As a matter of fact, such a "beyond" of the Lacanian death drive always remains within the symbolic order ("should we find anything else than the fundamental relationship between the subject and the signifying chain in what Freud names the beyond of the pleasure principle"?).[35]

As we shall see in Section 5.5, the Real of *jouissance*—that of the object *a*—is indeed always a Real-of-the-Symbolic.

Beginning from these presuppositions, Lacan also deduces that the death drive is precisely that which makes it *impossible* for the subject to return to the inorganic: Freud's Nirvana principle should indeed make us "smile" insofar as "nothing is less sure than returning to [the alleged] nothingness [of the pre-Symbolic]."[36] The case of suicides is paradigmatic here: the suicide's desire—which we could call the "death wish," in opposition to the death drive—that apparently is a desire to have done with the Symbolic—to exit from it in order to join the inanimateness to which, according to Freud, the evolution of life ultimately aspires—actually conceals a desire to be recognized by the symbolic Other as a suicide, as the one who rejects the Symbolic. . . . It therefore follows that "the more a subject affirms through the signifier that he wants to exit the signifying chain, the more he enters into it and becomes its part."[37] Beside the borderline case of suicides, it is more generally the dead as such who become for others "an eternal sign," says Lacan— "signs" which, I would add, the living can endlessly enjoy in their fantasies:[38] the dead continue to circulate between $ and *a* in the Other's fantasy, and thus never rejoin the primordial undead. I would also go so far as to propose that, for Lacan, the dead suffer language as, in different fashions, both psychotics and "pre-Oedipal" babies do. It goes without saying that in order to put forward these theses Lacan is here, unlike Freud, tacitly presupposing that the distinction between the organic and the inorganic is retroactively operative only from the standpoint of the Symbolic: outside of it there is only the undead; hence it is meaningless to talk about a *return* to the inorganic after the symbolic order as such has disappeared—after the death of the Symbolic—just as it does not make sense to refer to the animal's return to the inorganic.

To conclude my explanation of the role of the death drive in the functioning of the fundamental fantasy, I shall now briefly describe three different notions of death which are all present in Lacan's late theory of the subject:

(1) "Normal" death, *death "in reality."* This is merely a symbolic construction insofar as if, on the one hand, man as animal is always-already undead in the barred Real—human "life" is *per se* undead and "inorganic," as is that of all other "organic" entities—on the other hand, man as being of language continues to be present in the Other's fantasy as the symbolically *real* object of the Other's *jouissance*: this condition will persist as long as there is a symbolic order. Therefore, death "in reality" is ultimately nothing but the consequence of the symbolic order's inability to individuate the subject imaginarily—and thus of the subject's inability to individuate himself—beyond the visual unity granted by specularity. One could go as

far as suggesting that, according to Lacan, death "in reality" is, following a Leibnizian legacy, a mere "diminishing" of the body,[39] a loss of man's bodily height that prevents the Other from bringing about any new form of imaginary individuation. In fact, we know that Lacan undoubtedly considers man's erectile shape (his being a biped, as well as the stiffness of his penis) to be the natural "reservoir"[40] of his capacity to carry out specular identifications which are later symbolically united in a retroactive way. In other words, a subject can properly be individuated in reality only inasmuch as the three orders of the Imaginary, the Symbolic, and the Real maintain an extremely precarious reciprocal balance.[41]

(2) *Real death*, as distinct from death "in reality." This will coincide with the cessation of the subject's *post mortem* survival as an object of the Other's *jouissance*, and must logically be equated with his *symbolic death*. The latter is nothing but the total deletion of the subject from the field of the Other, the complete obliteration of "the dead from [the Other's unconscious] historical memory."[42] Once again, we witness here the strict interdependence between the Real, which is always a Real-of-the-Symbolic (as object of *jouissance*), and the Symbolic, which is always a Symbolic holed or supplemented by the Real.

(3) The symbolic death of the individual can logically occur only in concomitance with the *death of the Symbolic tout court*, which, following Sade, Lacan usually names the "second death." Yet these two interrelated notions, which are often confused by commentators, should be kept separate. In order to provide a credible example of the "death of the Symbolic," a permanent derailment of nature that will forever extinguish human life as (the registration of) the symbolic life of the being of language, Lacan repeatedly hints at the nuclear holocaust.[43] On the other hand, symbolic death is a strictly speaking unattainable state: Lacan exclusively refers to it by means of mythical examples which portray certain paradigmatic ethical figures. Symbolic death denotes the (im)possibility of leaving the Symbolic as an individual: this is certainly the case with Antigone who, in being placed alive in a tomb for her transgression of the law of the *polis*, should be regarded as a "still living corpse,"[44] as someone who is symbolically dead for the Other before being dead "in reality." As we can conclude from our analysis of psychosis and suicide, Lacan believes that, until there is a symbolic order, no-body (whether "alive" or "dead") can ever completely be "separated" from it. This last point is easy to grasp if we consider the Symbolic in terms of what Žižek pertinently defines as the (unconscious) "timelessness and spacelessness of the synchronous universal symbolic network of registration"[45] which will be operative until the end of time. Although the subject's symbolic death is achieved *stricto sensu* exclusively through the death of the symbolic order, what, on the other hand, Lacan deems possible on the in-

dividual level, and which accounts for the extraordinary importance he attaches
to the mythical examples of symbolic death, is a *temporary* separation from the
Symbolic—a momentary desubjectivizing permanence in the Real/void-of-
the-Symbolic, an undoing of the fantasy—which is logically followed by a new
symbolic reinscription.[46] This process should be considered as the ultimate ethical
achievement of psychoanalysis.

Before embarking upon a close investigation of the "components" of the fantasy
($, the object *a*, and the precise way in which they are related to each other through
desire), let us focus on its overall functioning by way of a simile. Here I expand
upon an example that Lacan himself provides as early as 1957:

> With fantasy we are in the presence of something that fixes and reduces to the sta-
> tus of a snapshot the course of memory, stopping it at a point called screen mem-
> ory. Think of a cinematographic movement that takes place rapidly and then
> suddenly stops at one point, freezing all the characters. This snapshot is distinc-
> tive of a reduction of the full scene . . . to what is immobilized in fantasy which
> remains loaded with all the erotic functions included in what [the full scene] ex-
> pressed and of which [fantasy] is the witness and the support, the last support that
> remains.[47]

How should we interpret this dense passage? What do we actually obtain from the
"reduced" phantasmatic snapshot? Two straightforward issues that remain implicit
in Lacan's account should be made clear: first, the film in question is inevitably, for
all of us, a *horror* film; secondly, we all want to watch horror films even if initially
nobody likes them. To put it bluntly, when the child freezes the shocking scene of
the film he is accidentally watching unaware of its traumatic content—when he
originally organizes the unbearable encounter with the Real of the desire-of-the-
(m)Other which causes anxiety—he both obtains a still that protects him from the
trauma (through the imaginary objectification of the scene) *and* lets himself be
partially traumatized (through the real scene which underlies its imaginary objectification). In other words, *thanks to* the mitigation of the screen/veil that "fixes"
what Lacan calls "the full scene," the child ends up "enjoying" what he has seen,
and wants to watch it over and over again. If, in the meantime, his parents confis-
cate the film, he will try to refind a similar scene in other films. . . . (To grasp what
Lacan is saying, think also about the way supposedly frightened children cover
their eyes with their hands while, simultaneously, peeping out avidly through the
gaps between their fingers. . . .)

The most important point to emphasize here is that the traumatic scene can be
formed only *retroactively* by the imaginary fixation of the still frame. The "course of

memory" can be memorized only thanks to the screen provided by the "screen memory." Initially, there is only the purely chaotic encounter with the desire-of-the-(m)Other, which is not subjectively experienced as such by the child. Strictly speaking, the real scene of the horror film will have become something more than a purely chaotic event—and thus something to be afraid of—only after it has been imaginarily frozen. In addition to this, the (retroactive emergence of the) real scene should now be regarded both as a lack, a reminder of the lost chaotic event that the child now desires as such, and precisely as lack, as the "witness" of the event, its "support that remains."[48]

If we translate all this into Lacanese, we are able to maintain the following: before the emergence of the fundamental fantasy $\$ \lozenge a$ through symbolic castration and the resolution of the Oedipus complex, before the retroactive sublimation of the lack in the (m)Other through the imaginary, albeit unconscious, function of the object a—the lack in the (m)Other being here nothing but the anxiety-provoking emergence of her desire during the second stage of the Oedipus complex—the subject's *desire*, as well as its real object, is *not* yet formed. The unconscious desire of the subject for the real object, for the lack which coincides with the desire of the Other, is ultimately dependent on the imaginary function of the fundamental fantasy: unconscious desire can desire only the lack beyond the screen/veil insofar as the screen/veil is present. Therefore, in order to desire the lack that (the) desire (of the Other) is, desire has to remain fundamentally unsatisfied; it has to continue to desire, to desire desire.

This elucidation—which, incidentally, also functions as an introduction to the next section of this chapter—is needed in order to answer, or at least to problematize further, a legitimate objection: if the real object of desire—or, more precisely, as should by now be evident, the real "object-*cause*"[49] of desire—is nothing but the desire of the Other as lack, why can the subject not desire it "directly"? Why is it necessary to keep on desiring the lack?

I shall go over this important argument once more: it is possible to desire the lack only insofar as it emerges as lack through the retroactive reification of the imaginary "veil" in the fundamental fantasy. The desire of the Other cannot be *desired* directly, and so one *repeats* one's desire for it. What happens when the subject faces it directly—as is the case at the moment of privation, as well as at the end of the psychoanalytic treatment, when symbolic castration is "consciously" assumed by the subject? This is precisely what Lacan calls "subjective destitution."[50] Given that desire is, by definition, the "essence" of the subject, we must also conclude that subjective destitution, a radical *manifestation* of desire, causes the *termination* of desire at the same time. In the rest of this book, my attempt to articulate this para-

dox of "pure" desire from different—albeit convergent—angles should always remain visible in the background.

5.2 THE SUBJECT OF THE FANTASY AND DESIRE

In Chapter 3, I analyzed in detail the way in which, during the so-called dialectic
of frustration, the child's demand—to be distinguished from a mere appeal/cry
relating to the satisfaction of biological needs—is constituted as an unconditional
and unsatisfiable demand for love. What the child actually demands is not the real
object that satisfies his needs, but the love of the one that can give him any object
as a gift, a symbolic object; in this context, "the [occasional] satisfaction of need
corresponds to nothing more than a compensation for the frustration of love."[51] In
the same chapter I also explained how, as a result of the dialectic of frustration, the
child both symbolizes his relation to the (m)Other for the first time and, for the
same reason, soon becomes utterly dependent on her alleged omnipotence. The
emergence of a subject who is no longer a "non-subject" (a-sujet) completely subjected (assujetti) to the (m)Other and her desire is possible only after the intervention of the law of the father that first deprives the mother—in the second stage of
the Oedipus complex—and successively castrates the child himself—in the third
and final stage of the Oedipus complex.

From what I have said so far, it is clear that desire stricto sensu, unconscious desire, consolidates itself only after the resolution of the Oedipus complex, which
simultaneously involves the formation of the fundamental fantasy and the sexuated subjectivation of the child. The question I shall now attempt to answer is: what
is the specific difference between the register of (pre-Oedipal and Oedipal) demand—most noticeably, the demand for love—and that of (post-Oedipal) desire?
My analysis mainly focuses on Lacan's seminal lesson XXI of Seminar V, which was
later reelaborated in the well-known article entitled "The Signification of the Phallus." More specifically, it is my intention to carry out a critical evaluation of the
formula according to which desire is "the margin, the result of the subtraction . . .
of the necessity [exigence] of need from [par rapport à] the demand for love."[52]

Most of the interpretations of this formula oversimplify it, and continuously
risk contradicting themselves, inasmuch as they render it tautologous with the formula of the demand for love. Indeed, desire is often simply described as the surplus produced by the articulation of need in demand—a perfect definition of the
demand for love. Obviously this cannot be regarded as an acceptable explanation
of desire, since the demand for love (and not simply "demand") is, in Lacan's formula, just one of the elements of the operation from which desire results.

Another mistaken interpretation is the one which is somehow the opposite of the one which reduces desire to demand. Although at one point in "The Signification of the Phallus" Lacan ambiguously asserts that "what is alienated in needs"—and constitutes primal repression "as it cannot . . . be articulated in demand"—nevertheless "appears . . . as desire,"[53] on the same page, he also unequivocally maintains that desire is definitely not just a repressed need. Lacan is extremely careful in distinguishing desire from repressed need as well as from the demand for love, even though he closely relates it to *both* of them. If, on the one hand, desire is not a mere prediscursive biological given that was repressed by the signifier—desire cannot be reduced to need alone—on the other, it is doubtless the case that desire is related to the repressed need in a way that the demand for love is not: "Desire is something that *gives back* the margin of deviation marked by the incidence of the signifier on needs."[54] By definition, desire remains beyond the "necessity of need," the "appetite for satisfaction"—after all, desire essentially looks for unsatisfaction—yet, at the same time, it also "recuperates"—in the unconscious—the needs that could not be satisfied through demand. As Guyomard remarks, desire "takes up again, at another level [that of the subject's *active* entrance into the Symbolic], the biological imperative of the satisfaction of needs."[55] If demand was defined in the pre-Oedipal dialectic between the mother and the child as that which lies beyond need, the desire of the post-Oedipal subject who has undergone symbolic castration is in turn defined by Lacan as that which "is located beyond demand"; "We need a beyond of demand insofar as . . . demand deviates, changes and transposes need":[56] such a beyond will be characterized by the fact that, in it, "the Other loses his predominance,"[57] his omnipotence.

Let us go through these difficult differentiations by means of a closer examination of the formula of desire. There is no doubt that, according to Lacan, desire is always to be understood as *sexual* desire.[58] We should keep this in mind when we are interpreting a specific sentence from Seminar V where Lacan states that "with respect to the demand for love, sexual need is going to become nothing but desire."[59] In other words, (sexual) desire is nothing but the post-Oedipal recuperation of sexual need at the level of the demand for love (which had "deviated" from sexual need). I believe that this quotation is far from contradicting the classic definition of desire as the result of the *subtraction* of need from the demand for love; on the contrary, I firmly regard such a definition as meaningful only if it takes into account what seems to undermine it. My suggestion is that the classic formula of desire means the following: "The state of *pure* desire"[60]—the abstract notion that expresses the function "desire" as fundamentally different from the functions "need" and "demand for love"—is equal to the *subtraction* of the necessity of need/appetite for satisfaction from the *post-Oedipal* demand for love only inasmuch as *really existing* desire (as fundamentally *sexual*) is equal to the *addition* of the necessity of need to the pre-Oedipal demand for love. Another way to express this formula would be to say that *pure* desire is equivalent to the subtraction of the *drive* from the demand for love: in fact, the drive represents precisely the appetite for satisfaction on the symbolic level, and drive is another name for "sexual desire." Conversely, we can equally conclude that "impure" (unconscious) desire is equivalent to the addition of the drive to the (pre-Oedipal) demand for love: the "impurity" of desire thus corresponds to that which, in consciousness, and especially the unconscious, is partially satisfied through demand, despite its unconditional character and the essentially unsatisfiable nature of desire.

Strictly speaking, desire applies only to a post-Oedipal scenario: in the end, commentators often fail to distinguish between desire and the demand for love precisely because they fail to acknowledge this important specification by relating (the child's) desire to the context of the pre-Oedipal dialectic of frustration. Yet at the same time, once we have assumed that desire is always post-Oedipal desire, and thus different from the pre-Oedipal demand for love, we can also show that desire overlaps with the demand for love, which is precisely what Lacan does in the following passage: "Desire presents itself as that which, in the demand for love, rebels against any sort of reduction to need, since actually the demand for love doesn't satisfy anything but itself, which is to say [pure] desire as an absolute condition."[61] In other words, the post-Oedipal demand for love is equal to the drive insofar as it partially satisfies need; it is equivalent to pure desire insofar as it does not satisfy need. At this stage, we can also see from a new standpoint why Lacan can say that desire satisfies itself precisely as unsatisfied desire: it is only insofar as desire is unsatisfied (pure desire) that the drive can satisfy itself (and desire) partially. The abstract function of pure desire, its "absoluteness," necessitates the drive, and vice versa. As we have already seen, when pure desire completely purifies itself of the drive, it can only cause the termination of desire itself.

Let us now take a step back and attempt to explain more exhaustively the transformation of the (pre-Oedipal) demand for love into desire: Lacan obtains the formula of desire only after what he himself calls a "second negation"[62]—of demand by desire—that follows the first negation—of need by demand. As Lacan has it, given the pre-Oedipal "alienation" of the child in the signifier, "we should ask ourselves what is the meaning of the fact that the human subject is able to take hold of the conditions that were imposed on him . . . as if they were made for him, and that he can satisfy himself with them."[63] In a few words, we could well argue that what is at stake for Lacan is a passage from the "*unconditionality*" of demand to the "*absoluteness*" of desire; such a change basically involves a *positivization of lack* on the part of the subject. The child manages to "positivize" the lack that surfaced with the unconditionality of the demand for love, and in so doing he subjectivizes himself and emerges as a desiring lack-of-being (manque-à-être). On the other hand, during the dialectic of frustration, the demand for love led the assujet simply to demand what the (m)Other demanded: the symbolic "beyond of satisfaction" was in that case exclusively demanded by demanding the contingent objects demanded by the (m)Other (with which the child also imaginarily identified). Such an inversion of the function of lack can take place only if the (m)Other is perceived as lacking, as desiring "beyond her demands,"[64] and such a lack is successively "organized" in the fundamental fantasy by the phallic signifier due to the subject's own symbolic castration. This is the reason why Lacan is able to speak of the "Aufhebung" of the phallus with regard to lack.[65]

To recapitulate: desire is an unconscious "beyond" of demand "where need regains the first place";[66] however, if, on the one hand, desire is necessarily "borrowed"[67] from the appetite for satisfaction of particular needs, and thus supersedes the negativity of the lack which is consubstantial with the unconditionality of demand, on the other hand it gives rise to an "absolute condition" which is "without measure" with respect to any particular need. More specifically, such a "condition" of desire should be regarded as a positivization of the lack that surfaced with demand, and "can be named absolute in that it is a necessity [exigence] for which the Other does not have to answer 'yes' or 'no.'"[68] In other words, the inversion of lack is that which allows subjectivation.

We should now ask a key question: how are we to account for everyday conscious desire? Lacan does not conceal the fact that "desire is necessarily articulated [in self-consciousness] through demand since we can approach it only by means of some sort of demand."[69] In other words, the diachronic dimension of conscious desire is to be identified with the dimension of post-Oedipal demand which, as in the pre-Oedipal scenario, depends on the demand of the Other. Although the subject has acquired a certain separation from the Other (and from his demands) which makes it possible for him actively to enter the Symbolic as a desiring manque-à-être, his desire is nevertheless necessarily repressed in the unconscious insofar as it was achieved only by paying the "ransom"[70] of castration. What is repressed in the unconscious, what generates the unconscious tout court and is somehow "veiled" in its own defensive mechanism, is first and foremost: (1) symbolic castration, the subject's assumption that, as a result of his attempt phallically to come to terms with the lack in the Other (A barred), with the Other's desire, he himself became a barred subject $; (2) the fact that the subject's ($) own desire ultimately relies on—and is caused by—such an unbearable lack.

We are therefore confronted with what Safouan, commenting on Seminar VI, calls "a forced neurotization of desire":[71] desire—and the subject's symbolic individuation—is possible (in the unconscious) only insofar as it is partly reduced to the demand of the Other (in self-consciousness). This is particularly visible in the case of the hysteric—"the subject for whom . . . it is difficult to establish a relationship [with the Other] that allows him to preserve his place as a subject"[72]—but should be regarded as universally valid for all subjects. Lacan thus speaks of a "fundamental situation of man between demand and desire"[73] which ultimately accounts for the fact that (1) desire is always the desire, or rather the demand, of *autre chose*, and consequently (2) the satisfaction of desire essentially consists of the preservation of its own unsatisfaction, since a subject remains a subject only insofar as—to use the full meaning of the denomination *manque-à-être*—he is a desiring *lack-of-being* that *wants-to-be*.[74]

As Lacan himself shows in a particularly dense passage of Seminar V, the phallic "structuration of the subject's desire"[75] by no means excludes demand. "It is thanks to the mediation of the phallic signifier that [the subject] is introduced *beyond* the relation with the [pre-Oedipal demand of the] Other," yet "as soon as that [beyond, desire] is constituted, from the moment the phallic signifier is there in the guise of [the signifier of] the desire of the Other, [the phallus] does not remain at this place but is integrated into the speech [and hence the demand] of the Other and comes . . . to occupy its place *on this* [conscious] *side*, in the original place of speech with the mother." As we shall soon see in greater detail, "it is there [on the conscious side] that it plays its role and assumes its [imaginary] function [as φ]."[76]

My reading of this passage is confirmed by Lacan's subsequent admission that "this beyond," the subject's desire as instigated by the Other's desire, "remains unconscious for the subject," and that "it is by now here [in self-consciousness] that the dialectic of demand takes place, without [the subject] knowing that this dialectic is possible only insofar as his desire . . . finds its place in a relationship with the desire of the Other that remains for him unconscious."[77] If one were to use Lacan's algebraic notations to express all this, one could propose that the unconscious desire of the subject in $\$\lozenge a$ is always more or less "masked"[78] by $\$$-D,[79] the fading of the (post-Oedipal barred) subject before the Other's demand. At this stage, it should not be too difficult to see why Lacan also designates $\$$-D as the algebraic notation of the *drive*: it is in fact only insofar as desire is partly submitted to the demand (of the Other) that the subject's drive can partially be satisfied; when one moves to "pure" desire, the fantasy is undone and the drive can no longer be satisfied.

What alternatives do we have to neurotic desire? Where should we locate the radical notion of "pure desire" in the context of the interplay between demand and (impure) desire? In analyzing the formula of desire, we came to the conclusion that

Positing a kind of general equivalence b.t. desire / the Ucs?

in its purest state "the [post-Oedipal] demand for love doesn't satisfy anything but itself, which is to say [pure] desire as an absolute condition."[80] In order to avoid any gross misunderstanding, it should be made explicit that this sentence is meaningful only if we assume that what the *purified* state of demand categorically *excludes* is precisely the request to be *loved*. Yet, at the same time, if "we can only approach [desire] by means of some sort of demand,"[81] then we must also assume that this will be valid *a fortiori* when *pure* desire is at stake. We should therefore ask ourselves the following crucial question: which sort of (purified) demand allows us to approach pure desire? (If not to reach it, since, as we have already seen, it elides itself.) I argue that, in its purified form, demand will be a demand beyond demand, a demand that demands nothing, or rather, demands nothingness itself, the void/ lack of the desire of the Other, and does not demand the demand of the Other— as happens in neurosis. In other words, pure demand, as an approximation to pure desire, does not demand to be loved back (to be recognized) by the Other, but simply desires what in the Other equally desires without demanding. Desire and love are structurally incompatible. Desire is the desire of lack, or, more precisely, "that which desire looks for in the Other is less that which is desirable [*le désirable*] than that which desires [*le désirant*], that which the Other lacks."[82] To put it differently, the pure desirer desires the desire of the Other, to be understood as that which in the Other desires (*le désirant dans l'Autre*), that is, the Other's lack. As Lacan notes, for this very reason, as a pure desirer I cannot desire the Other's desiring me, I cannot desire to be loved: if this happens, I "abandon desire."[83]

On a concrete level, pure desire will therefore be a demand that purely desires "*le désirant dans l'Autre.*" My final suggestion is that, in everyday life, such a transformation of demand into pure desire is paradoxically achieved when, instead of always demanding "something else," we contingently demand something specific in an inflexible way, at any price. Not giving up on one's desire, the well-known motto of Lacanian ethics, necessarily presupposes—and, in practice, problematically resolves itself into—not giving up on one's demand.

5.3 THE SUBJECT OF THE FANTASY AND THE OBJECT A

On the basis of my explanation in Section 5.2, it could rightly be suggested that Seminar V adopts a "panoramic" view of desire by analyzing the way in which it differs from need and the demand for love. On the other hand, Seminar VI is mainly concerned with the specific emergence of desire in relation to the object *a* in the fundamental fantasy. In this section, I shall first of all look at several crucial lessons from Seminar VI which focus on the precise dynamics of the relationship at work in the fundamental fantasy $\$\lozenge a$. I will then supplement these observations with an attempt to draw some final conclusions about the various significations which can be attributed to the object *a*: this will be done by referring to Seminar X which, as Safouan points out, "carries the theorization of the object *a* as far as possible."[84]

As we have already seen, the fundamental fantasy is nothing less than what structures the unconscious to be understood as primal repression: in this sense, it is both "fundamental," insofar as it constitutes the synchronic structure of the unconscious according to which the "true articulation between desire and its object"[85] should be understood, and "minimal," precisely insofar as it limits itself to providing a basic "imaginary support"[86] to desire by combining the barred speaking subject $ and the (unconsciously) imaginary object *a*. Lacan is thus able to say that the fantasy is "the locus of reference by means of which desire will learn to situate itself":[87] the subject's desire is not adjusted to a pregiven object, but must learn to adjust itself to a phantasmatic object. In other words, the fantasy is that which "introduces an essential articulation" within the original "non-opposition" of the speaking subject to the object (think of the way in which the child still identifies with the objects of the mother's demand during the dialectic of frustration).[88] Such a non-opposition is nevertheless even present in the fantasy itself, which is one of the reasons why the fantasy is repressed: this allows Lacan unhesitatingly to state that, since "the subject [as *manque-à-être*] is desire," making him pass through the object *a* "is as legitimate as making him pass through $."[89]

How should we understand this oscillating relationship between the subject and the object of the fantasy? The phantasmatic object is first and foremost the support which the subject gives himself insofar as he is a "failing" (*défaillant*) subject. As we have repeatedly seen from different perspectives, during the second stage of the Oedipus complex the child is confronted with the fundamental lack in the (m)Other—with the fact that his own demands cannot ultimately be recognized by the Other—and thus "fails in his certitude" of being the exclusive imaginary object of the (m)Other's love: at the same time, and for the same reason, the child is equally unable symbolically to "name himself as subject," he "fails in his designation as subject" precisely inasmuch as there is no Other of the Other, there is no signifier that "might guarantee the concrete consequences of any manifestation of the signifier," that is, the child's symbolic demand for love.[90]

The only way out of this impasse, the only way to constitute himself as subject, is for the child precisely to locate himself at the level of the lack of the Other as a failing/lacking subject. The object *a* serves this purpose insofar as it is the paradoxical object that represents the subject as lacking—or, more specifically, it is the *representation* of the lacking subject brought about by the representative function of the phallic signifier—and, in so doing, simultaneously institutes him as a "tension," a desiring *manque-à-être*. The most important point to emphasize here is that there is necessarily a price to be paid in order to transform the mere *failure of the subject* who is involved in the Oedipus complex into the *failing subject* that positively emerges when the complex is resolved: the subject's "mapping of himself as failing"[91] onto the object, the fact that the status of lack is reversed when the lacking subject who demands is transformed into the subject-of-lack who desires, must be paid for by the "ransom" of symbolic castration, the subject's (unconscious) assumption of his own structural failure as a subject. In other words, the object *a* is definitely that which allows the subject to name himself on the plane of self-consciousness through a personal pronoun—in this sense, the object *a* works as the means through which the subject's ego-ideal is subsumed "beneath" his ideal ego[92]—but it is concurrently that which can intervene to support this conscious naming only by endlessly representing the imaginarization of the subject's own castration on the plane of the unconscious, the synchronic plane of what is indeed repressed.

We should now be able to see why Lacan famously states that "the subject is only in the cut [*coupure*], in the interval."[93] Let us immediately ask the following question: is he here referring to the conscious ego or the unconscious subject? Although Lacan implicitly takes both levels into consideration, and avails himself of a single concept, for the sake of clarity it is probably easier to relate the subject's "being-in-the-interval" to self-consciousness and his "being-in-the-cut" to the unconscious. Diachronically, the subject as desiring *manque-à-être* is certainly to be identified with the (abstract, never concretely present) interval between demand as an expression of need and demand as demand for love.[94] Yet this classification *in absentia* is made possible only by the fact that, already on the synchronic level, "the subject encounters himself as cut" thanks to the support of "the form of cut" of the object *a* in the fantasy. In other words, the object *a* should be understood here as the detachable part of the subject, the so-called part-object (breast, feces, phallus) that allows him to symbolize on the imaginary plane the symbolic cut— or, rather, the cut in the Symbolic as such—as it surfaced at the moment of the privation of the mother, "the absence of the signifier."[95]

We could thus well argue that if the subject as cut is the one who is represented in the phantasmatic object at the moment of his own disappearance, then the subject is one (*le sujet est un*) in the unconscious insofar as he appears there as *pas-un*.[96] More precisely, the subject *continues* to make one in the unconscious fantasy precisely because, as failing/fading subject, he is not-one.[97] To put it differently, the subject can call himself "I" in self-consciousness—and thus value himself (*se compter*)—only because he repeats the act of counting himself (*se compter*) as not-one in the fantasy—where, in fact, the object *a* functions as a "lost name."[98]

Let us look at this issue of counting more closely. We have already explored from various standpoints the way in which symbolic identification is brought about by the phallic signifier which organizes the lack in the Other; the problem, however, is that the subject represses the fact that such an organization is not equivalent to an overcoming of lack: as Lacan says in Seminar IX, (primal) repression is generated by nothing but a literal miscalculation (*un erreur dans son compte*).[99] At the level of the unconscious, the identifying representation (one) of the subject's own failing in the object *a* necessarily institutes difference (not-one), and thus gives rise to the repetitive series 1, 1, 1, 1 . . . in which each "count" is started anew, each "go" is absolutely unique; repetition is the impossibility of repeating the primordial identification with pure difference. On the other hand, at the level of self-consciousness, the subject's naming of himself as "I" mistakenly adds 1+1+1+1 . . . and obtains 2, 3, 4 . . . —that is to say, the diachronic "temporal" continuity of his lived experience.

Let us attempt to reformulate the kernel of the difficult issues I have just raised in a somewhat simplified and illustrative way. When it comes to providing specific examples of fundamental fantasies, Lacan is not very eloquent: he usually prefers to confine his descriptions to the field of perversions (especially pathological masochism and fetishism) and reassess Freud's seminal texts on the formation of fantasies (first and foremost "A Child Is Being Beaten").[100] We should now dare to ask these straightforward questions: what kind of scene is staged in a "standard" phallic fantasy? In what precise sense is the emergence of the fundamental fantasy simultaneous with that of self-consciousness?

I do not think I am forcing Lacan's theories in suggesting that the object *a* in the "standard" phallic fantasy $$◊a$ must necessarily refer to the secondary (symbolic) identification with the father which promotes the formation of the ego-ideal.[101] More specifically, as we saw in Chapter 3, in secondary identification the child identifies himself with the symbolic father—embodied in the real paternal figure—as the one who has Φ, and who is thus able retroactively to signifierize the desire of/lack in the (m)Other. In and around Seminar VI, Lacan further specifies that secondary identification allows the child to proceed to a subjective assumption—and a parallel sexuation—which is inflected between "having" and "being," and is succinctly expressed by the formula "he is not without having it" (*il n'est pas sans l'avoir*). This is to say that when, at the resolution of the Oedipus complex, the child symbolically identifies himself with the father as bearer of Φ (by means of an imaginary alienating identification), he represents himself in the object *a* (the phallic *Gestalt*) precisely as "not being without having it."[102] The object *a* in fantasy is both an irreducible lack and the result of an organization of lack

159

effected by Φ; such a paradox is well expressed by the formula of secondary identification, which is perfectly calibrated in order to evoke the inevitable loss entailed
by subjectivation/sexuation; claiming that the child has it (Φ), as Lacan did in
Seminar V, is no longer a sufficient explanation, since having Φ necessarily entails
symbolic castration. Hence the child *has* Φ only insofar as he is *not* (the φ of the
mother). We can thus assume that the standard phallic fantasy is ultimately one
with the fantasy of castration—or, more precisely, $-\varphi$ is "*contained*" in the scene that
promotes secondary identification; such a scene is, for the same reason, repressed,
and constitutes the anchor of the unconscious.[103]

This conclusion concerning the standard fantasy seems to be confirmed by an
apparently unimportant remark made by Lacan in Seminar V apropos the perverse
fantasy of "A Child Is Being Beaten." As we saw in Chapter 3, Lacan believes he is
able to show that, despite a disturbance in the Oedipal relation with the mother
which hinders the emergence of the phallic *Gestalt*, a child can actively enter the
symbolic order—as a perverse masochist—through a fantasy of fustigation. The
child is in fact able to symbolize his predicament (the absence of love, and hence
of frustration, due to the presence of a sibling) through an imaginary signifier
(hieroglyphic) such as a stick or a whip which works as an alternative phallic signifier. "In being beaten, he is loved," says Lacan: in other words, this (phantasized)
act finally institutes the child as a subject of the signifier for whom "the question
of love exists," albeit in a negative manner.[104]

What interests us here is that Lacan later specifies that, insofar as he is beaten,
the child *is* the phallus φ *tout court*. The whip with which the child is being beaten
is the Φ which simultaneously castrates the child to be understood as φ: $-\varphi$ is thus
"contained" in the same scene that supports the symbolic identification with Φ.
This is what allows Lacan generally to maintain that, in the case of both perverse
and standard fundamental fantasies, "the phallus . . . is preserved [*qua* having Φ]
only insofar as it went through . . . castration," that is, the "*marking*" of the phallus
itself (*qua* not-being φ).[105]

So what about the emergence of self-consciousness in concomitance with the
establishment of the fundamental fantasy? In representing himself in secondary
identification as the one who "is not without having it," the child both subjectivizes himself, insofar as he has Φ "through" the father, and represents lack, insofar as he is not φ, by means of one and the same image. In so doing, the subject
pays with his being (φ) in order to sustain himself before a structurally lacking
Other, which therefore is itself sustained by the subject's own payment, the part of
himself which he imaginarily loses. By having Φ through the father, however, the
subject is able to give a "form" to the alienating imaginary identifications he had
previously acquired: the formation of the ego-ideal allows the amalgamation of his

various Ur-Ich, the consolidation of the ego *tout court*. In other words, the self-conscious ego emerges only insofar as one "has it" at the price of "not being it": this payment (castration) is precisely what is *concomitantly* repressed in the fantasy.[106] It goes without saying that beyond all objects of demand in self-conscious life, the subject ultimately seeks to take possession once again of that which he no longer is (φ) and which necessarily remains concealed for the ego.[107]

At this stage, we should be able to distinguish five overlapping functions of the object *a* which all depend on $\$\Diamond a$:

(1) The object *a* is the *imaginary representation of lack* in the fundamental fantasy, the image of the cut produced by Φ *qua* S (A barred); as such, it should also be understood as the consequence of castration $(-\varphi)$.

(2) The object *a* is the *detachable part-object* which is *imaginarily* cut from the subject and thus, by definition, "what one *n'a plus*";[108] contrary to (1) above, in this sense, the object *a* and the imaginary phallus φ are not mutually exclusive. In Seminar VI, Lacan explicitly defines the object *a* as the "effect" of castration brought about by Φ and the imaginary phallus as the "object" of castration;[109] this distinction, however, is complicated by the fact that part-objects are also called object *a* and, above all, one of the part-objects is precisely φ. (In addition to this, the pregenital part-objects, the breast and the feces, are retroactively phallicized through φ when the fundamental fantasy is formed.)[110]

(3) The object *a* is the *real lack* prior to its imaginarization in the fantasy; it is A barred before its signifierization, S (A barred), produces (1) above. In this sense, the object *a* is a real object that was lost: first and foremost, the maternal breast, whose loss is phallicized retroactively in the fundamental fantasy through φ, the only part-object which is not lost in the Real. One could well argue that functions (2) and (3) are, after all, expressing one and the same point; such a distinction, however, is pedagogically interesting insofar as it shows how Lacan—toward the end of Seminar VI, and especially in Seminar X—is progressively obliged to postulate a real dimension of object *a*, a Real *qua* lack-in-the-Symbolic, an "irrational remainder" which "is after all the only guarantee of the alterity of the Other."[111] It goes without saying that the first two (opposed) functions of the object *a* logically rely on the third.

(4) The object *a* is the *enigmatic desire of the* (m)Other;[112] it should be easy to see how this relates to function (3). The breast was originally lost by the child when the desire of the (m)Other caused primordial frustration; this desire was later perceived as such at the moment of privation, and retroactively signifierized/"mitigated"

after castration. The object *a* as desire of the (m)Other corresponds to a real lack for the subject, since it is itself a real lack in the (m)Other. This fourth function of the object *a* clearly demonstrates how it can be understood as the "cause" of the subject's desire, as that which lies "behind desire" in an "outside" which precedes any "interiorization."[113] After the emergence of the subject's desire, the desire of the (m)Other qua object *a* then becomes the *object* of desire.

(5) In self-consciousness, the object *a* should be related to what Lacan calls the *agalma*, the hidden precious object which is in the other more than himself, and the reason for which the subject ultimately desires him. This is nothing but the necessarily concealed part-object φ, the object which is always missing in self-consciousness, and can present itself only negatively as −φ; the most important point to grasp here is that the subject continuously projects onto φ as the non-specular remainder of the body a libidinal investment which surpasses the specular relation he maintains with his ideal ego.[114] Such an investment is operative both when the subject remains caught in the dialectic of demand—when he always demands "something else," and is not directly seeking the *agalma*—and when he explicitly desires the *agalma* as that which is in the other more than the other, the void in/of the other (his own desire).[115] As Safouan rightly observes, however, the *agalma* is, strictly speaking, different from the object *a* (or φ) qua hidden part-object: it is an *x* "which preserves its nature as *agalma* only insofar as the part-object, *a*, does not appear."[116] In other words, the *agalma* qua *x* is the "other side," the conscious side, of the part-object *a* qua real object which was *lost*; as Lacan says: "We are not always on the [unconscious] stage [of the fundamental fantasy], even though the stage stretches very far, even into the domain of our dreams. And as not on the stage and remaining on this [conscious] side of it . . . we find nothing but the lack at *x*."[117] On the other hand, the part-object *a* appears as such in self-consciousness when the empty place *x* of *agalma*, the direct consequence of −φ in self-consciousness, can be circumscribed (*cerné*) "by a certain edge, a certain opening . . . where the constitution of the specular image shows its limits." A "window" is thus opened onto the void; this means that the void is itself delimited and "materialized" in self-consciousness: Lacan defines the product of this process succinctly in terms of a "lack of lack" (the suspension of −φ), which functions as the "elective locus of anxiety."[118] I shall return to these intricate issues shortly.[119]

By recognizing functions (4) and (5) as overlapping, we could suggest that the subject, in desiring *agalma* as object *a*, desires nothing but the Other's desire as void/lack. Although Lacan acknowledges this as early as Seminar V—"desire is the desire of that lack which designates in the Other another desire"[120]—he usually does not point out how such a definition involves two opposed implications. If desire is the desire of the Other as desire of lack, this could apply equally to desiring the Other's desire as the object of one's fantasy which *represents* lack, and to the pure desire of the Other's desire as an irreducible real lack, as the prephantasmatic real void in the symbolic order which generated the subject's desire in the first place. It is indeed the case that the identification of the subject's desire with the Other's desire (as "mitigated" void) on the level of the "marionettes of fantasy" should not be confused with another, more "essential" level on which, despite phantasmatization, the desire of the Other remains unknown for the subject, and causes anxiety when it is encountered.[121]

From a slightly different standpoint, this clarification should also allow us to see how the subject's desire of the Other's desire in the fundamental fantasy is still a desire for *recognition*; consequently, it is incorrect to relegate the desire for recognition to the pseudo-Hegelian notion of *conscious* desire that Lacan embraced in the early 1950s. When Lacan says that desire is the desire of the Other's desire as lack, this does not necessarily exclude the possibility that this same desire is also, at the same time, a desire for *unconscious* recognition in the fundamental fantasy: due to the complex nature of the fantasy in which, paradoxically, lack is represented, unconscious desire is both a desire for lack and a desire to suture this lack. Insofar as lack is sutured in fantasy, the subject's desire as desire of the Other's desire as lack remains a desire for (phantasized) recognition—a desire to be desired or, better, loved by the Other. The subject's fundamental fantasy sutures lack only insofar as $ is at the same time the object *a* of the Other's desire (in the subject's fantasy).

To recapitulate: on the level of fantasy, the subject's desire is the Other's desire and, conversely, the Other's desire is the subject's desire: hence (1) the subject's desire is the object *a* of the Other's desire and, more importantly, (2) the subject's desire is ultimately the desire to be the object *a* of the Other's desire. On the contrary, pure desire desires "that which desires" (*le désirant*) in the Other, the real alterity of the Other which lies beyond the phantasmatic veil of unconscious recognition. All this can be reformulated by saying that the subject's desire of the Other as desire for the Other's desire *qua* lack is nothing but the desire for the Other as the desire to *reproduce* desire; one can continue to desire the Other's desire *qua* lack only if one continues to reproduce one's desire in $◇*a* (where *a* stands for the Other's desire as "domesticated" lack). Any direct attempt to face the Other's desire conceived as "raw lack" beyond fantasy unleashes anxiety and, as we have seen, this could entail the paradoxical termination of desire.

What precisely does Lacan mean when he states that the subject is the object *a* of the Other's desire, and that this condition should ultimately be regarded as the kernel of the subject's own phantasmatic desire?[122]

In Seminar X, Lacan clearly describes the fundamental fantasy as a "picture which is located over the frame [encadrement] of a window": the purpose of this absurd technique" is precisely "not seeing what one sees out of the window,"[123] the barred Other, the lack in the Other which emerged at the moment of privation. In Chapter 3, we examined the way in which the child is inserted into the symbolic dialectic of frustration long before realizing that the Other is barred; to begin with, there is a window insofar as protosymbolization, the first stage of the Oedipus complex, is initiated. At the onset of the second stage of the Oedipus complex, the child realizes that the window frames an abyss, and that he might easily fall out of the window (be engulfed by the mother): thus the scene depicted by the picture has the function of covering the abyss.

More importantly, in Seminar X, Lacan implies that such a "defensive" scene, whatever its particular traits in different subjects, always portrays the unspecularizable image of the other as *double*. In other words, the imaginary other is "seen" in the fundamental fantasy as the nonlacking image which owns the part-object lost by/castrated from the subject—the double is thus i′(a) + a, the imaginary other plus the object a. This emerges particularly clearly in Freud's famous case study of the Wolf Man, whose repetitive dream, Lacan says, provides us with an excellent example of the "pure fantasy unveiled in its structure":[124] a window is opened, wolves are perched on a tree and stare at the patient with his own gaze (as nonspecular remainder of his own body). Lacan also refers to a similar scene in Hoffmann's tale *The Sand Man*: the doll Olympia can be completed only with the eyes of the student Nathaniel.

These examples show how the lost part-object a, first and foremost the phallicized gaze, is precisely that which veils the void in the Other—his pure desire as A barred—who therefore appears as a double in the unconscious fundamental fantasy. In the fantasy, I see myself as the phallicized object of the Other's desire, I see myself in the Other in order not to "collapse" into his real desire: it is therefore no longer sufficient to talk about the subject's desire as the desire of the Other, insofar as we are here more specifically dealing with a "desire in the Other [Autre] . . . my desire enters into the antrum [antre] [for instance, the eye socket] in the guise of the object that I am."[125] At its purest, the object of my phantasmatic desire (as a defense) is thus the Other's desire in which I am myself an object.[126] This explains why the fantasy, despite being that which allows secondary identification and individuation *tout court*, is *per se* a structure based on a "radical desubjectivation" due to which "the subject is reduced to the condition of a spectator, or simply an eye."[127] In interpreting this quotation, we should avoid the risk of surreptitiously considering such a vision as a (specular) individuated action: as I have just demonstrated with the examples given above, the fantasy is, rather, an "interpassive" scene in which one "makes oneself be seen" by "his" gaze as lost part-object located in the double.

It is only in this context that we can make sense of the following enigmatic definition of fantasy provided in Seminar X: "I would say that the formula of fantasy $ desire of *a* can be translated as 'may the Other fade away, faint, before the object that I am as a deduction from the way in which I see myself.'"[128] What fades away in the visual interpassivity of the fantasy is undoubtedly the Other's desire as real lack, the real object *a*: Lacan can thus propose that the imaginarization of the object *a* in the (neurotic) fantasy defends the subject from anxiety "insofar as the [imaginary] object *a* is artificial [*postiche*]."[129] Yet at the same time—as I have already illustrated with the example of the frozen horror film—in "framing" anxiety, in being "the first remedy beyond *Hilflosigkeit*,"[130] the fundamental fantasy is also that which retroactively renders the Real of anxiety effective on the unconscious level; "It is the [subject's] constitution of the hostile as such,"[131] the birth of what Freud named "erotogenic masochism" and Lacan rebaptizes *jouissance*.

We should therefore distinguish three logical times of anxiety vis-à-vis the object *a* and the fundamental fantasy:

(1) The prephantasmatic leaning out of the window at the onset of the second stage of the Oedipus complex, the chaotic encounter with the desire of the (m)Other *qua* real object *a* that will have been perceived as such only after its mitigation in the formation of the fundamental fantasy. Here anxiety is both the mere "presentiment of something," Lacan says, but also the "pre-sentiment," the "terrible certitude" which precedes all (symbolically) deceitful sentiments and in reaction to which the initial doubt "what does the (m)Other want?" is formulated.[132] In this first sense, "[unstructured] anxiety is a sharp *cut*," the original emergence of A barred "without which the presence of the signifier, its functioning, its entrance, its mark [*sillon*] on the real would be unthinkable."[133]

(2) The "framing of anxiety" in the "picture" of the fundamental fantasy due to the imaginarization of the object *a*: here that which is hostile (*l'hostile*) is "tamed, placated, admitted,"[134] and becomes a guest (*l'hôte*). In order to frame the anxiety produced by the desire of the (m)Other, however, the subject must undergo castration, appear as an object in the Other, and "this is what is intolerable."[135] In other words, from this standpoint, what is fundamentally repressed in the fantasy is the revelation of the "non-autonomy of the subject";[136] this is why the subject is not without having it and can say "I" in self-consciousness only at the price of "not seeing it". . . .

(3) Anxiety *stricto sensu* that occurs when the signifier of lack, S (A barred), responsible for the framing of anxiety in the fantasy is itself missing, when castration ($-\varphi$)

is suspended due to the excessive proximity of the Other's real desire (beyond my fantasy). This is nothing but the uncanny moment when lack is itself lacking in self-consciousness. Undoubtedly, the diachronic dimension of demand is characterized by the metonymic empty place of *agalma*; lack is present in imaginary self-consciousness; this, however, by no means implies that we normally have an *image* of this lack. Anxiety emerges precisely when the subject acquires a "*positive*" image of lack[137]—when a "window" is opened onto the void concealed by his specular projections—and the *agalma*, "the absence where we are" beyond specularity,[138] is thus revealed in its true nature: a "presence elsewhere," a "pound of flesh," the part-object *a* (the image of lack) that I am for the Other's desire in my fantasy. Anxiety thus corresponds to the fleeting surfacing of the part-object, to the appearance of the double who gazes at the subject with the subject's own eyes. In other words, anxiety is the appearance of the disappearance of my own fantasy in self-consciousness, the intolerable appearance of my being nothing other than the phantasmatic object of the Other's desire: the "conscious" appearance of the fantasy thus necessarily coincides with its demise, and with the concomitant loss of self-consciousness. Here, it is important to emphasize that anxiety is not the "sentiment" experienced in disappearance but a signal that stages the risk of disappearing, being engulfed by the Other, the temporary appearance of what utter de-subjectivation might be. . . . [139] For one instant, the real desire of the Other (A barred) which primordially caused the loss of the part-object *a* emerges together with the part-object; for one instant, the object *a* is simultaneously perceived as both the object and the cause of desire.[140]

In one of the most important passages of Seminar X, Lacan criticizes Freud for identifying the anxiety of castration with the insurmountable impasse that necessarily terminates psychoanalysis. On the contrary, as we have just seen, Lacan believes that anxiety arises precisely when castration $(-\varphi)$ is suspended; indeed, the neurotic does not "recoil" from castration, since it is an "imaginary drama"[141] he was confronted with during the Oedipus complex and, after all, his own subjectivation relies on castration. What the neurotic refuses to carry out, and which causes anxiety, is the positivization of his castration.

How should we interpret such a distinction? I think we are obliged to acknowledge that here Lacan tacitly presupposes two notions of castration: in anxiety, *imaginary* castration $(-\varphi)$, which is nothing but the post-Oedipal dialectic of demand, is suspended, and thus potentially allows the full "*conscious*" assumption of *symbolic* castration, the real desire of the Other, which neurotics normally frame in the unconscious fantasy through repression. This reading seems to be confirmed by the fact that Lacan appears to suggest that the positivization of castration implies a (paradoxical) "guarantee" of the function of the Other as lacking, desiring Other. In other words, assuming symbolic castration means rendering one's own lack the counterpart of the (nonphantasmatic) lack in the Other: the subject thus gives the Other what he does not have—his real desire—instead of replying to his incessant demands.[142] In contrast to this, the neurotic does not "make of his castration what the Other [really] lacks" beyond the dialectic of demand.[143]

Although Lacan does not say it explicitly in Seminar X, castration in this second sense is nothing less than the aim of psychoanalytic treatment, a precursor of what in later years will appropriately be named the "traversing [qua undoing] of the fundamental fantasy." At this stage, however, one set of important questions remains unanswered: can we concretely circumscribe a *viable* "beyond" of neurosis? Is the ethical task of psychoanalysis to induce anxiety so that the subject may fully assume castration/"pure" desire?[144] And, most importantly, what is there to be done *after* the subject has assumed symbolic castration, positivized lack in self-consciousness, given that this same process necessarily involves (temporary) de-subjectivation? Despite the fact that a detailed examination of these ethical (and political) issues remains beyond the scope of my book, I shall nevertheless attempt to provide some introductory remarks in the next two sections, dedicated to the notion of *jouissance*.

5.4 Pure Desire, *Jouissance*, and the Ethics of Psychoanalysis

Throughout his discussion of anxiety in Seminar X, Lacan repeatedly affirms that the "framed" Real (of desire) with which the subject is in contact in the fantasy must necessarily be related to the *jouissance* of the Other.[145] In one important passage, he then specifies that "*jouissance* can know the Other only through this remainder, *a*";[146] in parallel, he proposes the existence of a "subject of *jouissance*" whom "one can isolate only in a mythical way," without ever knowing it.[147] This is to say that if, on the one hand, really existing *jouissance*, the *jouissance* that can be known, is present only in the Real-of-the-Symbolic, in the object *a* of the fantasy as paradoxical representation of lack, on the other, pure *jouissance* belongs to the mythical presymbolic Real. One could well argue that these two basic definitions of *jouissance* with regard to the Real already inform Seminar VII, and possibly provide its broadest framework. Indeed, toward the end of this seminar, Lacan openly makes the same point; he suggests that "the Other–thing . . . which lies beyond is . . . the libido," yet, simultaneously, "the only moment of *jouissance* that man knows occurs at the site where fantasies are produced."[148]

We have already analyzed the way in which Lacan discusses the notion of the real *das Ding* in Seminar VII. Now, we should reassess our previous examinations in light of the fact that the notion of the Real is inextricable from the notion of *jouissance* and, what is more, that their relationship is considered, first and foremost, from an ethical perspective. The ethics of psychoanalysis is nothing but an ethics of the Real, an ethics of the real desire of the subject who necessarily confronts himself with *jouissance*; the term "*ethos*" is thus indicated as the most appropriate name for the object *a*, the object-cause of desire.[149]

Lacan begins with two overlapping a priori assumptions which he thinks he can obtain from Freud's work:

(1) Ethics must be articulated from the standpoint of the subject's relation to the Real, since "in our activity, insofar as it is structured by the symbolic," the Real is precisely that which is "actualized" through "the moral law, the moral commandment."[150] From what we have already seen, I believe the term "Real" should here be related to the concomitant emergence of both everyday reality and the unconscious phantasmatic Real-of-the-Symbolic ("really existing" *jouissance*): these are in fact the two sides of the loss of the primordial Real which is exactly what "suffered" from the instauration of the signifier/law.[151]

(2) In opposition to the "optimism" expressed by any kind of "naturalist" eudaimonistic ethics, especially Aristotle's, which ultimately associates the Sovereign Good with happiness and pleasure, the inevitable demand for happiness all subjects express clashes with the fact that "absolutely nothing is prepared for [happiness], either in the macrocosm or the microcosm."[152]

This Freudian premise has profound consequences for all three terms of the Aristotelian equation: pleasure, happiness, and the Sovereign Good. First of all, extreme pleasure is dissociated from happiness, since it is "unbearable" for us;[153] happiness (as "moderated" pleasure) is not a biological given for man but something which should be located on the side of symbolic fictions: it requires a "lowering of tone of what is properly speaking the energy of pleasure."[154] In accordance with point 1 above, this "tempering"—provided by the law—is also what is needed to "move towards reality"[155] as opposed to the primordial Real of a supposedly pure *jouissance*: in other words, the Real of *das Ding* is the "support of an aversion" inasmuch as it is "an object which literally gives too much pleasure," painful *jouissance*.[156]

With regard to the Good, the third term of the Aristotelian equation, all this entails that Freudian psychoanalysis reverses the foundation of the moral law since, from its perspective, "there simply is no Sovereign Good."[157] More specifically, according to Lacan's interpretation of Freud, there is no Sovereign

Good since this is what the moral law, in founding itself, forbids as supremely evil for the subject: "The [barred] Sovereign Good is *das Ding*."[158]

Lacan does not hesitate to identify such a forbidden Sovereign Good in the sense of *das Ding* with the mother, the object of incest.[159] He also, more importantly, specifies that the (maternal) Thing is intrinsically inaccessible, even if it were not explicitly prohibited by the moral law.[160] What does this mean? Here we should remember how, in spite of the fact that Lacan often confuses these two terms, he definitely believes that the Thing is *not* the primordial Real: in the context of Seminar VII, the Thing is in fact a hole effected by the signifier in the primordial Real; hence, it is by definition a *loss of jouissance* which, as such, can only be always-already lost for the symbolic subject independently of any positive interdiction. In Seminar VII, however, this in no way contradicts the logical possibility of the existence of a mythical pure *jouissance*—mythically experienced by all children, "the subjects of *jouissance*," prior to their alienation in the Symbolic[161]—which is consubstantial with the primordial Real, and can thus be regained exclusively through symbolic death. As we have seen, symbolic death is, after all, possible only at the moment of the death of the Symbolic—the "Last Judgment,"[162] as Lacan has it—or in myths (e.g. Sadean fantasies) which project the possibility of exiting the symbolic order. Such a mythical return to the primordial Real would inevitably entail the disappearance of the Thing *qua* hole.

It is therefore easy to see why Lacan admits that if, on the one hand, the prohibition of incest can easily be accounted for in terms of the "utilitarian" necessity to exchange *daughters* in order to found new alliances, on the other hand, the question "Why doesn't a *son* sleep with his mother?"[163] can be answered only if one locates the prohibition of incest on the level of the phantasmatic unconscious relationship which man has with *das Ding*: "The desire for the mother cannot be satisfied because it is . . . the abolition of the whole world of demand, which is the one that at its deepest level structures man's unconscious. . . . The function of the pleasure principle is to make man always search for what he has to find again, but which he can never reach."[164] The key point to grasp here is not merely that the desire for the (m)Other *must not* be satisfied because this would entail our utter conscious and unconscious desubjectivation, but that the desire for the (m)Other *cannot* be satisfied because it would be the end of the mirage of "massive" *jouissance* generated by the Mother as *das Ding*. In other words, there is a perfect compatibility between the desire for incest as "fundamental desire"[165] and the repetition of the "unsatisfied" desire for the Other's desire as "mitigated" phantasmatic lack; the *desire* for incest, the desire for the mother as lost object (the Thing as hole), is indeed nothing but the desire to be desired by the (m)Other's desire as lack.

Conversely, the son's *consummation* of incest, the subject's plunging into the real lack in the (m)Other, does not entail any instantaneous return to primordial "massive" *jouissance*—in this sense, the law prohibits something which is already "inaccessible"—but a mere "psychotic" desubjectivation in the symbolic Other, where the subject will remain alienated (as an object of the Other's *jouissance*) literally until the "Last Judgment." . . .

I have repeatedly pointed out that what one finds in the place of the real object that cannot be refound is not just the self-conscious representation of the objects of everyday reality, but also the unconscious Real-of-the-Symbolic (the object *a*); Seminar VII primarily associates the latter with the superegoic *jouissance* of the commandment, which is something "intemperate" in itself—since it paradoxically becomes "crueller and crueller as we offend it less and less"[166]—and constitutes the other "obscene" side of the positive moral law. More importantly, Lacan shows how the "inner voice" of the superego which "substitutes itself" for the primordial Real—negatively represented in the Symbolic by the "dumbness" of *das Ding*—is its "opposite and the reverse," yet, unexpectedly, taken at its purest, it is also "*identical*" to it.[167]

This is where Kant's philosophy and Sade's novels come on the scene, and reveal their utmost ethical significance and danger. According to Lacan, both Kant and Sade attempt to force their way to the Real of the Thing—and thus return to the pure *jouissance* of the primordial Real—precisely by radicalizing the ambivalent nature of the superegoic commandment in opposite ways, by transforming it into a universal maxim to be understood as "pure signifying system."[168] Indeed, such an (asymptotic) purification of the Symbolic, the complete symbolization of the Real, can eventually achieve a *real-ization of the Symbolic*, its disappearance. . . . [169]

More specifically, Kant's ethics and Sade's "anti-ethics" similarly endeavor to exacerbate and finally break with the dialectic between law and desire as inherent transgression which Saint Paul expressed in the following way: "If it had not been for the law, I would not have known sin [transgression]."[170] The lack of mediation between law and desire in favor of one of the two should hypothetically give rise to either a pure *jouissance of the Law*, in the case of Kant, or, an—ultimately undistinguishable—pure *law of Jouissance*, in the case of Sade. In other words, the Kantian categorical imperative "Act in such a way that the maxim of your action may be accepted as a universal maxim"[171] is nothing but a reduction of the law to its pure form; the Sadean imperative "Let us take as a universal maxim of our conduct the right to enjoy any other person whatsoever as the instrument of our pleasure"[172] is nothing but the reduction of the law to its *object*, to the "right to *jouissance*."

Let us now focus on Kant. Lacan believes that, despite its structural impasse, Kantian ethics represents a historic preliminary step toward Freud's conclusion that there is no Sovereign Good. For Lacan, the kernel of Kant's ethics consists in directly applying the Sovereign Good to everyday life through the categorical imperative: given that, from this perspective, the good can only be identified with the Sovereign Good, there is no longer any hierarchy of goods, "morality becomes a pure and simple application of the universal maxim."[173] In other words, Kantian ethics refutes the servicing of (pathological) goods, the traditional position of Western morality: Lacan points out that this morality is founded on "modesty, temperateness . . . the middle path we see articulated so remarkably in Aristotle," and "concerns itself with what one is supposed to do 'insofar as it is possible.'"[174] Kantian ethics, on the contrary, revolves around an impossibility insofar as the "moral imperative is not concerned with what may or may not be done";[175] the strict application of the unconditional "Thou shalt" causes a void to surface at the place which was earlier occupied by the servicing of goods: as I shall explain later, psychoanalysis should make such a void overlap with pure desire.[176]

In order to follow Lacan's interpretation of the *Critique of Practical Reason* correctly, it is essential to emphasize here that the elimination of the gap between the Sovereign Good and the positive moral law in Kant also entails the obliteration of the space for inherent transgression coextensive with any morality; as Lacan repeatedly points out, without such a space—the ambiguous field of the Real-of-the-Symbolic—society is simply *impossible*: "We spend our time breaking the ten commandments, and that is why society is possible."[177] So what, after all, was Kant's project? Lacan's ingenious answer is: founding a new nature—"note that he [Kant] affirms the laws of a *nature*, not of a society. . . ."[178] In Kant, the moral law elevated to the function of the universal maxim is ultimately aimed at the impossible task of refounding Nature, the Thing. It is also in this sense that Lacan can state that, in Kant, "morality becomes a pure and simple object":[179] morality is the Sovereign Good *tout court* which, in turn, should perfectly correspond to the refoundation of the Thing, the recovery of the object which was always-already lost. On this basis, the link between the first two Critiques becomes clear: if, on the one hand, *The Critique of Pure Reason* should primarily be considered in terms of an enormous deconstructive task in which the Real is ultimately questioned in vain—*noumena* are as dumb as *das Ding*—on the other, *The Critique of Practical Reason* compensates for this silence with the commanding voice of the categorical imperative, with an exasperation of the superego which is, literally, meant to real-ize the Symbolic to the detriment of the dialectic between desire and the law. To recapitulate: Lacan believes that the ultimate impossible aim of Kant's philosophy as a whole is the "immanentization" of the Sovereign Good qua Thing through the categorical imperative.

At this stage, we should ask ourselves a naïve question: why does Kant (and Sade) plan a refounding of nature through ethics in the first place? We should now return to some of our earlier considerations regarding Lacan's interpretation of Descartes's notion of the nondeceiving God and the parallel birth of modern science. To put it bluntly, the "high point of the crisis of ethics"[180] marked by the work of Kant and Sade is nothing but a long-term reaction to the crisis of Aristotelian science, as well as the product of a dissatisfaction with respect to the new responses that Galilean–Newtonian science and Cartesian philosophy had already offered. The subtle argument elaborated by Lacan to interlink the history of ethics with that of (the philosophy of) science could be summarized in the following six points:

(1) Aristotelian *episteme* ultimately relied on a direct reference to nature, namely to the fact that celestial bodies seemed to follow a regular spherical trajectory in the sky, and "always returned to the same place": the universe was thus deemed to be structured around a concentric set of incorruptible celestial spheres at the centre of which resided a divine "immobile mover." On these premises, Aristotle was able to develop a philosophical system according to which there is a coincidence between God as "immobile mover"—the Thing which is the ultimate guarantor of both physics *and* metaphysics—and God as transcendent Sovereign Good.

(2) The crisis of Aristotelian science originates from a reversal of the relationship between the earth and the sky: Galilean physics ascends the sky (think of the invention of the telescope) and demonstrates that the celestial bodies "are by no means . . . incorruptible, that they are subject to the same laws as the terrestrial globe"; furthermore, "we know something else, we know that [celestial bodies] might not be in the same place,"[181] that they do not follow a spherical trajectory. This gives rise to the following set of abyssal questions: Does matter exist? How do we guarantee the "truthfulness of the Other"?

(3) Descartes's epochal answer to these interrogatives is: matter exists, and the Other is true insofar as, by definition, God is not a liar. As I have already explained, according to Lacan, the most important operation of Cartesian philosophy should be identified with the fact that it secures the Other to a nondeceptive a priori which is itself purely *symbolic*. In other words, although Descartes's nondeceiving God as the guarantor of the truthfulness of the Other continues to be associated with the Sovereign Good, in opposition to Aristotle's God, he is definitely no longer a real Thing: the objects of everyday reality are safe, but only at the price of introducing

a dualism (*res extensa–res cogitans*), a radical disjunction between the dimensions of physics and ethics (which also means between physics and metaphysics). Furthermore, this move paves the way for the later assumption that the Thing is in itself an unknowable *x*.

(4) Modern science—epitomized by Newton's law of gravity—fully assumes Descartes's conclusions, and proceeds to a systematization of the reversal of the relationship between sky and earth operated by Galileo.[182]

(5) Kant is dissatisfied with Cartesian science, and attempts to supplement it by means of an ethics at the heart of which the real Thing is to be reinstalled. As I said above, he intends to refound nature through the categorical imperative. This is why Lacan can affirm that the crisis of morality which occurs at the end of the eighteenth century is in strict relation to the fact that, at that time, the world of modern physics (the world of *phenomena*)—based as it was on Descartes's expedient, his separation of the Thing from the Sovereign Good—appears to be "completely sealed, blind and enigmatic."[183]

In other words, Kant reassesses the epistemological gap opened by the crisis of Aristotelian science in order to provide some definitive answers. More specifically, Lacan's reading of Kant presupposes that Kant completely rejects Descartes's dualism in favor of the thesis—shared by Lacan himself—according to which "the moral law is articulated [only] in relation to the real as such" (to be understood as both phenomenal reality and the unconscious Real-of-the-Symbolic).[184] As a consequence, the opacity of *phenomena* ("what does the Thing in itself look like beyond appearances?") was, for Kant, necessarily to be related to a thorough questioning of all positive moral laws. If we accept Lacan's suggestion that the phenomenal Real is, after all, "the guarantee of the Thing"[185]—the Thing is indeed a retroactive creation of the Symbolic[186]—it is easy to understand how, confronted with the opacity of the guarantor, the only possible way in which Kant could secure the Thing *qua* Sovereign Good was through its "precipitation" by means of an equation between the positive moral law and its universal form. This is also why we would be incorrect to consider Kant's move as a nostalgic return to the Aristotelian identification of the Thing with the Sovereign Good: one may argue, rather, that the utmost paradox of Kant's philosophy is to effect a sort of "Galileanization," a movement from sky to earth, of such an identification. . . .

(6) After Kant's desperate effort, Freud finally acknowledges the impossibility of positively reuniting the Thing with the Sovereign Good: the former is unknowable and always-already lost, the latter is forbidden and inaccessible *per se*. The assumption of these conclusions is a preliminary condition for the elaboration of any possible ethics.

What should interest us the most here concerning Kantian ethics is its unexpected link with a dimension of "massive" *jouissance*. Lacan juxtaposes the opposition between Kant's "pathological" *Wohl* and *das Gute* as the object of ethics to that between the pleasure principle that regulates unconscious life—the fundamental fantasy which *includes* inherent transgression[187]—and the Freudian *das Ding* whose "extreme good" the subject cannot stand.[188] Just as *das Ding* is "far beyond the domain of affectivity"[189] and, at its level, the subject can only "groan, explode, curse,"[190] so the establishment of a "natural society" through the implementation of the categorical imperative requires an elimination of the "realm of sentiment."[191] Lacan quotes a surprising passage from the second Critique in which Kant clearly states that the only correlative of the moral law in its purity is *pain*.[192] On the basis of what I have just said, we are confronted with a kind of suffering which is not simply unpleasant, since it cannot be related to "sentimental" pleasure in an oppositional way: the Lacanian name for this "pleasure in pain," this "outer extremity of pleasure [which] is unbearable to us,"[193] is nothing other than *jouissance*.

Kant's refoundation of a nature which is, in the end, essentially characterized by pure *jouissance*, finds a perfect parallel in Sade's theories, "for in order to reach *das Ding* absolutely . . . what does Sade show us on the horizon? In essence, pain."[194] The fundamental fantasy of Sade's novels can easily be identified with the infliction of eternal suffering on the other's body:[195] conversely, in order to endure eternal suffering, the body of the victim must be made immortal.[196] Most importantly, according to Sade, the immortality of the suffering body is the immortality of Nature: it is first and foremost Nature that enjoys through the continuous succession of generation and destruction that the sadist inflicts on the body of the victim. And as Lacan observes in Seminar XVII, this is precisely what makes libertine materialists of the end of the eighteenth century "the only authentic believers."[197] For them, Nature to be understood as matter is God; or, better, Nature is the *jouissance* of a "single [divine] being."[198] In other words, Sade is proposing a general equation between Nature as matter (a primordial Real which is a "totality"), God as the One *par excellence*, and *jouissance*. Crime is therefore perpetuated in the name of such a God; crime is the destruction that favors Nature's eternal regeneration; the sadist "follows Nature in its deadly operation, from which always new forms are reborn."[199]

Both Kant and Sade intend to reach the Thing—or, better, the primordial Real of unbearable *jouissance* beyond the law—precisely by means of an exasperation of the law itself. I believe it is in this sense that Lacan affirms that "transgression in the direction of *jouissance* only takes place if it is supported . . . by the forms of the law."[200] Here Lacan is definitely not just referring to the transgression structurally inherent to any form of positive law—the "partial" *jouissance* provided by any given fundamental fantasy, the "rut of a short and well-trodden satisfaction"[201]—rather, he is indicating how, by fully complying with the exponential strengthening of the superegoic imperative, one might *hypothetically* become an "infinite sinner" (*démesurément pécheur*),[202] as Saint Paul has it. However, Lacan reminds us once again that the point at which the Symbolic real-izes itself by means of a sort of self-saturation—a point where "the other's pain and the pain of the subject himself are one and the same thing"[203]—is a mythical one;[204] we may thus only conceive the logical *possibility* of a strengthening of *jouissance*.

We approach here what is possibly the main ambiguity of Seminar VII: Lacan definitely thinks that the Pauline dialectic between the law and desire (supplemented by inherent phantasmatic transgression/*jouissance*) can be overcome by a radical transgression carried out by the superegoic law itself; yet, at the same time, despite the fact that "whoever enters the path of uninhibited *jouissance* in the name of the rejection of the moral law . . . encounters [insurmountable] obstacles,"[205] Lacan also seems to imply that we can go beyond such a dialectic by means of a transgression which *opposes itself* to the superegoic law. In particular, the ethics of psychoanalysis does not "leave us clinging to that dialectic" of law and desire, and is concerned with a (pure) desire which, by eliminating morality, "transgresses interdiction" and "rediscovers the relationship to *das Ding* somewhere beyond the law";[206] elsewhere, Lacan adds that the "true duty" of psychoanalytic transgression is in fact "to go against the command" of the "obscene and ferocious figure" of the superego.[207]

Now, the big question is: how does the "transgressive" ethics of pure desire advocated by Lacanian psychoanalysis in Seminar VII concretely differ from the superegoic transgression of Sado–Kantian *jouissance*? Is such a distinction adequately defended, or do Lacan's arguments, rather, risk confusing these two kinds of transgression? Is such a confusion not a consequence of the very notion of ethical "transgression" aimed at an alleged "beyond" of the Symbolic—which, as I have already explained, in the context of Seminar VII, Lacan still inconsistently identifies with the "totality" of the primordial Real?[208]

Let us dwell on these questions. If, on the one hand, Sado–Kantian ethics represents for Lacan an important milestone in the history of ethics insofar as it has done with the servicing of goods (and, in so doing, resumes "the question of *das Ding*" in its relation to "whatever is open, lacking, or gaping at the centre of our desire"),[209] on the other hand, his appreciation of Kant and Sade should not be overestimated. The ethics of psychoanalysis is certainly anti-Kantian and anti-Sadean. One of the underlying leitmotivs of Seminar VII is precisely the necessity to distance the ethics of psychoanalysis from these two authors, and the awareness of how difficult it is to delineate such a demarcation in a clear way. Concerning Sade, Lacan thus preemptively claims that "it is extremely important to clear up [the] misunderstanding" according to which Sade "is our progenitor or precursor [and] as a result of our [analytic] profession, we are destined to embrace extremes."[210] As for Kant, Lacan unequivocally states that "however much we may hope that the [ethical] weight of [das Ding] will be felt on the right side, we find in opposition [on the 'wrong' side] the Kantian formula of duty."[211] Hence, we may infer that the ethical register that takes its direction from what is to be found on the level of das Ding can be articulated in two contrasting ways: what is ultimately at stake is whether, after the suspension of the pleasure principle and the servicing of goods, ethics is finally located on the "right" or on the "wrong" side of the line, the limit marked by the real hole in the Symbolic. While the superegoic transgression of both Kant and Sade literally aims—in an implicit or explicit manner—at what Lacan himself names the "point of apocalypse,"[212] the implosive self-saturation of the Symbolic—and thus could be accounted for as an ethics of radical evil insofar as it mythically plunges itself into the "unbearable" jouissance of the primordial Real—transgression is truly "ethical" when it aims at making pure desire, the Real-of-the-Symbolic, "the domain of the vacuole," appear as such, and therefore resists the paradoxical tendency of the superegoic moral law to real-ize the Symbolic.[213]

At this stage, we are thus able to formulate two overlapping general theses regarding the ethics of psychoanalysis: (1) it should oppose the oblivion and potential obliteration of the real lack in the Symbolic as noneliminable limitation and precondition of the Symbolic itself;[214] (2) it is inextricable from a psychoanalytic aesthetics aimed at temporarily disclosing the void of desire, the void in the symbolic Other, beyond specularity.

I therefore agree with De Kesel when he suggests that, for Lacan, Antigone is first and foremost an "image":[215] indeed, at the moment of being sentenced to enter her tomb alive for not having compromised her desire to bury Polynices, Antigone is attracted to and invested by an "unbearable splendour"[216] which, Lacan says, referring to the himeros enargès evoked by the chorus, "renders [pure] desire visible."[217] She is a representation of lack, and as such, one could well argue that, in the instant before vanishing, she literally embodies the object-cause of desire. On the one hand, the good of specular narcissism constitutes the first barrier that separates us from pure desire. On this level, "what I want is the good of the others in the image of my own," "my egoism is quite content with a certain altruism," thus "I can avoid taking up the problem of the evil I desire and that my neighbor also desires."[218] On the other hand, the beauty of the phantasmatic object a should be located on a second barrier;[219] on this level, "the beam of desire" is "redoubled":[220] it is both "tempered" by the effect of beauty and, at the same time, unable to be "completely extinguished by the apprehension of beauty"; that is to say, it continues its way where "there is no longer any object."[221]

Having said this, in opposition to De Kesel I believe that Antigone as an image of lack is also inevitably understood by Lacan as a *model* for the ethics of psychoanalysis as articulated in Seminar VII. This can easily be demonstrated by means of a simple syllogism. We are told that Antigone represents the "essence of tragedy";[222] we are also told that "tragedy is at the root of our [psychoanalytic] experience";[223] hence (the suicidal nature of) Antigone's act is at the root of Lacanian psychoanalysis. An aesthetic ethics cannot be reduced to an aesthetics: the centrality of Antigone's image can be extracted only from Antigone's own *act*. This does not, of course, imply that Lacan is content with locating suicide at the center of his ethics: on the contrary, he is certainly aware of this impasse. On the basis of what we have just seen, we may well agree with him when he states that "Antigone hanging in her tomb evokes something very different from an act of suicide."[224] Nonetheless, the fact remains that Antigone's ethical act, a precondition for desire's being made visible, is followed by her hanging. . . . Quite simply, at this stage, Lacan cannot find a better "image" for his ethics, one which would, after representing the representation of lack, represent the moment of symbolic reinscription instead of an irrevocable disappearance into the unrepresentable lack itself.[225]

In other words, in my opinion, Seminar VII ultimately fails to elucidate the way in which the Lacanian ethics of "pure" desire is distinct from the Sado–Kantian anti-ethics of "massive" *jouissance*. I would rather argue that such an essential distinction can be recovered in Seminar VII only retroactively, and in a germinal form, from the standpoint of what Lacan elaborates in later years. Let us approach this intricate matter in a roundabout way.

(1) Lacan says that the discourse of science which dominates the world nowadays is engaged in an ambiguous relationship with the Thing: although it "repudiates the presence of the Thing insofar as from [science's] point of view the ideal of absolute knowledge is glimpsed," this same ideal is "something that equally posits the Thing without accounting for it."[226] In other words, the mythical achievement of absolute knowledge would be perfectly equivalent to the real-ization of the Symbolic: science "posits the Thing without accounting for it" in the sense that the more it repudiates its presence as the real lack of the symbolic order, the closer it comes to returning to the primordial Real by means of a self-saturation. This is why, elsewhere in Seminar VII, Lacan can rhetorically ask: "Have we crossed the line . . . in the world in which we live?"[227] He believes that the possibility of the death of the Symbolic has become a tangible reality for us: one need only think of the impending threat of the nuclear holocaust and "an anarchy at the level of chromosomes."[228]

(2) The discourse of contemporary science—which, going by what I have just said, "forgets nothing by reason of its structure," and reveals for the first time the power of the signifier as such—is ideologically inextricable from the discourse "of the *general good*."[229] The general good should be understood as a "bourgeois fancy,"[230] a postrevolutionary[231] "politicization" of happiness which involves an enormous distortion of the Aristotelian service of the good: indeed, precisely insofar as it relies on the premise that "there is no satisfaction for the individual['s desire] outside of the satisfaction of all,"[232] it is by no means compatible with Aristotle's elitist morality of the master. Here Lacan is primarily interested in showing how the epistemological paradox of the discourse of science I have just summarized is echoed by a simultaneous ethical paradox: "The good cannot reign over all without an excess emerging whose consequences are fatal."[233] We thus obtain what Lacan calls "criminal good."[234] In other words, the discourse of science as the discourse of the general—or, better, potentially "universal"—good[235] refuses to carry out any destruction of goods—in the widest sense of the term—"consciously and in a controlled way"; a clear example of these practices may be recovered in the ritual ceremony of the potlatch, Lacan says, in which a variety of goods (consumer goods, luxury goods, goods for display) are destroyed in order to favor "the *maintenance* of intersubjective relations."[236] Such a refusal on the part of science makes it impossible to "discipline" desire insofar as desire "requires as its necessary correlative [controlled] destructions," and consequently leads to "massive destructions."[237] At its purest, the discourse of science as a discourse of the *universal* good follows the trajectory of Kantian ethics; as Lacan himself has it, "a renewal or updating of the Kantian imperative might be expressed in the following way, with the help of the language of electronics and automation: 'Never act except in such a way that your action may be programmed.'"[238]

(3) Antigone is the one individual who opposes herself to such a "criminal good" insofar as she makes an "absolute choice" which is motivated by no good.[239] On the other hand, Creon wants "to promote the good of all as the law without limits, the sovereign law, the [Sado–Kantian] law that passes the limit."[240] In other words, Lacan tacitly introduces the following proportion: Antigone : Creon = the ethics of psychoanalysis : the scientific discourse of the universal good. The most important point to grasp here is that Antigone deliberately embraces "second death"—symbolic death—only in order to resist the *hybris* of Creon's law, his "excessive," unreasonable decision to condemn Polynices' dead body to a second death. Antigone does not cede on her suicidal demand to bury Polynices because this is the only way in which she can make *desire* appear; in showing the void of pure desire through her splendor, she "saves" desire from Creon's strictly speaking totalitarian attempt to obliterate the Real-of-the-Symbolic, the lack of the law,

through the imposition of an (impossible) universal good turned into a "criminal" good.[241]

At this stage, we are therefore able to understand why Lacan enigmatically affirms that Antigone is attached to the limit of the *ex nihilo* which "is nothing more than the break that the very presence of language inaugurates in the life of man."[242] Hegel interpreted Sophocles' tragedy as the struggle between the law of the family (Antigone) and the law of the state (Creon). In opposition to this reading, Lacan identifies three different laws: the "transparent," normative *nomos* of Zeus; the unwritten laws of the "gods below" which represent Zeus's obscene side; a "certain legality" which is "not developed in any signifying chain or in anything else . . . a horizon determined by a structural relation [which] exists only on the basis of . . . language, but reveals [its] unsurpassable consequence."[243] It goes without saying that both the first and second kinds of law are ultimately represented by Creon; on the other hand, Antigone "denies that it is Zeus who ordered her to [bury Polynices]," and equally "dissociates herself" from the gods below. Antigone, rather, "establishes herself on the limit," the limit of the Symbolic, the Real-of-the-Symbolic, the *ex nihilo* unveiled as such.[244] Lacan thus affirms that Antigone acts exclusively in the name of the following right: "What is, is."[245] This mysterious affirmation immediately becomes clearer as we recall our discussion of the status of the Real in Seminar VI: the Real-of-the-Symbolic is the "elective point" of the relationship of the subject to his "pure being as subject." Not only does Antigone's positioning on the "radical limit" of the *ex nihilo* affirm the "unique value" of Polynices' being independently of any reference to the specific content of his actions, but, more generally, the heroine is also obliged to "sacrifice her own being in order to *maintain* that *essential* being" which is the very limit that Creon intends to obliterate. . . .[246] We must conclude that Lacan's aesthetic ethics is, at the same time, an ontological ethics, an ethics of the preservation of being as the void of the Symbolic.

(4) In my opinion, this is the climax of Lacan's clever use of *Antigone* to explain the ethics of psychoanalysis. Without a doubt, an elaborate attempt has been made to demarcate Antigone's (psychoanalytic) ethical act from Creon's (Sado–Kantian) "criminal good," one which is generally successful. Yet, at the same time, what remains unclear in this argument is the status of "massive" *jouissance* with respect to the "radical limit" of the *ex nihilo*, not to say its ethical implications with respect to pure desire. On this issue, Lacan repeatedly contradicts himself, and in various ways.

Problems are not limited to the paradox that, as we have seen, despite the fact that Antigone's act is clearly meant to "save" the Symbolic (being as such, the Real-of-the-Symbolic) against Creon's temptation to real-ize it, this ultimately amounts to her own symbolic annihilation—it has rightly been noted that Lacan thus unintentionally confuses "the assumption of the human condition," its finitude, symbolic castration, with "the apology of suicide as an ultimate, sublime form of the [ethics of] refusal."[247] More importantly, I believe that in Seminar VII we face an insurmountable deadlock concerning the economy and function of suffering. On more than one occasion, Lacan endeavors to dissociate pure desire from sheer pain. For example, he states that the pain that "defends the edge" of the field of desire does not correspond to its entire content; however, he never says anything about the nature of what, in this field, would not be painful.[248] He prefers to remind us that, after all, "the economy of [sado-]masochistic pain ends up looking like the economy of goods."[249] To put it bluntly, this means that pathological sadomasochism ultimately involves a "utilitarian" pain for the sake of pleasure and, as such, does not go beyond the pleasure principle. Beginning from this presupposition, in another lesson of Seminar VII, Lacan is then able to specify that Sadeanism (and hence, implicitly, Kantianism) is equivalent to the "divinization . . . of the limit in which being subsists in suffering";[250] in other words, Sado–Kantian pain would locate itself on the limit of the field of desire, and would serve the purpose of allegedly "defending" (the semblance of) being *against* the void of real desire. It is important to emphasize here that such a definition of Sado–Kantianism overtly contradicts the description of its functioning that Lacan provided earlier in Seminar VII. As we have seen, in that instance he correctly pointed out that Kant's categorical imperative (as well as Sade's command to enjoy) requires an elimination of the "realm of sentiment": they are both beyond the utilitarian economy of pain for pleasure, and what they finally achieve is the pain *in* pleasure of "massive" *jouissance*.[251] By definition, the suffering involved in "massive" *jouissance* cannot lie on the "limit" provided by the pathological masochism which services goods; conversely, if *jouissance* is found to lie within the field of desire, the latter is thus inextricable from pain, which is precisely what Lacan intended to deny. . . .

(5) I suggest that Lacan might offer his audience *too many* hints of topographical distinctions between Antigone's pure desire and Sado–Kantian "massive" *jouissance*. The field of pure desire is located *beyond* a margin—the barrier separating us from the Real-of-the-Symbolic—which, as we have just seen, is thought to be a defensive reification of pain and which, although Lacan does not state it explicitly, is (contradictorily) associated with "massive" *jouissance*. Yet at the same time, pure desire is also understood as an alternative way of temporarily inhabiting the limit/margin, one which is opposed to that of pathological pain. On this issue, Lacan's claim that Sadean suffering as a reification of the margin "is a stasis which affirms that *that which is* cannot return to the void from which it emerged"[252] should defi-

nitely be read together with his other claim, in a different lesson, that the only right invoked by Antigone's temporary occupation of the place of pure desire is "What is, is." In Sade's case, the *ex nihilo* is foreclosed: the "static" repudiation of the void through reified pain finally risks unwillingly losing being and returning to the primordial Real; in Antigone's case, on the contrary, the *ex nihilo* is affirmed as such: being as lack of being and desire as its metonymy are thus preserved.

Toward the end of Seminar VII, Lacan seems to be increasingly convinced of the fact that pure desire is to be located on a limit which is better understood as the ephemeral space of an "in-between" (see graph 5.3). Pure desire is no longer the ultimate beyond; however, the subject who accesses it cannot help continuing on his way to reach such an ultimate beyond. Antigone's desire finally aims at that which is beyond the limit that pure desire itself is: at the precise moment when pure desire appears as such in the guise of a "glow of beauty" and the limit (of the real lack of the Symbolic) is trespassed, "a certain relationship to a beyond of the central field [the zone 'in-between' of pure desire] is established, but it is also that which prevents us from seeing [the] true nature" of such a beyond.[253] As Lacan immediately indicates, such a beyond is nothing but "the inanimate condition . . . in which the death instinct is manifested";[254] Antigone's pure desire thus problematically identifies itself with "the pure and simple desire of death as such":[255] radical desire is radically destructive.[256]

In order to give a clear idea of what is possibly *the* structural deadlock of Seminar VII, we should observe that it is not a coincidence if Lacan does not further specify here the nature of such an "inanimate" beyond. Elsewhere in Seminar VII, however, in discussing a different issue, he is forced to lay his cards on the table—that is, to admit that his (inconsistent) postulation of a mythical presymbolic or postsymbolic *totality*, the "primordial Real," necessarily entails as its correlate the "massive" *jouissance* of the One. "That which lies beyond is not simply the

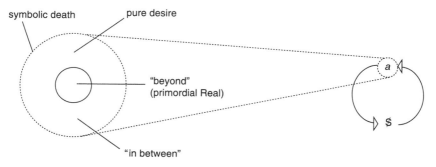

Graph 5.3

relationship to the second death," since "there is also the libido . . . the access to [massive] *jouissance*": this is normally obstructed by the "barrier" of the fundamental fantasy, "the only moment of *jouissance* that man knows."[257] In other words, Lacan is suggesting that the partial, "inherent" *jouissance* of the fundamental fantasy (socially conditioned by hegemonic ideologies) is *concretely* the only possible *jouissance* for man: in this sense, there is no Sovereign Good, not even in the guise of a radical evil which could initially appear to be "better" than the servicing of goods;[258] the task of psychoanalysis is to prepare the subject for assuming such a lack. This, however, does not exclude the possibility that there is "massive" *jouissance* in a pre- or postsymbolic "beyond" which is, as such, unknowable for man.

In an astonishing passage from Seminar V—a seminar which likewise presupposes the existence of a primordial Real as One—Lacan carries these matters to extremes, and ultimately turns the "inanimate" into a truly Sadean Nature with a capital N that enjoys *per se* through suffering: "If on the one hand the return to inanimate nature is effectively conceivable as a return to the lowest level of tension, to rest, on the other, nothing assures us that, in the reduction to nothingness of everything that arose and which is life, even there, as it were, it does not wag [*ça ne remue pas*], and the pain of being is not to be found at the bottom of everything. . . . Nothing proves that this pain comes to a halt in living beings, given all we now know about a nature which is variously animated, putrefying, fermenting, boiling."[259] My suggestion is that, in a similar fashion, throughout Seminar VII Lacan still presupposes the general equation between primordial Real, massive *jouissance*, and (pleasure in) pain due to his incomplete assumption of the logical consequences of the barring of the Other. He does not explicitly articulate such an equation because this would inevitably prove that, although Antigone's act is meant to "rescue" the Symbolic from the "criminal" universalization of the law, she nevertheless ends up embodying one of the most tangible fulfillments of the Sado–Kantian imperative.[260]

To conclude, one may well argue that if, on the one hand, the appearance of pure desire tacitly entails the subject's disappearance in primordial *jouissance*, on the other, the independence of the ethical act is, at least, formally preserved. All Lacan needs to do in later years in order to overcome the impasse of Seminar VII is to detach pure desire, the momentary disclosure of the real void of the Symbolic, from (the failure of) tragic transgression, and to indicate instead how the subtractive moment of ethics should be conceived as a precondition for a radically new symbolization. As we have seen, the death drive ultimately relies on the law of the *ex nihilo* as the "will" to begin all over again.

Contrary to Miller's claim that Seminar VII is problematic insofar as it introduces a "profound disjunction between the signifier and jouissance,"[261] I believe that, in Section 5.4, I demonstrated how, in this seminar, Lacan analyzes both the allegedly "massive" jouissance of mythical transgression and the "short satisfaction" of the jouissance which is structurally inherent to the superegoic component of any symbolic/signifying order. Furthermore, these two "degrees" of jouissance are intimately related, since the jouissance of transgression should itself be conceived, first and foremost, as the jouissance of the (Sado–Kantian) universalized Law.[262] In my opinion, the ambivalent status of jouissance in Seminar VII is, rather, the consequence of Lacan's mistaken assumption of the existence of a primordial Real as totality which, despite being relegated to a mythical pre- or postsymbolic domain, necessarily entails the postulation of a correlative "massive" jouissance. At this stage, Lacan has not yet completely overcome the (Sadean) idea that Nature is One (differential, "fermenting") being that enjoys per se: this notion structurally contradicts all theoretical (and clinical) elaborations which presuppose the a priori of the barring of the Other and the logically concomitant reduction of nature to the not-one of the undead.

Not without oscillations, in his late work Lacan progressively acknowledges that "inherent" jouissance is, in a radical sense, the only possible jouissance. We may well theorize the mythical horizon of an extrasymbolic condition, yet, at the same time, this very theorization is itself logically inconsistent with that of any increase in jouissance. In this final section it is therefore my intention to explain the different ways in which inherent jouissance functions, as well as to propose some preliminary remarks on the intricate issue of the individual subjectivation of jouissance: how should the subject resist the imposition of the superegoic—and always potentially criminal—imperative of the law? With this aim in mind, I shall now enumerate a series of fundamental theses regarding jouissance, adopting the privileged standpoint of Seminar XXIII (1975–1976): in my opinion, it is in this work that Lacan finally assumes the full consequences of the fact that there is no Other of the Other.

(1) To recapitulate some of the most important conclusions I drew in Chapter 4, we need to remember that the dictum "There is no Other of the symbolic Other" means primarily that, insofar as the symbolic Other is not legitimized by any Other external guarantor (the universal Law of the Name-of-the-Father), insofar as the Symbolic is not-all, real Otherness with respect to the Symbolic is no longer possible. In other words, in opposition to Seminar VII, finally, for Lacan, there is no

"primordial One" which was originally "killed" by the Symbolic; there is no "pure" primordial Real (no "real Real") beyond the dimension of the Real-of-the-Symbolic, that is, of the leftover of the Real which "holes" the Symbolic (in conjunction with the Imaginary). To go further, I must emphasize how, for Lacan, the "primordial One"—or "real Real"—is not-one precisely insofar as it cannot be "counted as One": it actually corresponds to a zero. In a key passage from Seminar XXIII, Lacan points out that "the Real must be sought on the side of the absolute zero," since "the fire that burns [the mirage of 'massive' jouissance] is just a mask of the Real."[263] We can think this 0 only retroactively from the standpoint of the "fake" symbolic/imaginary One (what Lacan calls a *semblant*):[264] even better, we can retrospectively think this 0 *as if* it were a One—the One *par excellence*—only from the standpoint of the "fake" One. 0 is *nothing per se*, but it *is* something from the determinate perspective of the "fake" One; the Thing-in-itself is *in-itself* no-thing: as Lacan says, it is *l'achose*.[265] In other words, the 0 equates with the always-already lost mythical jouissance of the "real Real": the "fake" One needs the "fake" *jouissance* of the object *a* in order to "make One"—to cork the hole in the symbolic structure—and thus retrospectively create the *illusion* of an absolute *jouissance* which was originally lost.

(2) *Jouissance* is "pleasure in pain." More specifically, this is *always* equivalent to the *jouissance* of the object *a*, which is a remainder of the Real which tears holes in the symbolic structure. The object *a* as the real hole in the Other is both the hole as presence of a surplus-leftover Real, as *jouissance* of the object *a*, *and* that hole as absence of the Whole Real (the primordial Real which was never there in the first place), that is, as absence of *jouissance*. Of what does this presence of a real leftover actually consist? At its purest, the *jouissance* of the object *a* as surplus *jouissance* (the partial drive) can only mean enjoying the *lack* of enjoyment, since there is nothing else to enjoy. This explains why, in Seminar XVII (1969–1970), Lacan can state: "One can pretend [*faire semblant*] that there is surplus *jouissance* [*jouissance* of the object *a*]; a lot of people are still seized by this idea."[266] *Jouissance* is suffering, since it is *jouis-sans*—to use a neologism which, to the best of my knowledge, was not coined by Lacan. Enjoying the lack of enjoyment will therefore mean suffering/enjoying the lack of the Thing, the fact that the Thing is no-thing (*l'achose*).

(3) One of the major tasks of psychoanalysis is to make the subject accept the real object *a* as lack. If *jouissance* is *jouis-sans*, enjoying "more" or "less" makes sense only from a perverse standpoint which takes the *presence* of *jouissance* for granted. There is only one fundamental difference at work here: one can either accept or fail to accept the lack that *jouis-sans* is. Even when the subject's fundamental fantasy (as barrier) is undone once and for all, as happens in the case of psychosis, what is at stake

is not an "increase" of *jouissance* but an incapacity of the Symbolic to manage the potentially destructive lack of *jouissance* that *jouis-sans* is. In other words, *jouissance* cannot be accumulated because it relies on lack; we cannot objectively accumulate lack, we can say that $(-1) + (-1) = -2$ only if we tacitly assume that -1 is something "more" than sheer lack—if from the very beginning, we deceitfully turn -1 into $+1$. . . . According to Lacan, the capitalist discourse epitomizes perversion precisely insofar as it pretends to enjoy the real object *a* (the lack) as accumulated *jouissance*.[267]

(4) *Jouissance* is a precondition of the inextricable relationship between the drive and desire. More precisely, the drive supplies a partial "masochistic" satisfaction of unconscious desire precisely through the dissatisfaction of *jouis-sans*. As a consequence, *jouissance* is generally a necessary precondition of human beings as desiring beings of language. Most importantly, *jouissance* (of the object *a*) is not only that which, so to speak, inevitably "accompanies" the signifier yet remains detached from it: *jouissance* also emerges in the signifier itself. The drive is not unspeakable, it "utters itself" in language in the guise of *jouis-sens*. Enjoyment (or, better, its lack) is also enjoy-meant. *Jouis-sans* also indicates a linguistic lack of *sense*, an intrinsic limitation of symbolic knowledge (*savoir*) as such; inasmuch as symbolic knowledge is not-all in the unconscious, it should also be regarded as a "means of *jouissance*."[268] The reason for this dual nature of *jouis-sans* is straightforward: the Symbolic (in its interplay with the Imaginary) in which the Real of the object *a* tears holes structures both the "libidinal" realm of desire/sexuality and the "epistemological" realm of knowledge. The basic Lacanian a priori for this parallelism can be found in the dictum according to which "The unconscious is structured like a language": desire and knowledge are the same unconscious linguistic structure, and both partake of *jouis-sans*. Putting together the "libidinal" acceptation of the object *a* with its "epistemological" counterpart, we may argue that the fact that there is no Other of the Other entails the "nonsense" (that is, the "epistemological" side of the object *a*) of the lack of *jouissance*, the lack of relation between the sexes (that is, the "libidinal" side of the object *a*).

(5) In his last Seminars, most noticeably in Seminar XXIII, Lacan avails himself of at least four different variants of the notion of *jouissance* which, in my opinion, should nevertheless all be linked, directly or indirectly, to the object *a*. The first variant concerns the phallic *jouissance* of the object *a* in the fundamental fantasy: Lacan uses the algebraic sign $J\phi$ to express it. In brief, this is the *jouissance* that allows the subject to "make One" as an individuated being of language, the noneliminable real supplement of phantasmatic symbolic identification. It is only on the basis of

a j'ouïs-sens that the barred subject is able to "hear" (ouïr) the sense of the symbolic order: we could render j'ouïs-sens as "I enjoy, therefore I can make sense."

The second variant relates to the jouissance of the Other under the hegemony of which we "make One" and "make sense"; this is therefore nothing but the ideological j'ouïs-sens which "corks" the holed symbolic structure itself. As Lacan observes as early as Seminar X, "j'ouïs" is nothing but the answer the subject gives to the superegoic commandment "Jouis!" ("Enjoy!").[269] It is easy to see that the jouissance of the Other is actually equivalent to phallic jouissance. The jouissance of the Other corresponds to ideological phallic jouissance considered, as it were, from the standpoint of structure, not from that of the (alienated) subject who is interpellated by a given ideology.

The third variant refers to what Lacan names Other-jouissance, which he denotes with the algebraic sign JA; in the early 1970s, Other-jouissance is famously associated with feminine jouissance. Other-jouissance should definitely not be confused with the jouissance of the Other. Should we then regard it as extrasymbolic? If, on the one hand, it is true that, in Seminar XX, Other-jouissance seems to indicate the pure jouissance of the Real beyond any symbolic contamination—indeed, it is located "beyond the phallus"[270]—on the other, it should be evident by now that such a definition of Other-jouissance is highly problematic for any serious attempt to develop a consistent theory out of Lacan's antistructuralist move. The first versions of the so-called Borromean knot—a topological figure which Lacan uses to represent the interdependency of the orders of the Real, the Symbolic, and the Imaginary in the subject (see graph 5.4 below)—show us precisely where the difficulty, if not the contradiction, lies:[271] JA (Other—feminine—jouissance) lies outside the ring of the Symbolic, but it is not outside all the rings. In other words, without the ring of the Symbolic it would not be possible to have the Borromean knot and, consequently, not even JA. The important point to grasp here is that feminine jouissance remains indirectly related to the Symbolic: the feminine not-all is ultimately both different from and dependent on the phallic Symbolic, precisely insofar as it stands as the not-all of the Symbolic, its constitutive point of exception. . . .[272] Consequently, JA cannot stand for the jouissance of the "real Real": in other words, there is no Other-jouissance given that there is no Other of the Other.

Lacan seems to become aware of this deadlock in Seminar XXIII, in which in fact J (A barred), a fourth variant of the notion of jouissance, takes the place of JA in the Borromean knot (see graph 5.5).[273] In one of the most important lessons of that year, Lacan says: "J (A barred) concerns jouissance, but not Other-jouissance . . . there is no Other-jouissance inasmuch as there is no Other of the Other."[274] The passage from the notion of Other-jouissance JA to that of the jouissance of the barred Other

J (A barred) epitomizes the distance that separates Saint Teresa's holy ecstasy, as referred to by Lacan in Seminar XX, from the "naming" of lack carried out by Joyce-le-saint-homme, as analyzed in detail in Seminar XXIII. In this seminar, JA (of Woman; of God) becomes impossible; however, feminine *jouissance* could be redefined in terms of J (A barred).[275] J (A barred) is therefore a (form of) *jouissance* of the impossibility of JA. Most importantly, I must emphasize that the *jouissance* of the barred Other differs from phallic jouissance *without* being "beyond" the phallus.

The elaboration of the notion of J (A barred) also has a significant repercussion for Lacan's late dictum according to which "Y a d' l'Un" ("There's such a thing as One").[276] In Seminar XX, Lacan seems to identify this One with JA, with the idea of a pure Real conceived of in the guise of pure difference, a fermenting Nature; although in Seminar XXIII he declares that JA is meant to designate the fact that there is a Universe, he nevertheless specifies that it is quite improbable that the Universe is, as such, a Uni-verse, that the Universe is a One (of pure, Other-jouissance).[277] That is to say, a pure, mythical Real—the undead—must be presupposed retroactively, but it cannot be counted as (a self-enjoying, divine) One, not even as the supposedly "weaker" One of pure difference.

At this stage, we should ask a crucial question: how does the *jouissance* of the impossibility of Other-jouissance, the *jouissance* of the barred Other, distinguish itself from "standard" phallic *jouissance*? After all, the latter is also, in its own way, a form of

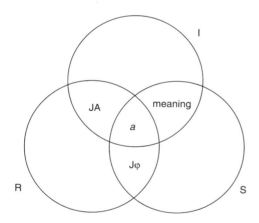

Graph 5.4

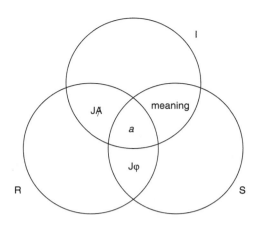

Graph 5.5

barred *jouissance*, of *jouis-sans*. . . . Lacan's straightforward answer is: phallic *jouissance* makes One, whereas J (A barred) makes the individual. If phallic *jouissance* (of the object *a*) makes the symbolic One, increasingly pre-tending to obliterate the lack, on the other hand, J (A barred), which also enjoys the object *a*, makes the individual who, as it were, develops "his own" Symbolic from that lack. Joyce is "the individual" for Lacan insofar as he succeeds in subjectivizing himself by (partially) individualizing the object *a*, the lack in the Symbolic;[278] the individual is not the ideological One, but stands for another modality of the One, another (nonpsychotic) way of inhabiting the Symbolic, "starting" from its real lack. In this way, the leitmotiv of the *ex nihilo* finds a new expression which goes beyond the "suicidal" figure of Antigone.

Here, I should particularly emphasize the way in which Lacan closely associates the emergence of J (A barred)—which he also more famously calls the *sinthome*—with the issue of the *naming* of the Real and the "marking" of *jouissance*, with the long-deferred question concerning the way in which the subject should bring about a reinscription in and a resymbolization of the Symbolic after he has temporarily assumed the real lack in the Other.[279] For Lacan, Joyce is indeed "*Joyce-le-sinthome*."[280] If, on the one hand, it is true that Joyce "abolishes the symbol"[281] (his "subscription to the [existing, hegemonic] Unconscious"),[282] on the other, it is equally the case that the "identification with the *sinthome*" (as the naming of one's Real) advocated in Lacan's last works as the aim of psychoanalysis could never amount to a permanent subjective destitution, a psychotic nonfunctioning of the Symbolic. In opposition to such a mistaken conclusion, I should stress that:

(1) Joyce is—to adopt a formula proposed by Leader—a "non-triggered" psychotic. He is initially "in between" neurosis and psychosis, and subsequently manages to produce a (partially) individualized Symbolic;

(2) neurotics can eventually turn their ideological symptom—the *jouissance* imposed by hegemonic fundamental fantasies—into a nonpsychotic *sinthome* when they undergo the traversal of the fundamental fantasy, the moment of separation from the Symbolic and the subsequent process of symbolic reinscription through a new, individualized Master-Signifier. This also means that Joyce, despite not being a psychotic, does not initially need to traverse any fundamental fantasy. Unlike neurotics, he is already separated from the Symbolic; instead, he needs to create his founding Master-Signifier. As Miller puts it: "[Joyce's] authentic Name-of-the-Father is his name as a writer . . . his literary production allows him to relocate himself in the meaning he lacked."[283]

To conclude, I would like to comment on two thought-provoking questions concerning the *sinthome*. The first is formulated by Hoens and Pluth in "The *sinthome*: A New Way of Writing an Old Problem." The second is found in Miller's seminal "The Six Paradigms of *Jouissance*." In both cases, the authors deliberately leave their questions open, possibly in order to indicate that we are confronted with what remains unconcluded in Lacan's work, and to urge new reinventions of his own reinvention of Freudian psychoanalysis.

Let us start with Hoens and Pluth, who ask: "From what point of view can the Name of the Father be seen as identical to the *sinthome*?"[284] As we have already seen while analyzing Seminar VII, by the late 1950s, *le Nom-du-Père* ceases to be exclusively a prohibitive *Non!-du-Père*; in fact, in the standard situation of neurosis, it also allows the regulation of an otherwise destructive *jouissance* through the symptom, its "No!" lets us (ideologically pre-tend to) enjoy (the lack which holes the Symbolic). What Lacan seems to further suggest with his later work on Joyce is that, in the case of "non-triggered" psychosis, this same regulation, which allows the subject to inhabit the social space, can eventually be carried out by the *sinthome* itself. In other words, the relativization of the Name-of-the-Father which follows the barring of the Other—the emergence of a structural lack—ultimately entails two complementary consequences as far as the symptom is concerned.

On the one hand, the Name-of-the-Father, insofar as it occupies a place which actually lies outside of its competence—since the lack belongs to the domain of the Real—can itself be considered as a symptom (hence in Seminar XXIII, Lacan states: "The Oedipus complex, as such, is a symptom").[285] On the other hand, "everything else that manages to orient and organize *jouissance*"[286] can carry out the containment action which is usually accomplished by the "standard" Name-of-the-Father if the latter does not function properly. Joyce's paternal metaphor was defective: it had to be supplemented by the writer. Thus, the name "Joyce" literally embodies a subjective placeholder for the lack in the Other, and it does so by means of a particular way of writing. The name "Joyce" is a "singular universal": Joyce reaches a substitutive version of the Name-of-the-Father—thus individualized and anti-ideological by definition—precisely by writing his *jouis-sens*.[287]

As for Miller, he reminds us that in his late work Lacan often suggested that the end of the psychoanalytic treatment should be understood in terms of a "getting by" with the symptom, a "know-how of the symptom." He is then led to the following question: "Does [the know-how of the symptom] entail the cessation of repetition or a new manner of repetition?"[288] I must point out that, for Miller, both alternatives exclude a priori the fundamental fantasy, since he strangely opposes *jouissance* "conceived as repetition" to *jouissance* "conceived as fantasy."[289] Even more unexpectedly, he opposes the know-how of the symptom to the *traversal* of the fundamental fantasy, defined as a mere "transgression which is put to work in analysis . . . an invitation to go in the direction of the void and of the destitution of the subject."[290]

I think that these sharp oppositions are extremely dubious and not sufficiently argued for. For instance, it is astonishing that Miller unhesitatingly proposes the assumption of the (repeated or unrepeated) symptom as the end of analysis without problematizing the fact that the symptom is by definition ideologized unless subjective destitution occurs. However, I believe that Miller's question remains extremely interesting if one reformulates it as follows: *after* the traversal of the fundamental fantasy, which is a necessary precondition for a nonideological know-how of the symptom, does the subject form a *new* fundamental fantasy? In other words, does the new way of desiring brought about by the *sinthome* include or exclude the (necessarily repetitive movement of a new) fundamental fantasy?

In my opinion, if the *sinthome* were to exclude the formation of a (radically new) fundamental fantasy, then it would be extremely difficult to articulate its precise status exclusively on the basis of Lacan's own work. In this case, I do not see how we could define it as something more accurate than a (nonpsychotic) overturning of the relationship between the Symbolic and the Real in favor of the latter—an "inverted" sublimation or, as Miller has it, "a Symbolic [that] remains very real."[291] Furthermore, what should we say about the political implications of this new kind of symbolic identification? To put it bluntly, apart from their partial compromise with the existing hegemonic Master-Signifier—Joyce certainly did not speak the way he wrote . . . —how do *sinthomes* communicate with each other if there is no common phantasmatic background at the level of the individual naming of the

Real? Is it not the case that a hypothetical society of fully *sinthomatic* beings of language—as opposed to phallic beings of language—would inevitably cause a fragmentation of the Symbolic into many Symbolics, and ultimately its complete demise?

On the other hand, I propose that if the *sinthome* were to include the formation of a new fundamental fantasy, and the "new manner of repetition" to which Miller refers corresponded to the emergence of a truly original fundamental fantasy—the unavoidable counterpart of a radically innovative Master-Signifier—then one can discern the outline of a politics which could deservedly claim to have inherited the legacy of Lacan's ethics of *jouis-sans*. The psychoanalytic community is not *per se* a political avant-garde; Lacanian psychoanalysis does not promote any specific Master-Signifier; however, it is clearly meant to pave the way for a new Master-Signifier which is compatible with its ethics.[292]

Let me recapitulate some important points before concluding. Insofar as the symbolic structure is universal only through a particular contingent Master-Signifier that hegemonizes fundamental fantasies, the subject's encounter with the real lack beneath his ideologized fundamental fantasy forces him to assume the lack in the universal. Conversely, the resymbolization of lack is therefore, by definition, always carried out at the level of the particular. More precisely, insofar as this is nothing but the specific moment at which the subject realizes that particularity is necessary if there is to be universality, it is here that the particular is turned into the individual. At this critical stage, the subject can either:

(1) *become his own name*, develop his own *sinthome*, while coexisting with the hegemonic Other. This solution inevitably implies a certain compromise with the senselessness of the ruling universal, a progressive diminishing of the awareness that the universal depends on the individual; such a realienation could be obviated only by periodically undergoing a new traversal of the fundamental fantasy through psychoanalytic treatment. Yet one soon realizes that this does not automatically imply a neat separation of the ethical and the political: in point of fact, an increase in the number of people who undergo Lacanian psychoanalytic treatment and ethically assume the inconsistency of the symbolic order, *jouis-sans*, would inevitably increase the chances of the success of a political force which does not aim primarily at obliterating lack;

(2) *name a movement*, promote a new Symbolic—resymbolized through one's individual Master-Signifier/*sinthome*—and struggle politically to establish its hegemony. This obviously presupposes (1) above: Marx-ism, for example, presupposes that Marx first made his own name *à la* Joyce. It goes without saying that such a direct

politicization of *jouissance* is compatible with Lacanian psychoanalysis only if the fundamental fantasy it sets up is radically *new*: in other words, a Master-Signifier is progressive and consequently worth fighting for only if it closely follows the temporary assumption of the real lack in the Symbolic, *jouis-sans*. At the risk of over-simplifying an intricate issue which is only introduced here, I would go so far as to suggest that any possible political elaboration of the extreme ethics of the *ex ni-hilo* should rely on the equation between what is new and what is good.[293]

Notes

Introduction

1. J. Lacan, *Le séminaire livre XVII. L'envers de la psychanalyse*, 1969–1970 (Paris: Seuil, 1991), p. 174.

2. A. Badiou, *Theoretical Writings* (London: Continuum, 2004), p. 119.

3. Quoted in E. Roudinesco, *Jacques Lacan* (New York: Columbia University Press, 1997), p. 211.

4. N. Chomsky, "An Interview," *Radical Philosophy* 53 (Autumn 1989), p. 32.

5. S. Žižek, *The Ticklish Subject: The Absent Centre of Political Ontology* (London and New York: Verso, 1999), p. 2.

6. See, for example, *Le séminaire livre XVII*, p. 139.

7. B. Burgoyne, "From the Letter to the Matheme," in *The Cambridge Companion to Lacan*, ed. J.-M. Rabaté (Cambridge: Cambridge University Press, 2003), p. 72.

8. In order better to distinguish their use as nouns from their common adjectival use, I shall henceforth always capitalize "Imaginary," "Symbolic," and "Real," with the noticeable exception of quotations from Lacan which do not capitalize them.

9. J. Lacan, *Le séminaire livre V. Les formations de l'inconscient*, 1957–1958 (Paris: Seuil, 1998), pp. 47–48.

10. J. Derrida, "Le facteur de la vérité," in *The Post Card: From Socrates to Freud and Beyond* (Chicago: University of Chicago Press, 1987), p. 462. J.-L. Nancy and P. Lacoue-Labarthe adopt a very similar stance: in introducing their book on Lacan, they state that "there is nothing here which presupposes . . . the idea or the horizon of an exhaustive and systematic 'interpretation' of Lacan's work" (*The Title of the Letter* [Albany: State University of New York Press, 1992], pp. 1–2).

11. For a reading which deems Lacan's notion of subjectivity to be largely compatible with Derridean deconstruction, see the work of P.-A. Rovatti, especially *Abitare la distanza* (Milan: Feltrinelli, 1994).

12. See M. Safouan, *Lacaniana: Les séminaires de Jacques Lacan, 1953–1963* (Paris: Fayard, 2001), p. 135.

13. This does not imply that the difference between neurosis and perversion *stricto sensu* is eliminated in Lacan's late work.

14. See, for example, Seminar VI, "Le désir et son interpretation," 1958–1959, unpublished, lesson of June 3, 1959.

15. See, for example, the enduring significance of the three kinds of lack with regard to the issue of identification as treated in Seminar IX, "L'identification," 1961–1962, unpublished (especially the lessons of February 28, 1962 and March 7, 1962), and the centrality of castration with respect to anxiety in *Le séminaire livre X. L'angoisse*, 1962–1963 (Paris: Seuil, 2004), especially pp. 55–68.

16. J. Lacan, *The Seminar. Book VII. The Ethics of Psychoanalysis*, 1959–1960 (London: Routledge, 1992), p. 129 (my translation).

17. Ibid., p. 101.

18. J. Lacan, *The Seminar. Book III. The Psychoses*, 1955–56 (London: Routledge, 1993), p. 180.

19. "Today, Lacan's own reinvention [of Freud's invention] is progressively hindered by its routine usage and it would be our duty to find again the space for reinvention" (J.-A. Miller, "I sei paradigmi del godimento," in *I paradigmi del godimento* [Rome: Astrolabio, 2001], p. 36).

CHAPTER 1 THE SUBJECT OF THE IMAGINARY (OTHER)

1. *The Seminar of Jacques Lacan. Book I, Freud's Papers on Technique, 1953–1954* (New York: Norton, 1988), p. 193.

2. The most important text of "ego psychology" remains H. Hartmann's *Ego Psychology and the Problem of Adaptation* (New York: International Universities Press, 1958). Lacan always insisted on the anti-adaptive aims of psychoanalysis (see, for example, J. Lacan, *Écrits: A Selection* [London: Tavistock, 1977], p. 24; J. Lacan, *Écrits* [Paris: Seuil, 1966], pp. 144–146), yet his attacks against the "autonomous ego" promoted by ego psychologists became increasingly explicit and caustic only in the mid-1950s (see, for example, *Écrits: A Selection*, pp. 131–133; *Écrits*, p. 490).

3. See, for example *Écrits: A Selection*, p. 22. Lacan thus also decisively distinguishes his notion of the ego from Kant's notion of the transcendental ego, of which Freud had not yet rid himself completely.

4. The ego is considered to be self-contained and self-identical by Cartesian philosophy, which Lacan repeatedly attacks for this reason (see, for example *Écrits: A Selection*, p. 1; *Écrits*, pp. 162–177). This critique of the Cartesian subject's self-transparency is *not* incompatible for Lacan with a "return to Descartes" (ibid., p. 163). Žižek has insisted upon the way in which, according to Lacanian psychoanalysis, it is possible to think the subject of the unconscious only against the background of the Cartesian subject (see, for example S. Žižek, *The Ticklish Subject: The Absent Centre of Political Ontology* [London and New York: Verso, 1999], pp. 1–2). For an excellent reading of Lacan's (and Freud's) Cartesianism, see the work of A. Sciacchitano, especially *Wissenschaft als Hysterie* (Vienna: Turia + Kant, 2002).

5. S. Freud, "On Narcissism: An Introduction," in *The Standard Edition of the Complete Psychological Work of Sigmund Freud* [henceforth SE], volume XIV (London: Hogarth Press and the Institute of Psychoanalysis, 2001).

6. *Écrits*, pp. 88, 188.

7. D. Evans, *An Introductory Dictionary of Lacanian Psychoanalysis* (London: Routledge, 1996), p. 20.

8. *Écrits: A Selection*, p. 21 (emphasis added).

9. "The mirror stage is not simply a moment in development. It also has an exemplary function, because it reveals some of the subject's relations to his image, in so far as it is the *Urbild* of the ego" (*The Seminar. Book I*, p. 74). Laplanche and Pontalis have attempted to clarify whether the mirror stage is better understood as a "stage" (*stade*) or as a "phase" (*phase*): "As Lacan has indicated himself, the word 'phase' [*phase*] is no doubt better adapted here than 'stage' [*stade*], in that it suggests a turning-point rather than a period in the process of psycho-biological maturation" (J. Laplanche and J.-B. Pontalis, *The Language of Psychoanalysis* [London: Karnac Books, 1988], p. 252). This is stated by Lacan in "Propos sur la causalité psychique" (1946) (in *Écrits*, p. 184). The problem is that twenty years later, in "Des nos antécédents" (1966) (ibid., p. 69), he declares the exact opposite: "[We have] incessantly kept on recalling in [psychoanalytic] practice a moment which is not of [infantile] history, a moment of configurative *insight*, and so we designate it as a stage [*stade*] even though it emerges in a phase [*phase*]." Despite terminological confusion, the argument remains sufficiently clear: the mirror stage does indeed emerge at a specific moment in the child's psychosexual development, but it cannot be confined to infantile history since it constitutes the subject's permanent imaginary structure.

10. The mirror stage was originally formulated by H. Wallon in his studies on the development of self-awareness in children (Wallon's key text on this topic is *Les origines du caractère chez l'enfant* [Paris: Presses Universitaires de France, 1949]); on Lacan's failure openly to acknowledge his debt, see M. Borch-Jacobsen, *Lacan: The Absolute Master* (Stanford: Stanford University Press, 1991), pp. 248–249. On the other hand, Lacan often mentions Bühler's experiments on child transitivism (see, for example, *Écrits: A Selection*, p. 5; *Écrits*, p. 180) as he also repeatedly defends his arguments by referring to Harrison's ethological experiments with pigeons: these demonstrate that "the animal's sight of its own image in a mirror is sufficient to unleash ovulation" (ibid., pp. 189–190). Lacan also refers to the work of other ethologists such as Köhler (on chimpanzees) and Chauvin (on grasshoppers).

11. R. Descartes, "Meditations on First Philosophy," in *Key Philosophical Writings* (Ware: Wordsworth, 1997), p. 135.

12. *Écrits*, p. 170.

13. See *The Seminar of Jacques Lacan. Book II, The Ego in Freud's Theory and in the Technique of Psychoanalysis, 1954–1955* (New York: Norton, 1991), especially p. 241.

14. "The ego really is an object" (ibid., p. 49).

15. "In the functioning of pairing mechanisms, ethologists have proved the dominance of the image, which appears in the guise of a transitory phenotype through the modification of the external appearance and whose manifestation serves as a signal, of a constructed signal, that is to say a *Gestalt* which sets the reproductive behaviour in motion." (*The Seminar. Book I*, p. 122; see also p. 138.)

16. Ibid., p. 138.

17. Lacan explicitly criticizes Darwin as early as 1938 in "Les complexes familiaux dans la formation de l'individu" (in *Autres écrits* [Paris: Seuil, 2001], especially p. 39). See also *Écrits: A Selection*, pp. 25–26; *The Seminar. Book I*, p. 177. Why is Darwin wrong? Because (1) human evolution is not based on (natural) adaptation; (2) human (disadapted) evolution does not depend on a particularly successful "struggle for life" ("Everything tells against this thesis of the survival of the fittest species," ibid., p. 177); the opposite is true: "the struggle for life" is a consequence of human—particularly successful—disadapted evolution. In Lacan's own words: "Aggressivity demonstrates itself to be secondary with respect to [imaginary] identification" ("Les complexes familiaux," p. 39); aggressivity cannot be explained in terms of a real vital rivalry ("the Darwinian idea according to which struggle lies at the very origins of life," ibid., p. 39). If Darwin's "myth" has been so popular, this "seems to derive from the fact that he projected the predations of Victorian society . . . and to the fact that it justified its predations by the image of a laissez-faire of the strongest predators in competition for their natural prey" (*Écrits: A Selection*, p. 26).

18. *Écrits: A Selection*, p. 4.

19. "It is worth noting, incidentally, that this is a fact recognized as such by embryologists [Lacan has Bolk in mind—see *Écrits*, p. 186], by the term *foetalization*, which determines the prevalence of the so-called superior apparatus of the neurax, and especially of the cortex, which psycho-surgical operations lead us to regard as the intraorganic mirror" (*Écrits: A Selection*, p. 4).

20. "The spatial captation manifested in the mirror stage [is] the effect in man of an organic insufficiency in his natural reality—in so far as any meaning can be given to the word 'nature'" (ibid., p. 4).

21. Ibid.

22. On this parallelism, the most important reference is Lacan's dialogue with Hyppolite in *The Seminar. Book I*, p. 148. Many years after formulating the mirror-stage theory, Lacan convolutedly expresses the same point in "Des nos antécédents" (p. 70). Here, in the new context of his theory of the subject of the Real, he states that the mirror stage should be reinterpreted, concisely speaking, as "the part for the whole": the whole (imaginary identification) can be achieved only at the price of the contemporaneous emergence of a correlated, inassimilable remainder or part (the images of fragmentation). There is no (image of the) whole without (an image of) the parts. Lacan seems to suggest that the notion of (the *imago* of) the fragmented body is nothing but an anticipation of the theory of the object *a*.

23. Lacan thinks that the hysteric's local paralyses are strictly related to the primordial unconscious image of one's fragmented body (see *Écrits: A Selection*, p. 5).

24. On the relationship between (primordial) aggressivity and the fragmented body, see *Écrits: A Selection*, pp. 11–12. Imagos of the fragmented body "represent the elective vectors of aggressive intentions" (while the specular *imago* represents the vector of narcissistic love).

25. See, for example, *The Seminar of Jacques Lacan, On Feminine Sexuality, The Limits of Love and Knowledge. Book XX, Encore, 1972–1973* (New York: Norton, 1999), p. 90.

26. See *Écrits: A Selection*, p. 24.

27. Ibid., p. 16.

28. Ibid., p. 7.

29. J. Lacan, *De la psychose paranoïaque dans ses rapports avec la personnalité* (Paris: Seuil, 1975), p. 253.

30. See *Écrits: A Selection*, p. 2; *Écrits*, p. 180; *The Seminar. Book I*, p. 163.

31. *Écrits: A Selection*, p. 27.

32. *The Seminar. Book I*, p. 171.

33. *Écrits: A Selection*, p. 17 (my translation).

34. *Écrits*, p. 88; see also *The Seminar. Book I*, p. 141.

35. Ibid., p. 121.

36. *Écrits: A Selection*, p. 3.

37. Ibid., p. 2.

38. This is why Lacan states that psychoanalytic theory "does not distinguish [secondary] identification from [primary] narcissistic identification: here the subject is equally assimilated by the object"; the only notable difference lies in the "constitution of a new object of reality, which opposes itself to a better formed ego" ("Les complexes familiaux," p. 54).

39. *The Seminar. Book I*, p. 137.

40. *Écrits: A Selection*, p. 22.

41. Lacan associates the ego-ideal with the introjection of the *imago* of the father in "Les complexes familiaux" (1938); by the time of his first Seminar (1953), the ego-ideal starts to be analyzed more explicitly in relation to the order of the Symbolic. Only around 1955–1957, however, will Lacan be able to reformulate the ego-ideal convincingly—still connected with the Oedipus complex and the subject's introjection of the Law—in terms of a privileged signifier defined as the Name-of-the-Father.

42. It is in this sense that we should read Lacan's apparently contradictory claim that the ideal ego "will also be the source of secondary identifications" (the ego-ideal) (*Écrits: A Selection*, p. 2).

43. See especially *The Seminar. Book I*, p. 134.

44. "Love doesn't happen with just any partner or just any image" (ibid., p. 182).

45. Ibid., p. 171.

46. Ibid., p. 126. Lacan also states that "the love object is confounded . . . with the subject's ego-ideal" (ibid., p. 112).

47. Ibid., p. 142. Lacan also defines the ego-ideal as "the other in so far as he has a *symbolic* relation to me [*moi*]."

48. Ibid. Of course this is not the case with the first love relation with the father: the ego-ideal is in fact formed by it; there is as yet no Symbolic to be perturbed.

49. Ibid., p. 176 (emphasis added).

50. Ibid., p. 177.

51. The two different ways in which this dictum can be understood seem to offer additional proof of love's separation from sheer narcissism: it is only desire as the desire to be recognized—and thus desired—by the other that can be related to love as I explained it above; on the contrary, desiring to destroy the other is synonymous with narcissism. In other words, love, unlike narcissism, presupposes a—minimal—recognition of the other's desire.

52. This is the oxymoron presupposed by recurrent, everyday expressions such as "I would like to be X."

53. See *The Seminar. Book I*, pp. 168–170.

54. Ibid., p. 174.

55. "Les complexes familiaux," p. 29.

56. *Écrits*, p. 179. Lacan discusses Merleau-Ponty's notion of consciousness in more critical terms in Seminar II (*The Seminar. Book II*, pp. 77–78); Merleau-Ponty is correct to emphasize the importance of a phenomenology of the Imaginary beginning with the *Gestalt*, but he is incorrect in relating it to a "notion of totality, of unitary functioning" which "leads him back to a vitalism . . . the idea of living evolution, the notion that nature always produces superior forms, more and more integrated." Merleau-Ponty thus fails to recognize the centrality of the Symbolic in man's successful disadaptation. Merleau-Ponty comments abundantly on Lacan's mirror stage in a university course entitled "Les relations avec autrui chez l'enfants" (Centre de Documentation universitaire, 1975). Lacan returns to Merleau-Ponty shortly after his death in "Maurice Merleau-Ponty," in *Autres écrits*, pp. 175–184.

57. With reference to Lacan's early theory of the subject, Miller writes that "the Lacanian twist is to transfer the phenomenological view of consciousness [*qua* intentionality] to the concept of the subject, that is, the subject of the unconscious. . . . What phenomenologists like Husserl and his French pupils, Sartre and Merleau-Ponty, developed through their concept of consciousness was the fundamental anti-objectivist or non-objectivist status of consciousness. . . . What had developed in phenomenology since Husserl was the concept of unconsciousness" (J.-A. Miller, "An Introduction to Seminars I and II—Lacan's Orientation Prior to 1953 (III)," in *Reading Seminars I and II—Lacan's Return to Freud*, ed. R. Feldstein, B. Fink, and M. Jaanus [Albany: State University of New York Press, 1996], pp. 26–27).

58. *The Seminar. Book II*, p. 177.

59. As Lacan himself observes, the most straightforward way to define complexes is by stating that the unconscious has its own "complex" logic, and does not amount to a reservoir of repressed, irrational drives. (See *The Seminar. Book I*, p. 65.)

60. See especially "Les complexes familiaux," pp. 28–29.

61. A. Di Ciaccia and M. Recalcati, *Jacques Lacan. Un insegnamento sul sapere dell'inconscio* (Milan: Bruno Mondadori, 2000), p. 82.

62. See "Les complexes familiaux," p. 34.

63. Ibid., p. 33. Consequently, "it is the refusal of ['ancient'] weaning that founds the positivity of the complex, that is to say, the *imago* of the feeding relationship which [the complex] tends to reestablish" (ibid., p. 31).

64. Ibid., p. 36.

65. Ibid., pp. 30–31. In "Les complexes familiaux," Lacan unequivocally stresses the cultural origin of *all* three complexes. I believe that this claim is insufficiently accounted for in this early work, and is thus incompatible with Lacan's discussion of the mirror stage as ultimately based on *Gestalten*. The precise coordinates of the interplay between the "instinctual" Imaginary and the "cultural" Symbolic in the three complexes is reelaborated and explained in detail in *Le séminaire livre IV. La relation d'objet, 1956–1957* (Paris: Seuil, 1994) through the triadic (and retroactive) sequence frustration–privation–castration.

66. "Les complexes familiaux," p. 43.

67. As early as 1950, Lacan sets out in a succinct manner the three fundamental, interconnected tenets of his future ethics of psychoanalysis: (a) following Saint Paul, "it is the law that creates sin"; (b) consequently, against Lombroso's criminology, "criminal instincts do not exist"—which is the same as stating, against Sade, that "there is no absolute crime"; (c) in parallel, following Freud's *Totem and Taboo*, Law is based on a primordial crime (see *Écrits*, pp. 126, 146, 149, 130).

68. The key text for Lacan's dialectical reading of psychoanalytic technique is "Intervention on the Transference" (1951), in *Feminine Sexuality: Jacques Lacan and the école freudienne*, ed. J. Mitchell and J. Rose (London: Macmillan, 1982).

69. "[A] vital crisis redoubles itself in a psychic crisis. . . . A vital tension resolves itself in a mental intention" ("Les complexes familiaux," p. 31).

70. In all complexes, there is indeed a strict connection between the rise of anxiety and the "precipitation" of the subject in an alienating identification. The crisis which precedes a given complex (its synthesis) is accompanied by anxiety: Lacan demonstrates how this point is derived from Klein (*The Seminar. Book I*, p. 69). Even in his later theories of the subject, Lacan will always link anxiety to what he will call "subjective destitution," and the consequent emergence of a new form of identification. In the early 1960s, Lacan will dedicate two consecutive years of his Seminar to the discussion of identification and anxiety.

71. "Les complexes familiaux," p. 41.

72. *The Seminar. Book I*, p. 146.

73. It is true that Lacan is, in general, heavily indebted to Lévi-Strauss's structural anthropology: however, the "structuralist" discussion of the Oedipus complex in "Les complexes familiaux" dates back to 1938 (in this article, Lacan briefly refers to the work of earlier anthropologists such as Frazer and Malinowski). It was therefore published eleven years before Lévi-Strauss's fundamental text, *The Elementary Structures of Kinship* (1949).

74. Miller, "An Introduction to Seminars I and II," p. 20.

75. Nobus similarly argues that, despite the development of Lacan's theories during the 1950s and 1960s, the notion of the mirror stage "did not involve a radical modification of the original description" (D. Nobus, "Life and Death in the Glass: A New Look at the Mirror Stage," in *Key Concepts of Lacanian Psychoanalysis*, ed. D. Nobus [London: Rebus Press, 1998], p. 120).

Chapter 2 The Unconscious Structured Like a Language

1. "The [symbolic] I is distinct from the [imaginary] ego" (*The Seminar of Jacques Lacan. Book II, The Ego in Freud's Theory and in the Technique of Psychoanalysis, 1954–1955* [New York: Norton, 1991], p. 8). "The subject is decentred in relation to the individual. That is what I is an [O]ther means" (ibid., p. 9).

2. "The law of man has been the law of language since the first words of recognition presided over the first gifts" (J. Lacan, *Écrits: A Selection* [London: Tavistock, 1977], p. 61).

3. See especially S. Freud, *The Interpretation of Dreams*, SE, IV–V; *The Psychopathology of Everyday Life*, SE, VI; and *Jokes and Their Relation to the Unconscious*, SE, VIII.

4. See *Écrits: A Selection*, pp. 148, 68.

5. J. Lacan, *The Seminar. Book III. The Psychoses, 1955–56* (London: Routledge, 1993), p. 167.

6. J. Lacan, *Le séminaire livre V. Les formations de l'inconscient, 1957–1958* (Paris: Seuil, 1998), p. 104. "Lacan's perseverance toward retaining the concept of the subject certainly ran against the grain of the time, especially in the days of a budding and flowering structuralism that seemed to have done away with the subject" (M. Dolar, "Cogito as the Subject of the Unconscious," in *Cogito and the Unconscious*, ed. S. Žižek [Durham: Duke University Press, 1998], pp. 12–13).

7. *The Seminar. Book III*, p. 241.

8. Ibid.

9. See especially *Écrits: A Selection*, p. 81.

10. At this stage, discourse can therefore be defined as an act of speech between (at least) two subjects. "Whenever Lacan uses the term 'discourse' (rather than, say, 'speech') it is in order to stress . . . the fact that speech always implies another subject, an interlocutor" (D. Evans, *An Introductory Dictionary of Lacanian Psychoanalysis* [London: Routledge, 1996], p. 44).

11. "Language entirely operates within ambiguity, and most of the time you know absolutely nothing about what you are saying" (*The Seminar. Book III*, p. 115).

12. *Le séminaire livre V*, p. 105.

13. B. Fink, *The Lacanian Subject* (Princeton: Princeton University Press, 1995), p. 38. However, Fink does not specify that the "I" understood as the "subject of the statement" is here exclusively the subject of the *conscious* statement. He fails to clarify the ambiguous and often misleading distinction between the "I" of the imaginary (the linguistic *pendent* of the ego) and the "I" of the unconscious.

14. This allows Lacan to affirm that there is a "paradox of the relation of language to speech" for which "the subject loses his meaning in the objectifications of discourse" (*Écrits: A Selection*, p. 70)

15. Ibid., p. 269.

16. Ibid., p. 166.

17. In "Cogito as the Subject of the Unconscious," Dolar comments in detail on Lacan's two allegedly opposed accounts of the cogito, both of which imply a choice between thought and being ("*either to think or to be*," ibid., p. 18). If the first account—which Dolar shows to overlap with Lacan's explanations in Seminar XI (1964)—locates thought on the side of alienated consciousness and being on that of an "impossible choice" which "would entail desubjectivization," the second account—which Dolar takes from Seminar XIV (1966–1967)—reverses these coordinates and suggests that "I cannot do otherwise but to choose being . . . a false being . . . which serves as the support of consciousness" (ibid., pp. 19, 28). While I generally agree with Dolar's argument, I nevertheless believe that the periodization he proposes is untenable: the "second" account is already present in "The Agency of the Letter" (1957) (see *Écrits: A Selection*, p. 166). In other words, the "two" readings of the cogito are always present in Lacan since, beyond terminological confusion, they both presuppose the general equation unconscious = "real" thought = "real" being. Badiou is therefore correct when he observes that, despite his repeated attacks against the "fundamental axiom of all philosophy" for which being is supposed to think, Lacan nevertheless recuperates this Parmenidean equation on the level of the unconscious: "But that the unconscious thinks, or, if you like, that 'it' thinks, is this really different to the philosophical idea according to which being thinks?" (A. Badiou, "Psychoanalysis and Philosophy," *Analysis* 9 [2000], p. 8).

18. See *The Seminar. Book III*, p. 240.

19. *Le séminaire livre V*, p. 103.

20. See *Écrits: A Selection*, pp. 48–50.

21. Ibid., pp. 49, 86.

22. *The Seminar of Jacques Lacan. Book I, Freud's Papers on Technique*, 1953–1954 (New York: Norton, 1988), pp. 274, 217, 256. Note that, in later years, Lacan will increasingly associate the term "intersubjectivity" with the *imaginary* relation between the ego and the other.

23. See *Écrits: A Selection*, pp. 88–90.

24. See, for example, ibid., p. 85; and J. Lacan, *Écrits* (Paris: Seuil, 1966), p. 41.

25. *The Seminar. Book III*, p. 24.

26. Ibid.

27. J. Lacan, *Le séminaire livre IV. La relation d'objet*, 1956–1957 (Paris: Seuil, 1994), p. 12 (emphases added).

28. On this issue, see S. Žižek, *Looking Awry: An Introduction to Jacques Lacan through Popular Culture* (Cambridge, MA: MIT Press, 1991), p. 181.

29. *The Seminar. Book III*, p. 112 (emphasis added).

30. Žižek, *Looking Awry*, p. 131.

31. See, for example, *Écrits*, p. 16.

32. The unconscious is deindividuated and understood as a locus as early as 1956. In Seminar III, Lacan states that calling the unconscious an internal dialogue "already falsifies everything," since "this so-called internal monologue is entirely continuous with the external dialogue" (*The Seminar. Book III*, p. 112).

33. Lacan still talks about the aim of analysis in terms of "reintegration and harmony, I could even say of reconciliation" as late as 1957 (see *Écrits: A Selection*, p. 171).

34. "The fact that the subject relives, comes to remember, in the intuitive sense of the word, the formative events of his existence, is not in itself very important. What matters is what he reconstructs of it. . . . When all is said and done it is less a matter of remembering than of *rewriting history*" (*The Seminar. Book I*, pp. 13–14; emphasis added; see also *Écrits: A Selection*, pp. 51–56).

35. Evans, *An Introductory Dictionary of Lacanian Psychoanalysis*, p. 192 (emphasis added).

36. See *The Seminar. Book III*, p. 113.

37. The old refrain according to which, in psychosis, the unconscious becomes conscious is certainly a simplistic way to express Lacan's theory of psychosis as expounded in Seminar III, but it is not completely incorrect. . . .

38. To be frank, Lacan seems to be aware of this problem when, as early as 1955, he admits that there is an "essential"—that is, structural and unsurpassable—level of resistance against recollecting repressed signifiers (even after undergoing psychoanalytic treatment) (see *The Seminar. Book II*, p. 321). But his continual call for a complete emancipation of full speech points in the opposite direction. The reader should also be reminded that the very denomination "full speech" is almost completely absent from Lacan's elaborations of the 1960s and 1970s.

39. *The Seminar. Book III*, p. 224 (my translation).

40. Ibid., p. 54 (emphases added).

41. Ibid., p. 36.

42. A. Lemaire, *Jacques Lacan* (London: Routledge, 1979), p. 13. Lemaire's outline of Saussure's linguistics is generally accurate. However, the author repeatedly confuses Lacan's writing of the sign (signifier over signified) with Saussure's (signified over signifier).

43. I owe the outline of the following threefold Lacanian subversion of the Saussurian notion of the sign to A. Di Ciaccia and M. Recalcati, *Jacques Lacan. Un insegnamento sul sapere dell'inconscio* (Milan: Bruno Mondadori, 2000), pp. 50–51.

44. *The Seminar. Book III*, p. 260.

45. However, the notion of the signified is not always clearly distinguished from that of signification.

46. *The Seminar. Book III*, p. 119.

47. See especially ibid., pp. 114–115.

48. See ibid., p. 263.

49. *Écrits: A Selection*, p. 153 (my translation).

50. *The Seminar. Book III*, p. 261.

51. M. Safouan, *Lacaniana: Les séminaires de Jacques Lacan, 1953–1963* (Paris: Fayard, 2001), p. 53.

52. *Le séminaire livre IV*, p. 47.

53. The signified that I attribute to what I or others say or think at any given moment in time can consciously be "lived" only in a single way. All that I say and all that I hear must necessarily have *for me*, at a given time, one univocal signification.

54. To exemplify the difference between the diachronic dimension of the conscious signifying chain (that of the signified) and the synchronic dimension of the unconscious signifying chains (that of the signifier), think of the uncanny experience we have when we listen to our own taped voice: literally, "we do not recognize our own words." This is to say that, as a consequence of the non-bi-univocal relation between the signifier and the signified, we (retroactively) actualize (render conscious) a virtual process of signification which was (unconsciously) synchronic to that which we (consciously) experienced at the moment when our voice was originally taped. Two conclusions can be drawn from this: (1) Virtual processes of signification are not lost: on the contrary, they are registered in the "other scene," the unconscious. The unconscious is a sort of tape recorder. (2) The existence of another scene implies that, at the level of the Symbolic, there are parallel signifying universes. Clearly, this is not just virtually valid at the intrasubjective level: suffice it to recall how our intersubjective daily experience with other human beings as beings of language is fundamentally based on misunderstandings. In other words, *the Other (subject) who always interprets my words in a way I did not intend him to interpret them already actualizes—* in that which is signified by him—*a fraction of "my" unconscious. . . .*

55. *The Seminar. Book III*, p. 167.

56. See, for example, ibid.

57. Ibid., p. 189.

58. I shall analyze this formula at the beginning of Chapter 5.

59. See especially R. Jakobson, *Essais de linguistique générale* (Paris: Éditions de Minuit, 1963).

60. For the following paragraph on Jakobson, I rely on Lemaire, *Jacques Lacan*, pp. 30–34.

61. In addition to associations of meaning (synonyms and antonyms), phonological associations are also possible.

62. Lemaire, *Jacques Lacan*, p. 30.

63. Ibid., p. 31.

64. This is why Juranville can state: "Lacan introduces the idea of the autonomy of the signifier. This certainly does not imply that the signifier may exist without the signified. But the signified is *produced* by the signifier" (A. Juranville, *Lacan et la philosophie* [Paris: Presses Universitaires de France, 2003], pp. 47–48).

65. See *Écrits: A Selection*, pp. 163–164.

66. I think that on the basis of my account it is possible to understand why Lacan enigmatically states that metaphor has "two sides" (*deux versants*), one of which is explicitly said to be metonymic (*Le séminaire livre V*, p. 44).

67. As we may clearly observe in schema 2.3, unconscious metonymy is not necessarily "vertical": here, the important point to grasp is that, whether "vertical" or "horizontal," the "linearity" of unconscious metonymic combinations is continuously fragmented and "redirected" by metaphor/repression.

68. Unconscious meaning is equal to the sum total of the signifying chains (made of signifiers) that constitute a subject.

69. Given that the unconscious is not "unidirectional," new signifiers can be contemporaneously added to *all* the signifiers in the unconscious signifying chains that have an associative (either metonymic or metaphoric) link with them.

70. See *Le séminaire livre V*, p. 28. On the distinction between "admitted" (*reçue*) and "new" signification, see M. Safouan, *Dix conférences de psychanalyse* (Paris: Fayard, 2001), pp. 100–101.

71. "We must in fact consider all human significations as having been generated metaphorically at some point" (*Le séminaire livre V*, p. 54).

72. For an overview of Laplanche's arguments, see his collaborative article with S. Leclaire, "The Unconscious: A Psychoanalytical Study," *Yale French Studies*, no. 48 (1972); for Lacan's critique of Laplanche's notion of the unconscious see, for example, his "Preface" to A. Lemaire's *Jacques Lacan*, esp. pp. xii–xiii.

73. On this issue, see especially *The Seminar. Book III*, p. 227.

74. "Metonymy exists from the beginning and makes metaphor possible. But metaphor belongs to a different level than metonymy" (ibid.). See also ibid., p. 225; *Le séminaire livre V*, pp. 64, 75.

75. *Écrits: A Selection*, p. 147.

76. Ibid., p. 161.

77. J.-A. Miller, "Préface," in *Joyce avec Lacan*, ed. J. Aubert (Paris: Navarin, 1987), p. 10.

78. *The Seminar. Book III*, p. 185. See also ibid., p. 199.

79. *Écrits: A Selection*, p. 194.

80. Freud's references to hieroglyphics are, on the other hand, more focused on the fact that the images that compose them are, like the images of dreams, "not intended to be interpreted but are only designed . . . to establish the meaning of some other elements" (S. Freud, "The Claims of Psycho-Analysis to Scientific Interest," in SE, XIII, p. 177; this passage is quoted and commented on by Lacan in *The Seminar. Book III*, p. 247). As Lacan remarks elsewhere: "Giving as an example Egyptian hieroglyphics . . . Freud shows us in every possible way that the value of the image as signifier has nothing whatever to do with its signification" (*Écrits: A Selection*, pp. 159–160). We would be wrong to think that here Lacan limits himself to underlining once again the way in which the imaginary level of language (the signified) depends on the symbolic level (the signifier). Indeed, he clearly refers to the *imaginary* dimension of the *unconscious* signifier—for instance, as it presents itself in the dream. The unconscious has itself an imaginary dimension which is not the conscious imaginary dimension of signification.

CHAPTER 3 OEDIPUS AS A METAPHOR

1. See J. Lacan, *The Seminar. Book III. The Psychoses*, 1955–56 (London: Routledge, 1993), p. 249.

2. J. Lacan, *Le séminaire livre V. Les formations de l'inconscient*, 1957–1958 (Paris: Seuil, 1998), p. 189.

3. J. Lacan, *Le séminaire livre IV. La relation d'objet*, 1956–1957 (Paris: Seuil, 1994), p. 199. See also ibid., pp. 53, 99; *Le séminaire livre V*, p. 163.

4. See *The Seminar. Book III*, pp. 147, 151; *Le séminaire livre IV*, p. 199. For an attack upon the notion of chronological psychogenesis, see ibid., p. 55.

5. *Le séminaire livre V*, p. 198.

6. The triadic sequence frustration–privation–castration is not without relation with the dialectical unfolding of the three complexes as expounded in "Les complexes familiaux."

7. Freud argues that around the age of five, both boys and girls believe that there is only one genital organ, the penis, and therefore suppose that those who do not possess it have been castrated.

8. *Le séminaire livre IV*, p. 63.

9. Ibid., p. 66.

10. Ibid.

11. Ibid., p. 67.

12. Ibid.

13. This very first symbolization, the scansion of the appeal/cry, is *not* actively assumed by the child insofar as it is basically a *direct* consequence of/reaction to the (visual) presence/absence of the symbolic mother. In other words, given the perfect homeostasis in which the child is supposed to live at this stage, given that the mother is always present/absent at the *right* time, the appeal/cry cannot "actively" be caused by internal need. Here the cry is always "joyful," it is not yet related to lack.

14. *Le séminaire livre IV*, p. 68 (emphasis added).

15. In this sense the relation with the object is effectively "direct."

16. *Le séminaire livre IV*, p. 68 (emphasis added). Lacan is not precise on one specific point: the mother is a symbolic agent and not, strictly speaking, a symbolic object. The symbolic object as such can emerge only when the symbolic mother does not answer the child's appeal.

17. Ibid.

18. Ibid., p. 69.

19. Ibid., p. 175.

20. Lacan himself evokes the "virtual" status of the Real in another passage of Seminar IV; see ibid., p. 32.

21. On the productivity of the lack of object, see ibid., pp. 36, 56.

22. See, for example ibid., p. 37: "Frustration is, as such, the field of unrestrained demands [*exigences*], with no law."

23. Ibid., p. 81; see also ibid., p. 192.

24. Ibid., p. 70.

25. Ibid. (emphasis added). See also ibid., pp. 30–31.

26. Ibid., p. 70. As we shall see in more detail at the end of this chapter, the imaginary phallus is also a privileged object for men.

27. Ibid.

28. Ibid., pp. 70–71 (emphasis added).

29. Ibid., p. 57. This should also explain why the pre-Oedipal relation is triadic for the mother whereas it is dual for the child (however, this duality relies on a third element that the child is not able to recognize).

30. Ibid., p. 71.

31. Ibid., p. 81.

32. On the fact that the existence of early vaginal masturbation cannot be disputed, see ibid., p. 97.

33. Some important passages of Seminar IV may be used to defend my claim: "All this happens at the level of the imaginary father. We call him imaginary equally because he is integrated into the imaginary relation which forms the psychological support of the relations with the fellow man, which are, properly speaking, relations of the species, the background of every libidinal capture as well as of every aggressive erection" (ibid., p. 220; see also ibid., p. 207).

34. "We should not forget that the phallus of the little boy is not much more valid than that of the little girl" (ibid., p. 193).

35. Where the second stage of the Oedipus complex is concerned, it is as a result more correct to state that the child identifies himself with the phallic *Gestalt* while competing with the imaginary father.

36. This is not sexuation proper: here, the child simply *identifies himself* with the *imaginary* phallus; sexuation is properly concluded only when he *locates himself* with respect to the *symbolic* phallus.

37. *Le séminaire livre IV*, p. 242.

38. Ibid., p. 243. For a clear-cut definition of anxiety, see ibid., p. 226. In Chapter 5, I shall return to the notion of anxiety and its relation to the Real.

39. M. Safouan, *Lacaniana: Les séminaires de Jacques Lacan, 1953–1963* (Paris: Fayard, 2001), p. 57.

40. The continuation of this quotation provides us with important clues about the child's individual entry into the Symbolic and, more generally, the "birth of the Symbolic" as such: "The erected stone gives us an example; another example is the notion of the human body insofar as it is erected. It is in this way that a certain number of elements, all related to corporal height and not simply to the lived experience of the body, constitute the first elements [of the signifier], taken from experience but completely transformed by the fact that they are symbolized" (*Le séminaire livre IV*, p. 51).

41. Ibid., p. 71 (emphasis added).

42. It is not completely correct to say that, at this stage, the mother is phallic for the child, since the phallus as + can emerge only against the background of its oppositional – with the advent of the phallic phase (when the mother is discovered to be deprived). During the dialectic of frustration, the child simply *ignores* the phallic *Gestalt*, and the mother is "non-deprived." Thus, the fantasy of a "positively" phallic mother is always retroactive.

43. "It is only . . . insofar as the round trip of the subject's profoundly aggressive tension toward the other [the father]—around whom the successive layers of what will constitute

his ego are knotted and crystallized—starts to be organized, that it is possible to intro-duce that which makes appear to the subject, beyond what he himself represents for the mother, the form of the love object which is caught, captured and kept in something which he himself *qua* object is not able to extinguish" (*Le séminaire livre IV*, p. 176).

44. *Le séminaire livre V*, p. 133.

45. See especially ibid., pp. 182, 198–199; *Le séminaire livre IV*, pp. 194, 196. This also explains why Lacan thinks that perverts, who remain stuck at this stage, alternatively identify with the mother *and* with the phallus.

46. *Le séminaire livre IV*, p. 71.

47. In order to understand Lacan's Oedipus complex it is therefore essential not to identify "primordial frustration"—which marks the *entry* of the child into the first stage of the Oedipus complex—with what is called "fundamental disappointment"—which marks the end of the first stage.

48. *Le séminaire livre IV*, pp. 81–82.

49. Ibid., p. 101.

50. Ibid.

51. Ibid.

52. Ibid., p. 142.

53. Ibid., p. 140.

54. Ibid., p. 223.

55. Ibid., p. 214.

56. Ibid., p. 155.

57. Ibid., p. 178.

58. *Le séminaire livre V*, p. 199.

59. *Le séminaire livre IV*, p. 101.

60. Ibid., p. 125.

61. Ibid., p. 126.

62. Ibid., p. 174 (emphasis added).

63. "It is at this level that one should understand the oral absorption and its so-called re-gressive mechanism, that can take place in any [adult] love relation" (ibid., p. 175).

64. Ibid., p. 184.

65. Ibid., p. 175.

66. In Seminar IV, this is also how Lacan explains the first formation of the superego, which is for him, in accordance with Kleinian theories, already begun in the child–mother relation.

67. *Le séminaire livre IV*, p. 188.

68. The mother, while perfectly satisfying the child's need, may "overload" his cries and turn them into signifiers, something as simple as "Look how happy he is, since I am such a perfect mum!"

69. *Le séminaire livre IV*, p. 131.

70. See S. Freud, *Beyond the Pleasure Principle*, in SE, XVIII, pp. 14–15.

71. Ibid., p. 15.

72. J. Lacan, *Écrits: A Selection* (London: Tavistock, 1977), p. 103.

73. Ibid., p. 104. See also *Le séminaire livre IV*, p. 51.

74. Ibid., p. 48.

75. See, for example, *Écrits: A Selection*, p. 189.

76. *Le séminaire livre IV*, p. 38.

77. "Think about what happens when you ask for a book in a library. You are told that it is missing from its place. . . . This means that the librarian lives in an entirely symbolic world!" (ibid., p. 38; see also ibid., p. 218).

78. Ibid., p. 123.

79. *Le séminaire livre V*, p. 202.

80. Ibid., p. 226.

81. *Le séminaire livre IV*, p. 224.

82. *Le séminaire livre V*, p. 226.

83. Ibid.

84. See, for example, ibid., pp. 165–166.

85. *Le séminaire livre IV*, p. 242. See also *Le séminaire livre V*, p. 193.

86. *Le séminaire livre V*, p. 194.

87. Ibid., p. 187.

88. Ibid., p. 190.

89. See ibid., pp. 192–193.

90. Ibid., p. 194. Kerslake overlooks this fundamental point when he claims that, in Lacan, the "primordial symbolization" of the "mother who 'comes and goes' . . . seems to take place *before*, that is, independently of, the law of the father" (C. Kerslake, "Rebirth through Incest: On Deleuze's Early Jungianism," *Angelaki: Journal of the Theoretical Humanities* 9, no. 1 [April 2004], p. 151). On the basis of this incorrect assumption—which, moreover, fails to take into consideration the retroactive nature of Lacan's account of the Oedipus complex—the author infers three highly misleading conclusions: (1) there are "dormant quasi-Jungian claims on behalf of the mother in Lacan's work" (ibid., p. 136); (2) insofar as Lacan disavows these claims, his "account of the Oedipus complex is open to 'problematisation' from within" (ibid., p. 136); (3) we should neatly distinguish the early Lacan of "Les complexes familiaux," who gives an important role

to the "maternal imago" (ibid., p. 147), and thus "is Jungian" (ibid., p. 148), from the later Lacan of Seminar V.

91. *Le séminaire livre V*, p. 194; see also ibid., p. 192.

92. Ibid., p. 188. This ambiguity may lead to the mistaken inference that there is an "incestuous" law of the mother which is entirely independent of the Father and, as such, extrasymbolic.

93. Ibid., p. 188.

94. Ibid., p. 189.

95. Ibid., p. 201.

96. Ibid.

97. Both of these dimensions should be considered as Lacan's rigorous rethinking of the Freudian notion of penis envy.

98. *Le séminaire livre V*, p. 194 (emphasis added).

99. *The Seminar. Book III*, p. 319.

100. See *Le séminaire livre V*, p. 195.

101. Ibid., p. 185.

102. See ibid., p. 193.

103. D. Evans, *An Introductory Dictionary of Lacanian Psychoanalysis* (London: Routledge, 1996), p. 129.

104. *Le séminaire livre V*, p. 186.

105. Ibid., p. 193.

106. *The Seminar. Book III*, p. 212 (emphasis added).

107. Ibid., p. 209 (emphasis added).

108. See *Le séminaire livre IV*, p. 204.

109. Ibid., p. 212.

110. Ibid., pp. 209–210.

111. Ibid., p. 210.

112. Ibid., p. 205.

113. *Le séminaire livre V*, p. 187.

114. "The real father is nothing but an effect of language" (J. Lacan, *Le séminaire livre XVII. L'envers de la psychanalyse*, 1969–1970 [Paris: Seuil, 1991], p. 147). Hence, the paternal symbolic function could also be embodied by a woman.

115. Ibid., p. 148.

116. *Le séminaire livre IV*, p. 206.

117. Ibid., p. 209.

118. Ibid., p. 206 (emphasis added).

119. Ibid.

120. Ibid., p. 209.

121. *The Seminar. Book III*, p. 171.

122. Ibid. (emphasis added).

123. Ibid., p. 96.

124. Ibid.

125. *Le séminaire livre IV*, p. 201.

126. Evans, *An Introductory Dictionary of Lacanian Psychoanalysis*, p. 181.

127. *The Seminar. Book III*, p. 96.

128. Ibid., p. 177 (emphasis added).

129. Ibid.

130. See *Le séminaire livre V*, p. 186.

131. *Le séminaire livre IV*, p. 204.

132. *The Seminar. Book III*, p. 176.

133. Ibid., p. 172.

134. Ibid., p. 176.

135. Ibid.

136. *Le séminaire livre IV*, p. 190.

137. See ibid: "Woman has much more difficulty than the little boy in providing an entrance for the reality of what comes to pass on the side of the uterus and of the vagina in a dialectic of desire."

138. Ibid., p. 153. This also explains the following apparently nonsensical statement: "The penis in question is not the real penis, but the penis insofar as woman has it—that is, insofar as she does not have it" (ibid., p. 152).

139. Ibid., p. 153.

140. Ibid., p. 190.

141. See ibid., p. 110.

142. Ibid., p. 203.

143. See ibid., p. 154.

144. It is against the background of *Gestalt* theory that one should interpret Lacan's sarcastic statement according to which the female sex is "less desirable than the male sex" be-

cause the latter is "provocative": such a provocation is nothing but phallic captation/captivation (see *The Seminar. Book III*, p. 176).

145. For a critical reading of such a "beyond," see Section 5 of Chapter 5 below.

146. See especially S. Freud, "Female Sexuality," in SE, XXI, pp. 223–243.

147. *The Seminar. Book III*, p. 176.

148. *Le séminaire livre V*, p. 195.

149. See S. Freud, "Some Psychical Consequences of the Anatomical Distinction between the Sexes," in SE, XIX, p. 256.

150. *Le séminaire livre IV*, p. 213 (emphases added).

151. See, for example *Le séminaire livre V*, p. 195.

152. See, for example *Le séminaire livre IV*, p. 213.

153. Ibid., p. 204.

154. Ibid., p. 213.

155. Ibid., pp. 213–214.

156. The reader should be reminded that, for Lacan, all relations to concrete objects in reality are filtered through the Imaginary.

157. *Le séminaire livre V*, p. 199.

158. See *Le séminaire livre IV*, pp. 30–31.

159. See *Le séminaire livre V*, p. 206.

160. Ibid., p. 174.

161. Ibid., p. 33 (emphasis added).

162. Ibid.

163. Ibid., p. 175.

164. Ibid.

165. Ibid.

166. Ibid. (emphasis added). This can fully occur only at the end of the third stage of the Oedipus complex. It is true that the child "can grasp quite early on what the imaginary x is and thus . . . make himself the phallus" (in the second stage of the Oedipus complex) (ibid.): at this stage, however, the phallus is not yet "completely accessible" given that it has not yet been associated with the Law/Name-of-the-Father; this is brought about by the real father only in the third stage of the complex.

167. For schema 3.3, see ibid., p. 176; for schema 3.4, the most well-known version of the paternal metaphor, see *Écrits: A Selection*, p. 200.

168. *Le séminaire livre V*, p. 17.

169. Safouan, *Lacaniana*, p. 104.

170. Ibid., p. 98.

171. *Le séminaire livre V*, p. 483 (emphasis added).

172. Safouan, *Lacaniana*, p. 92. J.-A. Miller is one of the few authors who have acknowledged that the phallus is also a signified: indeed, he entitled one of the passages of the seminal Chapter IX of Seminar V "The phallus as signified" (*Le séminaire livre V*, p. 161).

173. *Le séminaire livre V*, p. 240.

174. Literally, Lacan says that "the Name-of-the-Father has the function of signifying the signifying system as such" (ibid., p. 240); it is "the signifier that signifies that, within this signifier, the signifier exists" (ibid., p. 147).

175. The Name-of-the-Father is the signifier that "in the Other, insofar as it is the site of law, represents the Other" (ibid., p. 146).

176. Ibid., p. 199.

177. Ibid., p. 249.

178. Ibid., p. 196.

179. Ibid. (emphasis added).

180. Ibid., p. 155 (emphasis added).

181. Ibid.

182. Ibid.

183. *The Seminar. Book III*, p. 268.

184. Evans, *An Introductory Dictionary of Lacanian Psychoanalysis*, p. 149.

185. *Écrits: A Selection*, p. 303.

186. *The Seminar. Book III*, p. 268.

187. The ego-ideal could thus be said to be the quilting point *par excellence*.

188. *Le séminaire livre V*, p. 196.

189. See, for example, ibid., p. 175.

190. It is possible for other metaphoric substitutions to relate directly to the Real of a trauma only insofar as the fundamental fantasy generated by the paternal metaphor is traversed/undone, and a new fundamental fantasy emerges. This point will become clearer in Chapters 4 and 5.

191. This is something that Lacan began to articulate as early as his dialogue with Hyppolite regarding the Freudian notion of *Bejahung* in Seminar I (see *The Seminar of Jacques Lacan. Book I, Freud's Papers on Technique*, 1953–1954 [New York: Norton, 1988], pp. 54–61). Secondary repression presupposes the *Bejahung*, a certain symbolic mooring that distances the subject from the Real of the trauma.

192. J. Laplanche and J.-B. Pontalis, *The Language of Psychoanalysis* (London: Karnac Books, 1988), p. 334.

193. For Freud's notion of *Vorstellungsrepräsentanz*, see especially the articles "Repression" and "The Unconscious," both contained in SE, XIV. Lacan will explicitly discuss and originally appropriate this notion in his detailed comments on Freud's *Entwurf* in the first— and usually underestimated—part of Seminar VII (see J. Lacan, *The Seminar. Book VII. The Ethics of Psychoanalysis*, 1959–1960 [London: Routledge, 1992], pp. 57–62). I shall return to this notion in Chapter 4.

194. These issues are only introduced here. I shall analyze the notion of the fundamental fantasy in detail in Chapter 5 below.

195. Laplanche and Pontalis, *The Language of Psychoanalysis*, pp. 203–204.

196. Freud, "Repression," p. 148.

197. *Écrits: A Selection*, p. 286.

198. *Le séminaire livre IV*, p. 119.

199. "The Name-of-the-Father is the binary signifier that is primally repressed" (B. Fink, *The Lacanian Subject* [Princeton: Princeton University Press, 1995], p. 74).

200. See *The Seminar. Book III*, pp. 179–180, p. 172; "Becoming a woman and wondering what a woman is are two essentially different things. I would go even further—it's because one doesn't become one [because of an incomplete resolution of the Oedipus complex] that one wonders [becomes an hysteric] and, up to a point, to wonder is the contrary of becoming one" (ibid., p. 178).

201. Neurotics are not satisfied with these answers: insofar as we are all not fully satisfied with them, we are also all neurotics. At this stage, however, Lacan still believes that the phallic answer satisfies most of us. The two great categories of neurotics, hysterics and obsessionals, are not satisfied with the answers given apropos female sexuality and death respectively.

202. See *Le séminaire livre V*, p. 231.

203. These are substitutes for the standard phallic fantasy and, as such, remain phallic.

204. *Le séminaire livre V*, p. 253.

205. Against the background of Freud's "A Child Is Being Beaten" case study (see SE, XVII), in Seminar V, Lacan offers a paradigmatic example of such a disturbance which we could schematize in the following way: (1) the "imaginary place where the desire of the mother is located . . . is occupied" by a sibling; (2) a lack of maternal love corresponds to the impossibility of the child's beginning to symbolize: if the mother is always absent, her absence cannot trigger the process of symbolization that follows frustration; (3) the child finds himself a compensation, a "phantasmatic solution" that functions as a "symbolic act": the lack of love/presence of a rival is itself symbolized through an imaginary signifier (hieroglyphic) such as a stick or a whip; (4) the child actively enters the symbolic order on the basis of a "so-called masochistic fantasy of fustigation" (see *Le séminaire livre V*, pp. 240–241). "The sign of the stick . . . or of whatever else hits . . . is an element thanks to which even a disagreeable effect may become a subjective distinction. . . . What is at the outset a means to annihilate the rival reality of the brother, later becomes that through which the subject finds himself distinguished, recognized" (ibid., p. 253).

CHAPTER 4 THERE IS NO OTHER OF THE OTHER

1. J. Lacan, *The Seminar. Book VII. The Ethics of Psychoanalysis, 1959–1960* (London: Routledge, 1992), p. 52.

2. Ibid., pp. 103, 129 (my translation).

3. See, for example, ibid., p. 55.

4. Ibid., p. 54 (my translation).

5. Lacan's realization that the Thing is, first and foremost, real, and consequently dumb, does not mean that the unconscious ceases to speak: see, for instance, ibid., pp. 205–206. Miller was the first to emphasize how the existence of "another Lacan" (the Lacan of the Real) does not imply the negation of the thesis that "the unconscious is structured like a language." See especially J.-A. Miller, "D'un autre Lacan," *Ornicar?*, no. 28 (January 1984), pp. 49–57.

6. *The Seminar. Book VII*, p. 196.

7. See, for example, Seminar VI, lesson of November 12, 1958 .

8. See especially J. Lacan, *Le séminaire livre IV. La relation d'objet, 1956–1957* (Paris: Seuil, 1994), Chapter VII ; J. Lacan, *Le séminaire livre V. Les formations de l'inconscient, 1957–1958* (Paris : Seuil, 1998), Chapter XIII.

9. There are therefore four different phases in the evolution of the notion of fantasy: 1. The fantasy belongs only to perverse masochists (Seminars IV and V); 2. The paternal metaphor presupposes a standard, universal phallic fantasy, but Lacan does not assume it (Seminar V); 3. The fantasy is assumed as universal, but its masochism is still confined to perverts (Seminar VI). This is why Seminar VI discusses the fantasy almost exclusively as an imaginary formation, and consequently with almost no reference to the Real of *jouissance*; 4. The fantasy is universal and universally masochistic even in its standard, phallic version. The real (masochistic) role of the fantasy is presupposed by Seminar VII, but is only later developed in Seminar X (when the object *a* begins to be thematized also as a real object).

10. When *jouissance* is pompously introduced in Seminar V, it is exclusively referred to perverse masochism (see especially *Le séminaire livre V*, Chapter XIV). Yet in Seminar V, Lacan contradictorily admits that (nonpathological) perversion is a precondition of man as being of language . . . (ibid., pp. 78, 311).

11. Ibid., p. 463. Lacan also speaks of "the Other of this Other, that which allows the subject to perceive this Other, the locus of speech, as being itself symbolized." Miller has himself appropriately entitled one of the sections of this lesson (June 18, 1958) "L'Autre de l'Autre."

12. Seminar VI, lesson of May 13, 1959.

13. J. Lacan, *The Seminar. Book III. The Psychoses, 1955–56* (London: Routledge, 1993), p. 226.

14. J. Lacan, *Écrits: A Selection* (London: Tavistock, 1977), p. 201 (emphasis added).

15. Lacan indeed speaks of "partial delusions" even with reference to Schreber's case: ibid., p. 214.

16. Ibid., p. 217.

17. *The Seminar. Book III*, pp. 33–34.

18. How does the psychotic produce signification or signified if the signifier of signifiers is foreclosed? I believe it is not sufficient to argue that, in psychosis, "S2s have relations amongst themselves" (B. Fink, *The Lacanian Subject* [Princeton: Princeton University Press, 1995], p. 75). If in psychosis the relations between the S2s go beyond the dimension of the Real-of-language (the letter), if the psychosis is often latent, and the subject can thus manage to produce signification, he can do so only by means of a certain number of signifiers which both transcend the S2s and do not achieve the status of a proper S1. This would explain Lacan's statement according to which "for a human being to be called 'normal'" he has to acquire "a *minimal number*" of quilting points (*The Seminar Book III*, pp. 268–269; emphasis added). In other words, the psychotic is *not* without quilting points . . . . The psychotic forecloses the primordial (and qualitatively more important) quilting point produced by the paternal metaphor, but he nevertheless has (a quantitatively insufficient number of) other quilting points which, by definition, cannot be reduced to the status of S2; if this were not the case, he would simply be "completely crazy," he would not speak to us in our language. . . .

19. In Seminar III, Lacan literally says that "what is not symbolized returns in the real" (*The Seminar. Book III*, p. 86), and that "the object of a *Verwerfung* [foreclusion] reappear[s] in the real" (ibid., p. 190).

20. Ibid., p. 113.

21. M. Recalcati, "Follia e struttura in Jacques Lacan," in *aut aut*, 285–286 (May-August 1998), p. 151.

22. In psychosis, "the unconscious is present but not functioning" (*The Seminar. Book III*, p. 143).

23. Ibid., p. 250.

24. "Does the patient speak? If we did not distinguish language and speech, it's true, he speaks, but he speaks like those sophisticated dolls that open and close their eyes, drink liquid, etc." (ibid., p. 34).

25. Ibid., p. 250.

26. Ibid., p. 112. The unconscious is always "outside" but, in being outside, it is latent for neurotics, overt for psychotics.

27. I believe this is precisely the point which Grigg fails to emphasize in his otherwise excellent article on Lacan's evolving notion of psychosis (see R. Grigg, "From the Mechanism of Psychosis to the Universal Condition of the Symptom: On Foreclosure," in *Key Concepts of Lacanian Psychoanalysis*, ed. D. Nobus [London: Rebus Press, 1998], especially pp. 53–54, 56). Grigg correctly emphasizes that the Real returns in *reality*, and that what returns in reality are nothing but signifiers; on the other hand, he does not specify that the Real-of-language that returns corresponds to the *universal* (nonsymbolized) Symbolic, and thus risks confusing the Real-of-language with the primordial Real.

28. I will henceforth often use the phrase "universal Name-of-the-Father" to designate this universal level of the Law as such. This obviously does not exclude the possibility that the Name-of-the-Father also stands for the universal Law at the *individual* level of the subject's individual entrance into the Symbolic.

29. *The Seminar. Book III*, pp. 64–65.

30. Ibid., p. 69.

31. Ibid., pp. 69, 75.

32. Ibid., p. 37 (emphasis added).

33. Ibid., p. 64.

34. *The Seminar. Book VII*, p. 12.

35. See S. Freud, *Jokes and Their Relation to the Unconscious*, in SE, VIII, p. 115.

36. *The Seminar. Book III*, p. 64.

37. Ibid.

38. Ibid., p. 65.

39. Ibid., p. 66.

40. Ibid., p. 64. It goes without saying that here the religious undertones of the notion of the Name-of-the-Father find their justification.

41. Ibid., p. 65. Such an "act of faith," Descartes's *certainty* that he is not deceived by God, presupposes the sublation of the strictly speaking psychotic position according to which "God certainly deceives me." In Cartesian philosophy, this is nothing but so-called "hyperbolic doubt": "What if God is deceiving me all the time?". . .

42. Ibid.

43. Ibid., p. 64.

44. Ibid.

45. For example, Lacan clearly relies on his notions of the Name-of-the-Father and the phallus when he analyzes historically disparate (and premodern) cultural phenomena such as ancient comedy (in Seminar V) and courtly love poetry (in Seminar VII).

46. See *Le séminaire livre IV*, p. 51. Lacan admits: "I'm speaking about the history of humanity as a whole" (ibid., p. 50).

47. To put it bluntly, it is only at this moment that the stone with which "prehistoric" man grinds his food will have become a tool. . . .

48. J. Lacan, *Le séminaire livre XVII. L'envers de la psychanalyse, 1969–1970* (Paris: Seuil, 1991), p. 135.

49. *The Seminar. Book VII*, pp. 66–67 (emphases added).

50. *Le séminaire livre IV*, p. 211.

51. For an account of Lacan's reelaboration of Freud's use of myths, see D. Leader, "Lacan's Myths," in *The Cambridge Companion to Lacan*, ed. J.-M. Rabaté (Cambridge: Cambridge University Press, 2003), pp. 35–50.

52. *Écrits: A Selection*, pp. 310–311 (emphasis added).

53. *Le séminaire livre IV*, p. 219 (emphasis added). See also *Le séminaire livre V*, p. 367.

54. For Lacan's own use of this expression, see, for example, "Preface to the English-Language Edition," in The Seminar. Book XI. The Four Fundamental Concepts of Psychoanalysis (London: Hogarth Press and the Institute of Psychoanalysis, 1977), p. xli; Le séminaire livre XVII, pp. 56–57.

55. This was the title given by Lacan to his interrupted Seminar of 1963.

56. See Lacan's considerations on Gide's perversion in Le séminaire livre V, pp. 258–261.

57. Ibid., p. 317 (emphasis added).

58. Ibid.

59. Ibid., p. 316.

60. Ibid., p. 367.

61. Ibid., p. 312.

62. Écrits: A Selection, p. 311.

63. Ibid., p. 316 (my translation; emphasis added).

64. Ibid., pp. 316–317.

65. J. P. Muller and W. J. Richardson, Lacan and Language (New York: International Universities Press, 1982), p. 409.

66. J.-A. Miller, "La suture: éléments de la logique du signifiant," in Un début dans la vie (Paris: Gallimard, 2002), p. 108.

67. See, for example, Seminar XXI, "Les non-dupes errent," unpublished, 1973–1974, lesson of April 9, 1974.

68. The locution Real-in-the-Symbolic ("le réel dans le symbolique") and symbolic Real ("le réel symbolique") are used by Lacan himself, especially during the years in which he problematized the notion of the Other of the Other: see, for example, Le séminaire livre IV, p. 209; Le séminaire livre V, p. 12; Seminar VI, lessons of May 20, 1959 and June 3, 1959.

69. The Seminar of Jacques Lacan. Book I, Freud's Papers on Technique, 1953–1954 (New York: Norton, 1988), pp. 121, 137.

70. Such a sign is ambiguous, since it could easily be read misleadingly as the "Real-that-is-barred-by-the-Symbolic," whereas what I wish to denote is quite the opposite: the Real that will have been barred by the Symbolic was always already barred in itself.

71. See Le séminaire livre IV, p. 31.

72. See, for example, Le séminaire livre V, p. 246.

73. Well-known formulas such as "the real has no fissure" and "there is no absence in the real" undoubtedly refer to this second meaning of the Real (see, for example, The Seminar of Jacques Lacan. Book II, The Ego in Freud's Theory and in the Technique of Psychoanalysis, 1954–1955 [New York: Norton, 1991], pp. 97, 313).

74. The Seminar. Book III, p. 186.

75. Le séminaire livre IV, p. 31.

76. Ibid.

77. Ibid.

78. Ibid. (emphasis added).

79. Ibid., p. 33.

80. To be more precise, Lacan is using the term *Wirklichkeit* in two ways: (a) as "the whole of what effectively happens," everyday reality, which undoubtedly "happens," together with the Real-of-the-Symbolic; (b) the Real-of-the-Symbolic as that which normally happens without being identified in reality. I will henceforth use *Wirklichkeit* in this second, narrower sense.

81. *Le séminaire livre IV*, p. 32.

82. Ibid.

83. Ibid., p. 33.

84. Ibid., pp. 32–33.

85. Ibid., p. 33.

86. Ibid., p. 46.

87. Ibid., p. 45.

88. Ibid., p. 44.

89. Ibid.

90. Ibid., p. 43.

91. Ibid., p. 46.

92. My inference is supported by the fact that Lacan adds that this "uncultivated character" may end up thinking that "it is perhaps the sprite of the current who plays tricks . . . and transforms the water into light" (ibid). This image cannot help reminding the reader of Schreber's trickster God.

93. Ibid.

94. Ibid. (emphasis added).

95. See ibid. Lacan also hints that the power station can be built only—the Holy Spirit can intervene only—if "the matter that will come into play when the machine comes on already presents itself in nature in a privileged manner, or to tell you everything, in a signifying manner" (ibid., p. 44): here I refer the reader to Section 3 of Chapter 3 above, and my discussion of the phallic *Gestalt* as something which is already in nature, as well as to the discussion in Chapter 1 of the "privilege" that a disadapted Imaginary is for humans. For the way in which each subject develops from being "an uncultivated character" to becoming an "engineer" of the power plant (Lacan's own words), the reader should refer to my treatment of the Oedipus complex in Chapter 3.

96. Seminar VI, lesson of May 13, 1959.

97. Ibid.

98. Ibid.

99. Ibid.

100. Ibid. Lacan also states that "this whole development of knowledge, with what it involves in terms of . . . the function of the object, is the result of a choice" motivated by a specific "position of desire," the "desire to know."

101. Ibid.

102. Seminar VI, lesson of May 20, 1959.

103. Ibid.

104. Ibid. Lacan similarly argues that "the subject does not locate himself simply in terms of discourse, but also indeed in terms of some real[ities]" (Seminar VI, lesson of May 27, 1959).

105. Seminar VI, lesson of May 20, 1959.

106. For the location of the "Real as real" at the unconscious level, see Seminar VI, lesson of May 27, 1959.

107. Ibid. "Being is properly the real insofar as it manifests itself at the symbolic level" (Seminar VI, lesson of June 3, 1959).

108. Seminar VI, lesson of May 27, 1959.

109. Ibid. These definitions are accompanied by the following statement: "It is only too obvious that the real is not an opaque continuum." This sounds like an open dismissal of Lacan's early theory of the Real as "that which has no fissures." In parallel, Lacan again attacks the "philosophical tradition"—Aristotle in primis—since he believes that it always based its systems on the presupposition that "the relationship of the cutting of the real to the cutting of language . . . is only a question of the overlapping of one system of cutting by another system of cutting." On the other hand, Lacan implicitly suggests that the cutting of the Real depends on the cutting of language: this is proved by the fact that contemporary science (as the epitome of the cutting of language) has recently reached what Lacan calls the "disintegration of matter.". . .

110. Ibid.

111. See The Seminar. Book VII, p. 132.

112. One might well argue that the unconscious Thing "that speaks" in the articles of the mid-1950s is nothing but die Sache, the representation of the Thing on the symbolic level which, in Seminar VII, Lacan makes every effort to oppose to the dumbness of the real das Ding (see ibid., pp. 43–46).

113. Ibid., p. 118.

114. Ibid., p. 121 (my translation). See also p. 163.

115. Ibid., p. 118 (emphases added).

116. Ibid., p. 121 (my translation).

117. Ibid., pp. 202–203. The Thing is by definition inaccessible, since when one mythically accesses it, one automatically returns to the primordial Real, the Thing qua hole disappears . . . .

118. See J. Lacan, Le séminaire livre XXIII. Le sinthome, 1975–1976 (Paris: Seuil, 2005), p. 12.

119. *The Seminar. Book VII*, p. 63 (emphasis added).

120. For the mother as Thing, see especially ibid., pp. 67–69. Lacan's (inconsistent) transcendent stance in connection with this notion is in any case far more multifaceted than that of the vast majority of its commentators. First of all, critics usually fail to acknowledge that such a stance applies almost exclusively to Seminar VII; secondly, they fail to recognize that the Thing is the *negation* of the primordial Real; thirdly, they innocently tend to think the presymbolic whole of mother and child in terms of an actual union between two distinct subjects which is later interrupted by the intervention of the father (the symbolic law). (For an exemplary mistaken account of the mother–child "real" relationship, see B. Lichtenberg Ettinger, "Weaving a Trans-subjective Tress or the Matrixial *sinthome*," in *Re-Inventing the Symptom: Essays on the Final Lacan*, ed. L. Thurston [New York: Other Press, 2002], pp. 83–109.)

121. *The Seminar. Book VII*, p. 57.

122. The Thing is described as "the *cause* of the most fundamental human passion" in ibid., p. 97.

123. Ibid., p. 70 (my translation).

124. Ibid., p. 55.

125. Ibid., p. 20.

126. Ibid., p. 223.

127. These arguments from Seminar VII are also valid for the following Seminars if only one substitutes object *a* qua lost object for the transcendence of the lost Thing.

128. J.-A. Miller, "Extimité," in *Lacanian Theory of Discourse: Subject, Structure, and Society*, ed. M. Bracher (New York: New York University Press, 1994), p. 26.

129. *The Seminar. Book VII*, p. 71. See also ibid., pp. 101, 139, 198.

130. Ibid., p. 71.

131. M. Safouan, *Lacaniana: Les séminaires de Jacques Lacan, 1953–1963* (Paris: Fayard, 2001), p. 138.

132. *The Seminar. Book VII*, p. 112 (my translation).

133. Ibid., p. 99 (my translation).

134. This level of the Imaginary should not to be confused with the imaginary object of self-conscious ego-logical knowledge.

135. *The Seminar, Book VII*, p. 99 (my translation).

136. Ibid., p. 118. D. Porter's far from impeccable English translation of Seminar VII omits this important phrase altogether.

137. One should, strictly speaking, distinguish "the Other thing" (*l'Autre chose*) from the other thing (*autre chose*) in which the Thing is found: the Thing is essentially a transcendent Other thing inasmuch as it is never completely refound in the other thing(s) in which it is found. Thus this transcendent *Autre chose* "is at the same time *la Non-chose*" whose "Non- is certainly not individualized in a signifying way" (ibid., p. 136, my translation); as we have seen, the Non-Thing *qua* hole is indeed outside of the signifier.

138. A. Di Ciaccia and M. Recalcati, *Jacques Lacan. Un insegnamento sul sapere dell'inconscio* (Milan: Bruno Mondadori, 2000), p. 196.

139. *The Seminar. Book VII*, p. 111.

140. Ibid., p. 112.

141. See ibid., p. 99.

142. Ibid.

143. Ibid., p. 118.

144. Ibid., p. 119.

145. Ibid., p. 122.

146. Ibid., p. 120. This will also be valid later when the notion of the undead replaces that of the primordial Real: the undead is clearly not a *nihil*, which is always paired with some-thing.

147. Ibid., p. 213 (emphasis added).

148. Ibid.

149. *Le séminaire livre IV*, p. 48; see also *The Seminar. Book VII*, p. 213.

150. J. Derrida, "Le facteur de la vérité," in *The Post Card: From Socrates to Freud and Beyond* (Chicago: University of Chicago Press, 1987), p. 464.

151. Ibid., p. 477 (my translation; emphases added).

152. *The Seminar. Book VII*, p. 213.

153. Ibid. (my translation; emphasis added).

154. See, for example, *Le séminaire livre IV*, p. 50.

155. Ibid.; see also *The Seminar. Book VII*, p. 214.

156. Ibid., p. 214.

157. See *Écrits: A Selection*, p. 287.

CHAPTER 5 THE SUBJECT OF THE FANTASY . . . AND BEYOND

1. J. Lacan, *Le séminaire livre V. Les formations de l'inconscient, 1957–1958* (Paris: Seuil, 1998), p. 179.

2. Ibid., p. 122.

3. Ibid., p. 179.

4. Ibid., p. 256.

5. Ibid., p. 189.

6. "The subject does not have a signifier that represents him" (ibid., p. 157).

7. Ibid., p. 99.

8. J. Lacan, *Le séminaire livre X. L'angoisse, 1962–1963* (Paris: Seuil, 2004), p. 104.

9. See Seminar IX, lesson of December 20, 1961.

10. See, for example, J. Lacan, *Écrits: A Selection* (London: Tavistock, 1977), p. 316; J. Lacan, *The Seminar. Book XI. The Four Fundamental Concepts of Psychoanalysis* (London: Hogarth Press and the Institute of Psychoanalysis, 1977), p. 207.

11. *Écrits: A Selection*, p. 316. S. Žižek efficaciously analyzes the various meanings of this formula in *For They Know Not What They Do: Enjoyment as a Political Factor* (London and New York: Verso, 1991), pp. 21–27.

12. *Écrits: A Selection*, p. 316.

13. See, for example *Le séminaire livre X*, p. 31.

14. See, for example, J. Lacan, *Écrits* (Paris: Seuil, 1966), p. 848.

15. The signifier kills the undead Thing, and thus gives rise to the nonsignified of death, to "that limit of the signified which is not reached by any human being." In this sense, the death drive should also plainly be understood as "the fact that we realize that life is uncertain and ephemeral" (J. Lacan, *Le séminaire livre IV. La relation d'objet, 1956–1957* [Paris: Seuil, 1994], pp. 48, 50).

16. Such a mythical birth of the Symbolic cannot be repeated at a universal level: nevertheless, it is repeated in the particular each time a child successfully resolves the Oedipus complex, as well as each time an analysand traverses his fundamental fantasy and proceeds to a radical reconfiguration of his symbolic coordinates.

17. See J. Lacan, *The Seminar. Book VII. The Ethics of Psychoanalysis, 1959–1960* (London: Routledge, 1992), p. 212.

18. Seminar IX, lesson of February 28, 1962.

19. Seminar VI, lesson of June 3, 1959.

20. See, for example, *The Seminar. Book VII*, p. 90.

21. Recalcati points out that the conservative function of the death drive problematizes Freud's widely accepted—not least by Lacan himself—libidinal dualism (M. Recalcati, *L'universale e il singolare: Lacan e l'al di là del principio di piacere* [Milan: Marcos y Marcos, 1996], p. 28). For my part, I am not completely convinced that this conservative function of the death drive really applies to Freud: too many issues remain indeterminate in Freud's own account of this notion. . . . It is doubtless the case, however, that such a Lacanian interpretation of the death drive undermines Lacan's own alleged fidelity to Freud's dualism, and paves the way for a form of monism that would distinguish itself from the ingenuousness of Jung's unitary life energy.

22. See, for example *The Seminar. Book XI*, p. 168.

23. If on the one hand, Lacan defines *jouissance* as the (partial) "satisfaction of the drive" (*The Seminar. Book VII*, p. 209), on the other, the (partial) drive itself should be understood as the (partial) satisfaction of desire.

24. S. Freud, *Beyond the Pleasure Principle*, in SE, XVIII, p. 63.

25. J. Laplanche and J.-B. Pontalis, *The Language of Psychoanalysis* (London: Karnac Books, 1988), p. 102.

26. Lacan makes the same point in *Le séminaire livre IV,* p. 47.

27. Nevertheless, Lacan acknowledges that Freud's notion of the death drive as the Nirvana principle is "very suspect in itself" (*The Seminar. Book VII,* p. 212).

28. Ibid., p. 211 (emphasis added).

29. Ibid., p. 212 (emphasis added).

30. Ibid., p. 211. In this sense, Lacan also claims that the dimension of the death drive is "that of the subject. It is the necessary condition for the natural phenomenon of the instinct in entropy to be taken up at the level of the person" (ibid., p. 204).

31. Ibid., p. 209.

32. Ibid. "Remembering, historicising, is coextensive with the functioning of the drive in what we call the human psyche."

33. Ibid., p. 212 (my translation).

34. Ibid., p. 134.

35. *Le séminaire livre V,* p. 246.

36. Ibid.

37. Ibid., p. 245.

38. Ibid.

39. "There is never either complete generation or total death in the strict sense. . . . What we call *generation* is unfolding and growth; just as what we call *death* is enfolding and diminution." It goes without saying that Leibniz applied this notion only to the nonhuman body (*Monadology,* in *Philosophical Texts* [Oxford: Oxford University Press, 1998], p. 278).

40. See *Le séminaire livre IV,* p. 51.

41. We could provocatively argue that there is only one structural distinction between a pre-Oedipal baby—or *a fortiori* a fetus—and a dead person, namely that the big Other is able to individuate imaginarily only the former. The more clearly we can identify the "human" shape of the fetus—thanks to technological innovations—the earlier we tend to consider it as "alive." Apart from this, the fetus and the dead person are both symbolically alive for the big Other, and equally unable to individuate themselves.

42. S. Žižek, *The Ticklish Subject: The Absent Centre of Political Ontology* (London and New York: Verso, 1999), p. 379.

43. See, for example, *The Seminar. Book VII,* pp. 232–233.

44. Ibid., p. 268.

45. S. Žižek, *The Art of the Ridiculous Sublime* (Seattle: W.C. Simpson Center for the Humanities, 2002), p. 20.

46. Or by a permanent desubjectivation in the Other's fantasy, as in the case of psychosis, which ultimately corresponds to a complete alienation in the Symbolic.

47. *Le séminaire livre IV,* pp. 119–120.

48. As for this "realization" of lack, Lacan writes: "One could say that with the presence of a curtain, that which is beyond it, as lack, tends to realize itself as an image. Absence is painted on the veil" (ibid., p. 155).

49. See, for example, *Le séminaire livre X*, p. 120.

50. Of course, at the moment of privation we are dealing with a subject-to-come. Therefore subjective destitution is, strictly speaking, valid only *after* the resolution of the Oedipus complex.

51. *Le séminaire livre V*, p. 188.

52. Ibid., p. 382. In "The Signification of the Phallus," this formula is rendered as "desire is neither the appetite for satisfaction [*appétit de satisfaction*], nor the demand for love, but the difference that results from the subtraction of the first from the second" (*Écrits: A Selection*, p. 287).

53. Ibid., p. 286 (my translation).

54. *Le séminaire livre V*, p. 381 (emphasis added).

55. P. Guyomard, *La jouissance du tragique* (Paris: Aubier, 1992), p. 23.

56. *Le séminaire livre V*, p. 381.

57. Ibid., p. 382.

58. "The other great generic desire, that of hunger, is not represented [in the unconscious]" (*Écrits: A Selection*, p. 142). I should point out that hunger is not represented in the unconscious only if it is considered *independently* of sexual desire.

59. *Le séminaire livre V*, p. 383.

60. Lacan spells this out just before providing his audience with the formula of desire (ibid., p. 382; emphasis added). The formula deals with *pure* desire.

61. Ibid. Lacan is tacitly using three different and logically consecutive formulas: (1) demand for love = demand − necessity of need; (2) "impure" desire, i.e. desire + drive, = (pre-Oedipal) demand for love + (conscious and, above all, unconscious) necessity of need; (3) "pure" desire = (post-Oedipal) demand for love (i.e. "impure" desire) − (conscious and, above all, unconscious) necessity of need.

62. Ibid.

63. Ibid., p. 252.

64. Ibid., p. 359.

65. Ibid., p. 344.

66. Ibid., p. 382.

67. "How could we desire anything if we were not to borrow the raw material from our needs?" (ibid.).

68. Ibid.

69. Ibid., p. 330.

70. See Seminar VI, lesson of May 13, 1959.

71. M. Safouan, *Lacaniana: Les séminaires de Jacques Lacan, 1953–1963* (Paris: Fayard, 2001), p. 135.

72. *Le séminaire livre V*, p. 364.

73. Ibid., pp. 363–364.

74. See ibid., pp. 364–365. "Want-to-be" is the translation of "*manque-à-être*" that Lacan himself proposed.

75. Ibid., p. 367.

76. Ibid. (emphases added). The same point is elaborated in a more convoluted fashion in "The Signification of the Phallus," where Lacan seems to suggest that desire is both *beyond* demand *and within* it (*Écrits: A Selection*, pp. 286–287).

77. *Le séminaire livre V*, pp. 367–368.

78. On the "masking" of desire, see especially ibid., pp. 319–327.

79. See *Le séminaire livre X*, p. 80.

80. *Le séminaire livre V*, p. 382.

81. Ibid., p. 330.

82. Seminar IX, lesson of February 21, 1962.

83. Ibid.

84. Safouan, *Lacaniana*, p. 231.

85. Seminar VI, lesson of May 13, 1959.

86. Seminar VI, lesson of May 27, 1959.

87. Seminar VI, lesson of November 12, 1958.

88. Ibid.

89. Seminar VI, lesson of May 13, 1959.

90. Ibid.

91. Ibid.

92. Seminar VI, lesson of November 12, 1958.

93. Seminar VI, lesson of May 20, 1959.

94. Such an interval is yet another elaboration of the distinction between the subject of the statement and the subject of the enunciation. It goes without saying that demand can also be expressed "mentally"; therefore being-in-the-interval should not ingenuously be understood as the "silent" subject. . . .

95. Seminar VI, lesson of May 20, 1959.

96. See especially Seminar VI, lesson of June 3, 1959.

97. "Lacan brings back the cut, the gap, into the One itself"; this One-with-a-gap is to be opposed to both the notion of "One-substance" and to that of "radical Otherness." See S. Žižek, *Organs without Bodies: Deleuze and Consequences* (London: Routledge, 2004), p. 33.

98. Seminar VI, lesson of June 3, 1959.

99. Seminar IX, lesson of March 7, 1962.

100. See *Le séminaire livre IV*, pp. 111–121; *Le séminaire livre V*, pp. 233–243.

101. "The image of the ideal Father is a phantasy of the [standard] neurotic" (*Écrits: A Selection*, p. 321).

102. For the sake of clarity and conciseness, I shall refer here only to the boy, but my exposition is equally valid *mutatis mutandis* for the girl, who, Lacan says, "is without having it" ("*elle est sans l'avoir*"). At the moment of symbolic castration, the girl, like the boy, renounces being the imaginary phallus of the mother and, by identifying with the father, does not have the phallus as a form of having it. This makes woman the phallus-of-man. Note, however, that woman, despite being the phallus of man, is *not* the phallus *tout court*: Lacan does not say "*elle l'est*" but "*elle est sans* . . .": it is only as an inflection of the "without" that woman is the phallus-of-man. . . .

103. "The phantasy contains the −φ, the imaginary function of castration under a hidden form" (*Écrits: A Selection*, p. 322).

104. *Le séminaire livre V*, pp. 345–346.

105. Ibid., p. 308.

106. In Seminar VI, Lacan admits that "the object *a* [qua representation of lack] plays [in the fantasy] the same role of mirage as . . . the image of the specular other plays with respect to the ego" (lesson of May 27, 1959). See also *Écrits: A Selection*, p. 314.

107. "In the case of the neurotic, the −φ slides under the $ of the phantasy to the advantage of the ego" (*Écrits: A Selection*, p. 323).

108. *Le séminaire livre X*, p. 139.

109. Seminar VI, lesson of May 13, 1959.

110. "The phallus is the last in a series of figurations of the *objet a* that display a conspicuously imaginary character. . . . The phallus is not merely one figure of the *objet a* among others but assumes a special status" (R. Boothby, *Freud as Philosopher* [London: Routledge, 2001], p. 273).

111. *Le séminaire livre X*, p. 37.

112. See Seminar VI, lesson of June 3, 1959; *Le séminaire livre X* , p. 35.

113. *Le séminaire livre X*, pp. 120–122.

114. See ibid., pp. 50–52, p. 74.

115. These are clearly two different subjective positions: on the one hand, the subject continues to demand always new things, but he considers each demand as "what he really wants"; on the other hand, the subject (temporarily) assumes the impossibility of satisfying his demand for love, and by saying "No, it's not that . . ." to what the other offers him, he approaches pure desire (of the void). In other words, it is imperative to make a distinction between new imaginary identifications that are the consequence of mere frustration—in everyday life "there are as many [narcissistic] masks as there are forms of unsatisfaction" (*Le séminaire livre V*, p. 333)—and those which follow the (reciprocal)

experience of "*falling* in love," the fleeting moment in which the Real as void, the *agalma*, pierces the imaginary-symbolic veil of reality and appears in self-consciousness. Ultimately, this is precisely the difference between relating to the Other's demand (demanding something of him, being frustrated in our demand, and consequently identifying with him) and temporarily relating to the pure desire of the Other (and thus purely desiring). I have elaborated these points in "*Le Ressort de l'Amour*: Lacan's Theory of Love in his Reading of Plato's 'Symposium,'" in *Angelaki: Journal of the Theoretical Humanities* 11, no. 3 (2006): "Encounters with Ancient Thought," ed. J. Sellars.

116. Safouan, *Lacaniana*, p. 240. Or, rather, only insofar as the object *a* rapidly disappears after temporarily emerging. . . .

117. *Le séminaire livre X*, p. 127.

118. Ibid., pp. 127–128.

119. In his first detailed analysis of the object *a* in Seminar VI, Lacan clearly associates the "privileged" part-object which retroactively signifierizes pregenital part-objects with the phallic *Gestalt*. This is certainly no longer a case a few years later (suffice it to recall here that the phallic *Gestalt* does not figure among the four part-objects accurately described by Lacan in his discussion of the drive circuit in Seminar XI). So how should we understand the hidden part-object *a* (or φ) which creates the illusory "optical effect" of *agalma* as the ultimate object of desire in conscious life? In being that which, by definition, lies beyond specularity, the hidden part-object *a* (or φ) is nothing but the *gaze*. For Lacan, the gaze qua *a* is one with the phallic part-object which is imaginarily lost when the fundamental fantasy and individuation simultaneously emerge through castration; the gaze is the privileged "genital" object *a* that retroactively phallicizes (the loss of) the two kinds of "pregenital" object *a* (the breast and the feces). In other words, there is no all-encompassing genital/phallic drive *per se* but, rather, genitality—post-Oedipal desire—is sustained by the partial scopic drive (and by the invocatory drive which revolves around the voice as part-object): one "phallically" falls in love with the *je ne sais quoi* which lies beyond the eyes (or the voice) of the beloved. . . .

120. *Le séminaire livre V*, p. 329.

121. *Le séminaire livre X*, p. 14.

122. It should be specified that the subject is the object of the Other's desire in the *subject's* own fantasy. Although the subject is, at the same time, an object in the Other's own fantasy—in which the Other's desire ultimately consists of being the object of the subject's desire as phantasized by the Other—it is nevertheless clearly the case that the Other's own fantasy remains as unknowable for the subject as the Other's pure desire.

123. *Le séminaire livre X*, p. 89.

124. Ibid.

125. Ibid., p. 61.

126. "The object *a* is this distinctive object that I put in the place of the Other's lack . . . it is the nonconfessable object that I am myself in the [phantasmatic] scenario which fascinates and fixes my desire" (M. Borch-Jacobsen, "Les alibis du sujet," in *Lacan avec les philosophes* [Paris: Albin Michel, 1991], p. 310).

127. *Le séminaire livre IV*, p. 125.

128. *Le séminaire livre X*, p. 62.

129. Ibid., p. 63.

130. In Seminar X, Lacan refines his early theorizations of the Hilflosigkeit as a mere biological given: if the child is a biologically helpless animal, he completely depends on the
(m)Other, and becomes aware of his helplessness precisely when he is confronted with
the (helpless) desire of the (m)Other.

131. Ibid., p. 91.

132. Ibid., p. 92.

133. Ibid. (emphasis added). If anxiety first of all depends on a "cut," then it is not sufficient to state that "it is not the removal of the maternal breast but its proximity that an-
guishes the child" (J. Ansaldi, *Le Discours de Rome suivi de L'angoisse, Le Séminaire X* [Nîmes:
Théétète Éditions, 2004], p. 54). The proximity of the breast certainly causes—or will
have caused—anxiety during the second stage of the Oedipus complex when the
mother attempts to "engulf" the child; however, it is only the (logically antecedent) removal, the cut of the maternal breast at the moment of primordial frustration, that
retroactively generates anxiety in relation to the emergence of the desire of the
(m)Other. Anxiety originates on the verge of a bond which excludes separation only
because it relies on a prior separation which excludes any bond.

134. *Le séminaire livre X*, p. 91.

135. Ibid., pp. 122–123.

136. Ibid., p. 60.

137. "The source of anxiety is the rising of lack in a positive form" (ibid., p. 75).

138. Ibid., p. 60.

139. "Anxiety is already a protection . . . anxiety develops by letting a danger appear, whereas
there is no danger at the level of the final experience of Hilflosigkeit" (*The Seminar. Book VII*,
p. 304; my translation).

140. Lacan's definition of anxiety *stricto sensu* in terms of the "lack of lack" pitilessly refutes
Derrida's claim according to which, in Lacan's "phallogocentric" theory of the subject,
"something is missing from its place, but the *lack* [the phallus] *is never missing* from it"
(J. Derrida, "Le facteur de la vérité," in *The Post Card: From Socrates to Freud and Beyond* [Chi-
cago: University of Chicago Press, 1987], p. 441; emphasis added). Derrida's problem
is that he completely misses the dimension of the Real in Lacan insofar as he always considers lack as an intrasymbolic element guaranteed by the Other of the Other. His considerations on Lacan's "fear" of acknowledging the anxiety-provoking power of
literature are equally belied: "[Lacan] forecloses this problematic of the double and of
Unheimlichkeit without mercy. And does so, doubtless, in order to deem it contained in
the imaginary . . . which must be kept rigorously apart from the symbolic. . . . What
thus finds itself controlled is *Unheimlichkeit*, and the anguishing disarray which can be
provoked . . . by references from simulacrum to simulacrum, from double to double"
(ibid., p. 460). For his part, in commenting on Hoffmann's tales, Lacan speaks of the
"essential dimension which the field of fiction provides for our experience of the *Un-
heimlich*. In reality, the latter is fleeting. Fiction shows it in a much better way, it even produces it as an effect. . . . This is a kind of ideal point but it is very precious for us since
this effect allows us to see the function of fantasy" (*Le séminaire livre X*, p. 61).

141. Ibid., p. 58.

142. Ibid. As Safouan writes, the function of the Other is thus guaranteed "in what in him is irreducible to transparency" (Safouan, *Lacaniana*, p. 235).

143. *Le séminaire livre X*, p. 58.

144. Harari recalls that, in Seminar XI, Lacan will point out that "the anxiety of the analysand should be administered in doses by the analyst" (R. Harari, *Lacan's Seminar on "Anxiety": An Introduction* [New York: Other Press, 2001], p. 4).

145. See, for instance, *Le séminaire livre X*, pp. 76, 96.

146. Ibid., p. 203 (emphasis added).

147. Ibid.

148. *The Seminar. Book VII*, p. 298 (emphasis added).

149. See J. Lacan, *Television: A Challenge to the Psychoanalytic Establishment* (New York: Norton, 1990), p. 39.

150. *The Seminar. Book VII*, p. 20.

151. Lacan also affirms that "reality is precarious. And it is precisely to the extent that access to it is so precarious that the commandments which trace its path are so tyrannical" (ibid., p. 30).

152. Ibid., p. 13.

153. See ibid., p. 80.

154. Ibid., p. 13.

155. Ibid.

156. Ibid., pp. 53–54.

157. Ibid., p. 70.

158. Ibid.

159. Ibid., pp. 70, 67.

160. Ibid., p. 159.

161. Primordial *jouissance* as exposed in Seminar VII is not to be understood in terms of a union between the child and the mother *qua* Thing: we are dealing here with an "unlimited totality." Once again, one should be reminded that the Thing is only a retroactive creation of the Symbolic.

162. Ibid., p. 294.

163. Ibid., p. 67 (emphasis added).

164. Ibid., p. 68 (my translation).

165. Ibid., p. 67.

166. Ibid., p. 89.

167. Ibid., p. 55 (my translation; emphasis added).

168. Ibid., pp. 55, 316.

169. Before Lacan, J.-B. Botul had himself brilliantly operated a Sadeanization of Kant in a series of outstanding lectures delivered in 1946 to a group of "Kantian integralists" at New Königsberg, Paraguay: "I suggest that in Kantianism, as is the case with all moralities which aim at the universal, there is a germ of perversion. . . . At the end of the day, it is possible to reverse Kantian morality point by point. . . . One then obtains a set of rules which we have known closely in this barbarous twentieth century: 'Kill in such a way that your killing could serve as a model for the entirety of humanity'" (J.-B. Botul, *La vie sexuelle d'Emmanuel Kant* [Paris: Fayard, 2000]).

170. Epistle to the Romans 7:7, in *The Holy Bible: New Revised Standard Version* (Nashville, TN: Thomas Nelson Publishers, 1990).

171. *The Seminar. Book VII*, p. 76.

172. Ibid., p. 79.

173. Ibid., p. 70.

174. Ibid., p. 314.

175. Ibid., p. 315.

176. All this is valid *mutatis mutandis* for Sade's anti-ethics of "evil sought for evil's sake" (ibid., p. 197).

177. Ibid., p. 69. See also ibid., pp. 77–78.

178. Ibid., p. 77.

179. Ibid., p. 70.

180. Ibid., p. 76.

181. Ibid., p. 75.

182. It is therefore not a coincidence that the law of gravity is precisely the law that systematizes the way in which the earth "attracts" the sky.

183. Ibid., p. 70.

184. Ibid., p. 76.

185. Ibid.

186. This, of course, is something that Kantian philosophy does not assume.

187. Since "the field of the pleasure principle is beyond the pleasure principle" (*The Seminar. Book VII*, p. 104).

188. Ibid., p. 73. "The pleasure principle as an unpleasure principle, or least-suffering principle . . . is calculated . . . to keep us a long way from our *jouissance*" (ibid., p. 185).

189. Ibid., p. 103.

190. Ibid., p. 73.

191. Ibid., p. 79.

192. Ibid., p. 80.

193. Ibid.

194. Ibid.

195. Ibid., p. 261.

196. See ibid., p. 202.

197. J. Lacan, *Le séminaire livre XVII. L'envers de la psychanalyse, 1969–1970* (Paris: Seuil, 1991), p. 74.

198. Ibid., p. 75.

199. Ibid. A perfect overlapping of Kant's "masochistic" ethics with Sade's "sadistic" anti-ethics is possible only because, at the desubjectivized level of "massive" *jouissance*, "the other's pain and the pain of the subject himself are one and the same thing" (*The Seminar. Book VII*, p. 80). The same reflexivity of *jouissance* is equally operative in Sade's novels at the level of the relationship between torturers and tortured.

200. *The Seminar. Book VII*, p. 177; see also ibid., p. 195.

201. Ibid., p. 177.

202. Ibid. (my translation).

203. Ibid., p. 80.

204. "The overthrowing of the order of the Law . . . can only take place through the elaboration of a myth" (B. Baas, "Le désir pur: à propos de 'Kant avec Sade' de Lacan," in *Jacques Lacan: Critical Evaluations in Cultural Theory*, ed. S. Žižek [London and New York: Routledge, 2003], p. 51).

205. *The Seminar. Book VII*, p. 177.

206. Ibid., p. 84.

207. Ibid., p. 7.

208. As Lacan himself will have it in Seminar XVII, "one transgresses nothing" (*Le séminaire livre XVII*, p. 19).

209. *The Seminar. Book VII*, p. 84.

210. Ibid., p. 191.

211. Ibid., p. 108.

212. Ibid., p. 207.

213. Ibid.

214. A. Zupančič is correct when she claims that "an ethics of the Real is *not* an ethics oriented towards the Real, but an attempt to rethink ethics by *recognizing* and acknowledging the dimension of the Real . . . as it is *already* operative" (*Ethics of the Real: Kant, Lacan* [London and New York: Verso, 2001], p. 4; emphases added). The problem with her remarkable book, however, is that it progressively parts from this initial programmatic statement; in my opinion, Zupančič overestimates Lacan's appreciation of and compatibility with Kantian ethics: indeed, for Lacan himself, the latter is precisely an ethics *toward* the Real. . . .

215. M. De Kesel, "An Image, Not an Example: Some Statements on Lacan's Aesthetical Ethics," unpublished paper.

216. *The Seminar. Book VII*, p. 247.

217. Ibid., p. 268 (my translation). On this issue, see also F. Regnault, *Conférences d'esthétique lacanienne* (Paris: Seuil, 1997), p. 92.

218. *The Seminar. Book VII*, p. 187 (my translation).

219. On how beauty should be located at the level of the fundamental fantasy, see ibid., p. 239.

220. Ibid., p. 248 (my translation).

221. Ibid., p. 249.

222. Ibid., p. 247.

223. Ibid., p. 244.

224. Ibid., p. 286.

225. Commentators usually fail to acknowledge that, in Seminar VII, Lacan prudently follows Descartes's ethical legacy, and repeatedly specifies that he is proposing a *provisional* ethics, one which is expressed "in the form of a question" (ibid., p. 109), "in an experimental form" (ibid., p. 319), and could lead to an impasse (ibid., p. 192). Safouan is therefore perfectly correct when he maintains that, against Lacan's will, the *ne céder pas sur son désir* "was soon turned into an imperative," and thus "recuperated by the superego" (Safouan, *Lacaniana*, p. 155).

226. *The Seminar. Book VII*, p. 131 (my translation).

227. Ibid., p. 231.

228. Ibid., p. 232.

229. Ibid., p. 236 (emphasis added).

230. Ibid., p. 303 (my translation).

231. See ibid., p. 292 (in relation to the French Revolution) and p. 318 (in relation to the Russian Revolution).

232. Ibid., p. 292.

233. Ibid., p. 259.

234. Ibid., p. 240.

235. See ibid., p. 318.

236. Ibid., pp. 234–235 (emphasis added).

237. Ibid., p. 235.

238. Ibid., p. 77.

239. Ibid., p. 240.

240. Ibid., p. 259.

241. Here, the image of Polynices' scattered limbs being abandoned to the dogs and the birds as a consequence of the *hybris* of the law is clearly meant to evoke the state of our bodies following nuclear holocaust. . . .

242. Ibid., p. 279.

243. Ibid., p. 278.

244. Ibid.

245. Ibid., p. 279.

246. Ibid., pp. 279, 283 (emphasis added).

247. Guyomard, *La jouissance du tragique*, p. 86.

248. *The Seminar. Book VII*, p. 239 (my translation).

249. Ibid.

250. Ibid., p. 262 (my translation).

251. On Kant's and Sade's similar "apathetic" rejection of all sentiments, see Baas's excellent analysis in "Le désir pur," especially pp. 40–41. "Apathy *qua* negation of sensitivity leads beyond pleasures, beyond pleasure *tout court*, [and achieves] what [Sade] names 'sovereign *jouissance*.'"

252. *The Seminar. Book VII*, p. 261 (emphasis added).

253. Ibid., p. 281.

254. Ibid.

255. Ibid., p. 282.

256. Ibid., p. 216.

257. Ibid., p. 298.

258. Ibid., p. 217.

259. *Le séminaire livre V*, p. 246.

260. Further proof of this ambiguity is provided by the fact that Antigone seems also to embody the epitome of scientific discourse: at one point, Lacan says that she possesses a "kind of *complete* self-knowledge" (*The Seminar. Book VII*, p. 273; emphasis added; the term "complete" is curiously absent from the English translation). B. Baas has himself emphasized the proximity between Antigone ("apathetic figure *par excellence*") and Sadean heroines (see "Le désir pur," p. 61).

261. J.-A. Miller, "I sei paradigmi del godimento," in *I paradigmi del godimento* (Rome: Astrolabio, 2001), p. 18.

262. There is another fundamental problem with Miller's reading: he never problematizes the equation between (Antigone's) pure desire and the *jouissance* of transgression. As I have shown, this equation is precisely what, for good reasons, Lacan desperately and unsuccessfully attempts to disprove in Seminar VII.

263. J. Lacan, *Le séminaire livre XXIII. Le sinthome*, 1975–1976 (Paris: Seuil, 2005), p. 121.

264. "The one is conceivable only from the existence and the consistency that the body has insofar as it is a vase" (ibid., p. 18).

265. *Le séminaire livre XVII*, p. 187. Here Lacan identifies "*l'achose*" with what he calls "*l'insubstance*," and says that these two notions "change completely the meaning of our materialism."

266. Ibid., p. 93.

267. See, for example ibid., pp. 92–95.

268. Ibid., p. 57. "'Llanguage enjoys'" (*lalangue jouit*) (J.-C. Milner, *For the Love of Language* [Basingstoke: Macmillan, 1990], p. 131).

269. *Le séminaire livre X*, p. 96.

270. *The Seminar of Jacques Lacan, On Feminine Sexuality, The Limits of Love and Knowledge. Book XX, Encore, 1972–1973* (New York: Norton, 1999), p. 74.

271. Graph 5.4 represents a synthesis of the different versions of the Borromean knot proposed by Lacan in Seminar XXII, "R.S.I.," 1974–1975, unpublished (see lessons of January 21, 1975 and January 14, 1975).

272. "The feminine 'non-All' does not mean that there is a mysterious part of woman outside the symbolic, but a simple absence of totalization" (S. Žižek, *The Puppet and the Dwarf: The Perverse Core of Christianity* [Cambridge, MA: MIT Press, 2003], p. 68).

273. See *Le séminaire livre XXIII*, p. 55.

274. Seminar XXIII, lesson of December 16, 1975. This passage has been modified beyond recognition in the Seuil version of Seminar XXIII. I rely here on the version provided by the *École Lacanienne de Psychanalyse*.

275. In this way, it would be easy to think of Joy-cean *jouissance* as a thorough reelaboration of the *jouissance* of the mystic which Seminar XX had already paired up with feminine *jouissance*. It then also becomes clear why Lacan's recurrent parallelism between Joyce and a saint is far from being gratuitous ("Joyce-the-sinthome is homophonous with sanctity"; J. Lacan, "Joyce le symptôme," in *Le séminaire livre XXIII*, p. 162).

276. See, for example, *The Seminar. Book XX*, p. 5.

277. *Le séminaire livre XXIII*, p. 64. Lacan also unequivocally states: "I would say that nature presents itself [*se spécifie*] as not being one. From this then follows the problem of which logical procedure [we should adopt] in order to approach it" (ibid., p. 12).

278. "Joyce identifies himself with the *individual*" ("Joyce le symptôme," p. 168).

279. As for the strict relation between the *sinthome* and a particular form of *jouissance*, Lacan writes: "Joyce is in relation to *joy*, that is, *jouissance*, written in the *llanguage* that is English; this en-joycing, this *jouissance* is the only thing one can get from the text. This is the symptom" (ibid., p. 167).

280. Ibid., p. 164.

281. Ibid.

282. Ibid.

283. J.-A. Miller, "Lacan con Joyce: Seminario di Barcellona II," *La Psicoanalisi*, no. 23 (1998), p. 40.

284. D. Hoens and E. Pluth, "The *sinthome*: A New Way of Writing an Old Problem," in *Re-Inventing the Symptom: Essays on the Final Lacan*, ed. L. Thurston (New York: Other Press, 2002), p. 13.

285. *Le séminaire livre XXIII*, p. 22.

286. A. Di Ciaccia and M. Recalcati, *Jacques Lacan. Un insegnamento sul sapere dell'inconscio* (Milan: Bruno Mondadori, 2000), p. 108.

287. The *sinthome* could thus also be defined as "positive" *jouis-sens* and opposed to "negative," ideological *jouis-sens*. The latter should be identified on two different levels: (a) a general level for which, as we have seen, all (phallic) knowledge is tacitly a "means of *jouissance*"; (b) particular instances in which the ideological conjunction between hegemonic signifiers and *jouissance* explicitly emerges in *jouis-sens*. In these cases, we are confronted with an idiotic, conformist language which sides with a necessarily idiotic Other. In other words, although it openly discloses the lack in the hegemonic Other, negative *jouis-sens* does not work subversively in order to denounce it; on the contrary, it fully participates in the Other's ideological homogenization by providing it with a linguistic discharge for its structural and inadmissible *jouissance*. This is why we get so-called "dirty words": blasphemy and insults might also belong to this category, or, to provide some more prosaic examples, expressions such as "cool," "you know," "check it out," "I was like . . .". It goes without saying that their common feature is compulsive repetition.

288. Miller, "I sei paradigmi del godimento," p. 32.

289. Ibid., p. 31.

290. Ibid., p. 32.

291. J.-A. Miller, "Préface," in *Joyce avec Lacan*, ed. J. Aubert (Paris: Navarin, 1987). With regard to Joyce's writing, Miller also adds that it provides us with "a topology in which the Symbolic, as place of the Other, neither overhangs the Imaginary, nor even encircles the Real as impossible, but enters into the formation as one of the three" (ibid., p. 12). These pronouncements are extremely suggestive, but also rather vague.

292. "Nobody has ever observed how it is rather curious that the discourse of the analyst produces nothing but the discourse of the master" (*Le séminaire livre XVII*, p. 205).

293. As for this last point, a detailed study of the possible connections between Lacan's ethical subject and Badiou's political subject as expounded in *Théorie du sujet* (Paris: Seuil, 1982) would be necessary.